The Work of Many Hands: Card Tables in Federal America 1790–1820

Benjamin A. Hewitt

Patricia E. Kane

Gerald W. R. Ward

The Work of Many Hands

Card Tables in Federal America 1790–1820

1982

Yale University Art Gallery

New Haven · Connecticut

This book has been published in conjunction with an exhibition held at
the Yale University Art Gallery, 25 March–30 May 1982.

This publication has been made possible by a planning grant from the National
Endowment for the Humanities, a federal agency, and by a grant from
The Barker Welfare Foundation in memory of Catherine Barker and
Charles V. Hickox.

Design & Typography by Howard I. Gralla

Drawings by John O.C. McCrillis

Composition in the Fournier types by Michael & Winifred Bixler
and by The Press of A. Colish

Composition of the backmatter in Baskerville types by Typographic Art

Printed by the William J. Mack Company

Bound by Mueller Trade Bindery

Production Supervision by Yale University Printing Service

Contents

One of the primary functions of a university art museum is to present exhibitions which are the result of important new research. "The Work of Many Hands: Card Tables in Federal America," breaks new ground in the field of American decorative arts. Based upon Benjamin A. Hewitt's ten-year computer study of one specific furniture form, it is unprecedented in its statistical method of analyzing American furniture. Drawing upon his professional training as a psychologist and aided by grants for time at the Yale University Computer Center, Dr. Hewitt undertook this pioneering study as a labor of love. He gave greatly of his own resources, both in time and travel, to make it a reality. The Yale University Art Gallery has also been a beneficiary of his generosity through gifts in recent years of nine Federal-period card tables, seven of which are documented. As a result of Dr. Hewitt's donations, Yale now has the largest collection of documented Federal-period card tables in any public institution.

The scope of the study has been broadened with essays by Gerald W.R. Ward on card playing in Federal America, and by Patricia E. Kane on price and design books of the late 18th and early 19th centuries. These essays provide information based upon traditional written and pictorial evidence as a counterfoil to Dr. Hewitt's statistical approach. The exhibition and catalogue show the importance and relevance of studying material objects as a key to understanding our past culture. The innovative approach of this study opens new avenues for scholars in the field of American decorative arts.

Plans for the exhibition and its catalogue were initiated in 1979 as a cooperative effort of the staff of the American Arts Office at the Art Gallery and Richard Beard, coordinator of the Yale Center for American Art and Material Culture. The preliminary phase was funded by a National Endowment for the Humanities planning grant awarded in 1980 at which time Patricia E. Kane, curator of American decorative arts, assumed responsibility for directing the project. She has been aided by Barbara McLean Ward, exhibition coordinator, who saw to the many administrative details involved in completing this endeavor, and Gerald W.R. Ward, assistant curator of American art. Lisa Jandorf, National Museum Act Intern 1979–80, helped with research and planning during the early stages, Virginia L. Wagner, National Museum Act Intern 1980–81, completed much of the important organizational work, and David Barquist, National Museum Act Intern 1981–82, participated in planning the exhibition design and installation.

Students participated in many facets of the exhibition. Deborah Binder and William Goodman, both Yale undergraduates; Thomas S. Michie and Gordon Sands, Marcia Brady Tucker fellows; and John Adams and Lisa Koenigsberg, Rose Herrick Jackson fellows, conducted essential research and contributed in many other ways to bring various phases of the project to completion.

Grateful thanks are given to members of the Art Gallery staff. Kathleen Giglietti, secretary to the curator of American decorative arts, and Marion Sandquist, secretary to the assistant curator, typed the bulk of the numerous drafts of the manuscript. Ilene Markell typed the charts with remarkable accuracy. Ethel Neumann, secretary to the Director, came to the aid of the American Arts Office by assisting with the final typing. Other members whose time and skills were critical are: Diane Hoose, business manager; Rosalie Reed, registrar, and her staff; Louisa Cunningham and William Cuffe, Rights and Reproductions; Janet Saleh Dickson, curator of Education; Janet Gordon, assistant curator of Education; and Caroline Rollins, coordinator of Membership, Sales, and Publications.

Helpful advice from many scholars and curators has to be acknowledged. Discussions with Charles Hummel of the Winterthur Museum, and Damie Stillman, Professor of the History of Art, University of Delaware, were key in formulating the goals of the exhibition and catalogue. Jules D. Prown read all of the essays and gave unstintingly of his insight and experience. William B. Keller, author of the voluminous catalogue of the Cary Collection of Playing Cards at Yale University, provided guidance in the selection of playing cards for the exhibition and for illustrations in the book. Vincent Ciulla Design made recommendations concerning the format of the exhibition and its presentation. Anne Wilde skillfully edited the publication and prepared the index. The beautiful and immensely helpful drawings for the book are the work of John O.C. McCrillis. The book was expeditiously produced under the direction of Greer Allen; and Howard I. Gralla, designer, has taken a great diversity of material and created an elegant book design which enhances the written word. The exhibition installation was designed by Margaret Morton and Thomas J. Morton with skill and understanding and was brought to reality by Robert M. Soule and his staff.

Finally, we must express our thanks to the National Endowment for the Humanities for providing a planning grant for this exhibition without which the crucial preliminary work could not have been undertaken. We are grateful to William Barnabas McHenry for his support of our project. We are also grateful to the following individuals and institutions that have been willing to part with their objects for the duration of the exhibition:

American Antiquarian Society; The Baltimore Museum of Art; The Beinecke Rare Book and Manuscript Library; The Brooklyn Museum; Thomas and Rebecca Colville; Connecticut Valley Historical Museum; The Currier Gallery of Art; The Diplomatic Reception Rooms, Department of State; Gracie Mansion; Hammond-Harwood House; The Henry Francis du Pont Winterthur Museum; Benjamin A. Hewitt; Historic Deerfield, Inc.; Kaufman Americana Foundation; Mr. and Mrs. John M. Keese IV; The Lewis Walpole Library; Litchfield Historical Society; Mr. Robert L. McNeil Jr.; Timothy Fuller Marquand; The Metropolitan Museum of Art; Museum of Fine Arts, Boston; Museum of the City of New York; New Hampshire Historical Society; New London County Historical Society; Robert and Barbara Sallick; Patrick M. Spadaccino Jr.; Mr. and Mrs. Randolph Staudinger; Wadsworth Atheneum; The Webb-Deane-Stevens Museum; and John Whitmore.

Much needed support in the preparatory phases was provided by a grant from the DeWitt Wallace Fund. Very generous gifts from The Barker Welfare Foundation in memory of Catherine Barker and Charles V. Hickox and from Eileen Bamberger, S. Sidney Kahn, B.A. 1959, William L. Bernhard, B.A. 1955, and Catherine Cahill have made the book possible. We are grateful to the Friends of American Arts at Yale for funding the exhibition.

ALAN SHESTACK
Director

Preface

At the time I was becoming seriously interested in collecting American furniture, I studied furniture books, magazine articles and advertisements, and auction catalogues to learn as much information as possible about the kinds of antiques I was buying. I had two reasons for doing so: I had made some costly mistakes because I didn't have enough knowledge to question the origin and date on some of the price tags; more important, I realized that I could enjoy collecting only if I knew what I was doing.

Unfortunately I did not find answers that satisfied me. Some writers made statements about regionalism without documenting their sources, and experts sometimes contradicted one another. I reached the conclusion that the empirical information I was reading and picking up from talks with dealers and collectors might be unreliable because it could not be verified.

Then in 1966 I read Charles F. Montgomery's *American Furniture: The Federal Period.* It was a book of verified facts that were immediately useful. His approach appealed to me as a psychologist because it was scientific; he had used microanalysis to identify wood species, and he had devised ways of quantifying some of his data to indicate the probability that certain characteristics would be found on furniture from various regions. His catalogue entries defined how he identified the origin of these items. He described how he analyzed the 407 pieces of undocumented furniture in his catalogue and substantiated his attributions; he showed how many of the 84 pieces of documented furniture in the catalogue reflected regional preferences for ornament, style, materials, and construction methods.

At the time, I regretted that he had not written about the Queen Anne period which appealed to me more than the Federal. But being generally interested in furniture, I began using his information, became increas-ingly self-confident in my buying, and ultimately became so fond of Federal furniture that it is the only kind I collect.

In 1970 Mr. Montgomery came to Yale as Curator of the Garvan and Related Collections of American Art and professor of the history of art. Because I was then a researcher in the psychology department I was eligible to audit his courses. I did so for two years, during which my talks with him and his colleagues increased my interest in furniture research. He and I had many discussions about regionalism, and these led to speculations about new ways of identifying origins. He regretted that early in his career his records of the characteristics of documented furniture had not been systematic enough to collate and reveal regional distinctions. One day he made the statement that sparked this study: "What we need are norms—as you have in psychology—where you compare the characteristics of people in different occupations, schools, or college majors." I saw readily how this could be accomplished.

Undertaking this study would use my training and experience in a new and exciting field. I foresaw my role as solving ambiguous problems which had challenged me since World War II when I was a cryptographic analyst of Japanese codes, and as using such familiar techniques as developing codes and systems for research, similar in kind to what I had been doing at Yale.

We concluded that the research design (which is detailed in the text) would entail matching the characteristics of undocumented furniture with those of documented furniture so as to build sizable regional groups whose characteristics we could then tally for inter-regional comparisons. To ensure consistent data we decided to study this one form of furniture because so many card tables were known to be documented. In the fall of 1971 I developed the codes and the system to fol-low.*

*The codes and system by which the data were accumulated are available at a nominal fee from the American Arts Office, Yale University Art Gallery.

In the winter of 1972 I began to gather data. For more than five years about half my time was spent on fascinating trips to museums and private collections along the east coast, to the mid- and far west, and to Hawaii. By the summer of 1977 information about most of the 400 tables in the study had been collected. Mr. Montgomery and I decided that the time had come to bring the study to a conclusion because fewer documented tables were emerging (data about 65 of the 75 in the study had been gathered). In 1978, when the statistical analysis was completed and only the tallying of frequencies and the summarizing of findings were ahead, Montgomery died suddenly. Even though he would have retired that year, he had planned for this exhibition and book, with which he had intended to help me because we had recognized that in the decorative arts I was inexperienced and lacked formal training.

Patricia E. Kane succeeded Charles as curator of American decorative arts. Without her determination to have the findings published in conjunction with an exhibition at Yale, this book would not have been written. Although Miss Kane and I started the planning in 1978, I needed first to check my interpretations of the findings against contemporary documentary information. Miss Kane and Jules D. Prown, professor of the history of art, reviewed my report of the latter study with the conclusion that it was congruent with my major conclusion—that regional characteristics reflect the high degree of specialization and standardization within the furniture industry.

In planning the book and the exhibition we aimed to relate card tables to the people who used them and to develop an understanding of the popularity of this form of Federal furniture, the subject of Gerald W.R. Ward's essay. We also aimed to consider the influence of design books on the development of styles of card tables and to determine how price books provide information about their manufacture and their craftsmen, the focus of Miss Kane's essay. The American Arts Office of the Art Gallery and the Center for American Art and Material Culture applied for a planning grant from the National Endowment for the Humanities under which we moved ahead on July 1, 1980.

Since then, writing up the findings has been the work of many hands. Patricia Kane, Barbara McLean Ward, exhibition coordinator, and I are responsible for organizing and writing the essay "The Regional Characteristics of American Federal-Period Card Tables." I deeply appreciate the many personal and professional sacrifices they made to accomplish this task and their willingness to share with me so much of their knowledge of American social, economic, and furniture history, through which I developed a firmer grasp of the conclusions I had reached.

Many people read one or more drafts of the essay. Especially helpful were the suggestions of Charles Hummel and Brock Jobe at the outset and of Mr. Ward, assistant curator, who painstakingly reviewed each draft. I thank James Leggio for his suggestions on organization. For their helpful suggestions about revising the final draft I am indebted to Professor Prown; David Barquist, National Museum Act intern; and Gordon Sands, Marcia Brady Tucker fellow. Other colleagues who provided many helpful suggestions were Dr. Bessie Lee Gambrill, W. Scott Braznell, and Patrick M. Spadaccino Jr. Most of my conclusions were first tested in public at workshops sponsored by the Friends of American Arts at Yale, and I am grateful to the Friends for their encouragement and advice.

For helping to compile the catalogue Mrs. Ward's efforts are gratefully acknowledged; she gave meticulous attention to documentary details and provided important editorial assistance in organizing the materials. Raymond MacDougall, dealer and genealogist, expeditiously produced a wealth of important information about the interrelationships of Salem cabinetmakers through his research of Samuel Barnard, a hitherto unknown maker whose superb craftsmanship in the single known example of his output (cat. 19) is established. I am indebted to Florence M.

Montgomery for reading the catalogue and making so many important suggestions.

Virginia L. Wagner, National Museum Act intern, contributed importantly to many phases of the book by compiling illustrative materials and charted information, by making perceptive suggestions about its organization, and by communicating effectively with so many lenders.

Gathering information about so many card tables would have been impossible without the cooperation of numerous collectors, museums, and dealers. Because so many collectors asked to remain anonymous I chose not to acknowledge any by name. Curators in all of the museums were extremely helpful. A few on whom I imposed excessively were J. Peter Spang at Historic Deerfield, Inc.; Brock Jobe, when he was at the Museum of Fine Arts, Boston; Wendy Cooper, when she was at the Brooklyn Museum; William V. Elder III at the Baltimore Museum; Marilynn Johnson Bordes at the Metropolitan Museum of Art; Charles Hummel and Nancy Richards at the Henry Francis du Pont Winterthur Museum; and Clement Conger, at the White House and Diplomatic Reception Rooms of the U.S. Department of State.

Among the many dealers who allowed me to use information about tables they owned, or who helped me locate documented tables, were Nancy Stiner, Kenneth Hammitt, Richard French, Israel Sack, Inc., Benjamin Ginsburg, Bernard Levy, Philip Bradley, and Robert Trump.

Charles Parsons' help enabled me to see most of the documented New Hampshire card tables in the study. I want especially to thank him for apprising me of tables as he found them, for sharing his vast knowledge and research with me, for driving me from one end of the state to the other, and for introducing me to so many people with heirlooms of great importance to this study.

I am indebted to the staff of the Decorative Arts Photographic Collection of the Henry Francis du Pont Winterthur Museum for providing information about the ownership of many documented tables, and to Bradford Rauschenburg of the Museum of Early Southern Decorative Arts for contributing documentary evidence of piecework turners in Charleston.

For essential help with the statistical and data-processing stages of the study, I thank Professor John Hartigan, chairman of the Yale statistics department, for defining appropriate statistical procedures for the analyses. For their competent help as statisticians and programmers I am thankful to Diccon Bancroft, Joseph Vitale, and Anthony Wong, and especially to Wendy Madsen, a volunteer, for her extraordinary competence in programming data and in meticulously documenting the interrelationships of the many computer programs.

For providing vital information about cabinetmaking practices I am indebted to Nicholas Kotula, John Whitmore, and the late Chauncey Whitmore, and I thank John Whitmore for recognizing tables which were important to this study and for getting permission from their owners for me to examine them.

Professor Prown made arrangements for Yale to donate computer time to this project, and the American Arts Office printed the forms on which data about tables were recorded and underwrote some of the photographic expenses during the data-gathering stage. I am particularly indebted to Alan Shestack for raising the funds to make this publication possible, and to the Friends of American Arts for their sponsorship of the exhibition.

Marion Sandquist of the American Arts Office volunteered many thoughtful services, which included typing letters to collectors and museums. Last but very importantly I want to thank Kathleen Giglietti, secretary to the curator of American decorative arts, for so competently typing the manuscript and also for reducing so many mountains to molehills.

BENJAMIN A. HEWITT
Guest Curator

The Work of Many Hands: Card Tables in Federal America 1790–1820

Card table, Massachusetts, 1760–
1780. *Primary wood*: mahogany.
Secondary woods: white pine,
maple. H. 72 cm; W. 91 cm;
D. 88 cm. Mr. and Mrs. Stanley
Stone.

*Card tables in the Chippendale
style, such as this superb Massachusetts example, were the immediate stylistic predecessors of
Federal-period card tables. Sunken
wells for counters and squared
corners for candlesticks were
typical features of these earlier and
more specialized tables. In addition, this table is ornamented with
a needlework panel depicting a
card game in progress.*[1]

1. Charles F. Montgomery and
Patricia E. Kane, eds., *American
Art, 1750–1800: Towards Independence* (Boston: New York
Graphic Society, 1976), p. 163, no.
114; also see no. 115, an accompanying pole screen.

"Avarice and Conviviality": Card Playing in Federal America

Gerald W. R. Ward

Hundreds, perhaps even thousands of American Federal-period card tables have survived, and they represent only a fraction of the enormous total produced in their own time. The heavy demand by customers in the rapidly increasing population was met by Federal cabinetmakers in two principal ways. They satisfied most clients with standard ready-made tables, while the requirements of wealthy and demanding patrons also allowed cabinetmakers to make distinctive (and more costly) customized and custom-made tables. No form of Federal furniture other than chairs has come down to us in such quantity as card tables.

Why were card tables so popular in Federal America? How, when, and where were they used? What games were played on them, and by whom? What are the possible explanations for what must be considered a virtual craze for card playing and gambling during these years? Tentative answers to these and related questions are offered in this essay from the point of view of the user rather than that of the maker of the tables. Based primarily on traditional forms of written and pictorial evidence, this approach serves as a counterfoil to Benjamin A. Hewitt's statistical study based firmly on the three-dimensional objects. In conjunction with Patricia E. Kane's discussion of cabinetmakers' price books and design sources, these three studies suggest the rich possibilities inherent in the study of American decorative arts objects from all points of view, and their value to students of American history.

It should immediately be said that card tables and card games were far from new in the Federal period. Card playing, although severely legislated against both in the north and the south, was not an unknown activity even in 17th-century puritan New England. A sure indication that cards enjoyed at least some popularity there is the fact that students at Harvard College in 1655 could be disciplined for "Drunkenesse, Fighting, Rayling, Swearing, Cursing, Lying, filthy Speaking, prophanesse, Revelling, playing at Cards or Dice, or such like."[1] In the 18th century, as religious and civil restrictions against playing with "the Devil's picture book" were somewhat relaxed, the tables themselves (fig. 1) tell the story of card playing's increasing acceptability. The first American card tables recognized as such today were made in the late 1720s in what has come to be called the Queen Anne style, and New York card tables in the rococo style are among the outstanding achievements of early American furniture.[2] By the eve of the Revolution, card playing was firmly established as a social diversion, although still regarded with considerable skepticism among conservative circles in New England. Even though sober young men such as John Adams might scoff at those who "waste their bloom of life at the card or billiard table among rakes and fools," the custom was widespread in fashionable homes and entrenched in taverns.[3]

The constraints against leisure activities were loosened even further after the Revolution, and card games became one of the

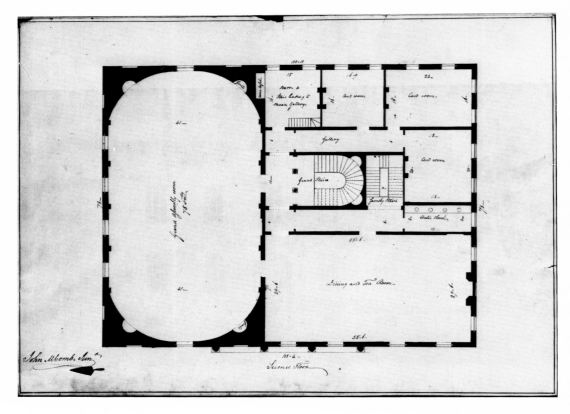

FIG. 2.
Plan by John McComb Jr.
(1763–1853) for the second floor
of the Tontine City Tavern,
New York, ca. 1793. Courtesy of
the New-York Historical Society, New York City.

*Each of the urban centers in Fed-
eral America sported an assembly
hall, public tavern, or club, where
people gathered for dancing, card
playing, and entertainment.
McComb's plan for the New York
version of such an establishment
included three "card rooms" on the
second floor, in addition to the
"grand Assembly room" and the
"Dining and Tea Room." Similarly in the Salem, Massachusetts, Assembly House, opened
in 1783, card tables were found in
the drawing rooms.
On the night of January 16, 1783,
there were "about 90 persons at
the assembly; 41 ladies and 28
gentlemen draw for dancing; the
rest repair to [the] gaming-table."[1]*

*Even the backwoods town of
Charleston, Virginia (now West
Virginia), boasted an inn where
everyone assembled for similar
festivities. The English traveler
Thomas Ashe recorded his experi-
ences there in 1806: "I entered the
ballroom, which was filled with
persons at cards, drinking, smok-
ing, dancing, etc. The music consisted of two bangies, played by
negroes nearly in a state of nudity,
and a lute, through which a
Chickasaw breathed with much
occasional exertion and violent
gesticulations. The dancing ac-
corded with the harmony of these
instruments. The clamour of the
card tables was so great, that it
almost drowned every other."[2]*

1. *The Diary of William Pynchon
of Salem*, ed. Fitch Edward Oliver
(Boston: Houghton Mifflin, 1890),
p. 141. The writer would like to
thank Damie Stillman for bringing
the Tontine City Tavern drawing
to his attention.
2. *Travels in America, Performed in
1806* (New York, 1811), letter 11,
as quoted in Allan Nevins, ed.,
*American Social History as Re-
corded by British Travellers* (New
York: Henry Holt, 1934), p. 62.

principal ways in which the postwar generation indulged its newfound freedom. The
Federal era was marked by significant changes
in the social life of Americans. It witnessed,
for example, the beginnings of the American
theater, a proliferation of dancing assemblies,
publication of the first American novels, an
increase in the consumption of alcohol, and
the adoption of revealing dress for fashionable women.[4] Older and more traditional
members of society battled against this introduction of "luxury" and moral laxness, but
as Henry Adams aptly noted, many people
in the Federal period insisted that "in this
world they must be allowed to amuse themselves, even though they were to suffer for it
in the next."[5]

Card playing was not restricted to any
particular class or segment of society, although certain games had distinct social con-
notations. Indeed, card playing cut across
economic, social, and geographic boundaries
to such an extent that it can be considered almost a universal form of recreation. From
the White House to the most rugged tavern
in the back country, card games enjoyed
great popularity. Mrs. Anne Royall even
noted in her travels that the debtors confined
to Salem's jail were happily singing and playing cards while serving their time.[6] Naturally
there were differences between the ambience
of a loo party in a Washington drawing
room and a card game in Edenton, North
Carolina, where a cardsharper named Thomas
Penrise, when detected in his attempt to
cheat some drunken sailors, started a scuffle
in which he "gouged out three eyes, bit off
an ear, tore a few cheeks, and made good his

retreat."[7] Although cards were perhaps the only link between these two settings, their presence in each is a good indication of the widespread enthusiasm for card playing, remarked upon by many contemporary observers of the social scene.

Although a game of cards might take place almost anywhere, three principal locations were particularly favored. Card parties in private homes became increasingly fashionable; cards were also featured at the assembly houses in the larger cities, and, along with other forms of gambling and sport, were popular in taverns throughout America. Each of these three settings deserves attention.

Ritual card parties were an established part of social life in urban Federal America. As early as 1781, Rebecca Franks of Philadelphia visited New York and wrote home to her sister that "few New York ladies know how to entertain company in their houses unless they introduce the card tables." Twenty years later, Sally Otis of Boston registered a similar observation about society in Alexandria, Virginia. Writing home to her sister, she stated "The Evening closed as usual with cards (the only amusement here known among the men)." Jane Mesick found in her study of society during this era that cards were generally featured during the two periods each day—in the early afternoon and after the evening meal—when fashionable hostesses received callers in both northern and southern cities.[8]

Following English practice, and the great success of the resorts at Bath and elsewhere, American cities and towns erected assembly houses for dancing, card playing, exhibitions, concerts, and other entertainments (fig. 2). In Philadelphia, Francisco de Miranda noted in 1784 that an assembly was held every two weeks at the City Tavern. There, he observed, "the dance begins at seven o'clock and lasts until two or three in the morning. Those who do not like to dance play cards on tables prepared for that purpose in nearby rooms."[9] New York City and Salem were similarly equipped, and Richmond would

have been, had Benjamin Latrobe's 1798 plan for a proposed theater, hotel, and assembly building been realized. Latrobe's design specified three rooms for cards, including one reserved for "Private Card parties."[10] Boston boasted the famous (or infamous) "Tea Assembly," or "Sans Souci Club," organized in the winter of 1784–85. Here, much to the dismay of the older generation, subscribers could dance and play cards at twenty tables until midnight (fig. 3). Later, Charles Bulfinch's Boston theater, built in 1793–94, included "spacious card and tea rooms."[11]

Taverns were the third common setting for cards. Numerous travelers commented upon the prevalence of card playing and gambling at these establishments (fig. 4). In New York a law was passed in 1788 which made tavern keepers subject to fine and imprisonment if they permitted card playing, cockfighting, and gaming, or kept dice, billiard tables, or shuffleboards in their houses, a sign that such activity was rampant. And it was probably in a tavern where "Tricket," the unrepentant gambler portrayed in *The Gamester* (Philadelphia, 1800), "spent his hours in greedy wishes, hopes, and fears; in rage, in oaths, and curses, over his cards, with the tankard at his side, often drained by the thirsty passion burning in his stomach, and raging in his mind."[12]

Different styles of card tables were used in these different settings. High-style tables were originally owned only by relatively well-to-do people and were most likely to be found in fashionable homes. Contemporary inventories record that card tables might be found in several different locations in a house, although generally in a room of some elegance and formality. Aaron Burr, for example, kept "2 Inlaid card Tables" in the "Blue or drawing room" on the first floor of his New York townhouse, but also had a pair of card tables in his upstairs hall.[13] Jerathmiel Peirce of Salem kept his "2 mahogany Card Tables" in the drawing room, which had been remodeled by Samuel McIntire in

FIG. 3.
Unknown artist, *Avarice and Conviviality, or the Union of Elegance and Inelegance*, published in England, ca. 1795. The Lewis Walpole Library.

This English view provides an approximation of a bustling card room in a fashionable American assembly hall or club. For example, the Sans Souci Club, founded in Boston in the winter of 1784–85, was said to contain twenty card tables for the pleasure of its patrons, at which bets larger than a quarter were not allowed. Tea, coffee, and chocolate were provided to the players free of charge, but wine, punch, and lemonade had to be purchased.[1]

1. Charles Warren, "Samuel Adams and the Sans Souci Club in 1785," *Massachusetts Historical Society Proceedings* 60 (1927): 322.

FIG. 4.
Thomas Rowlandson (1756–1827), *A Game at Put in a Country Alehouse*, published in London, 1799. The Lewis Walpole Library.

Put was a simple game played by two, three, or four players, but generally by two, as seen in this print. The rustic setting for this game is a reminder that card games could be played on almost any horizontal surface and in any surroundings. Taverns and inns were particularly important settings for card playing in Federal America. The English traveler Isaac Weld Jr. noted, for example, that gambling in Richmond was rampant. "I had scarcely alighted from my horse at the tavern," he wrote, "when the landlord came to ask what game I was most partial to, as in such a room there was a faro table, in another a hazard table, in a third a billiard table, to any one of which he was ready to conduct me. Not the smallest secrecy is employed in keeping these tables;

they are always crowded with people, and the doors of the apartment are only shut to prevent the rabble from coming in. Indeed, throughout the lower part of the country in Virginia, and also in that part of Maryland next to it, there is scarcely a petty tavern without a billiard room, and this is always full of a set of idle low-lived fellows, drinking spirits or playing cards, if not engaged at the table. Cock-fighting is also another favourite diversion. It is chiefly, however, the lower class of people that partake of these amusements at the taverns; in private there is, perhaps, as little gambling in Virginia as in any other part of America. The circumstances of having taverns thus infested by such a set of people, renders travelling extremely unpleasant."[1]

1. *Travels Through the States of North America, and the Provinces of Upper and Lower Canada, During the Years 1795, 1796, and 1797* (London, 1807), vol. I, p. 191.

the Adamesque style in 1801. The wealthy William Bingham of Philadelphia had "3 Card Tables" and "1 Lottery table" in the "Front Room up stairs S.W. Corner" of his mansion, while Thomas Jefferson's White House had a total of five mahogany card tables in 1809: a pair in the "Lady's Drawing-Room," another pair in the "President's Drawing-Room," and a single example in the "President's Sitting Room." Wendell Garrett found in his study of Newport interiors from 1780 to 1800 that gaming tables were for the most part located in bedchambers, while Edward S. Cooke Jr.'s study of Salem Federal inventories found card tables listed almost invariably in first-floor rooms.[14] And, as Cooke and others suggest, furniture was no doubt moved from room to room as the occasion required. This would apply particularly to small objects such as card tables, for as defined by Thomas Sheraton, a table was primarily a movable piece of furniture.

Several factors which have nothing to do with card playing help explain why card tables were produced in such large numbers during the Federal period. Perhaps the most important of these is the significant use of such tables as elements of decoration in the symmetrical arrangement of furnishings in the Federal domestic interior. They were frequently made in pairs and placed against the walls of the room, flanking a window, doorway, or fireplace, and perhaps standing under looking-glasses. They thus functioned when not in use much as pier or side tables. The close relationship between Salem pier tables and card tables, and the rarity of American Federal pier tables, suggests this use of card tables as objects of ornament.[15] The tables were simply placed against the wall, with their top leaf down. On many tables, the pictorial inlay visible on the leaf when it is in the closed position is ample evidence of this practice. When needed, the lightweight tables were simply carried, or in the case of those tables with casters, wheeled to the desired position, and opened for play.

Being both portable and versatile, however, and relatively inexpensive as well, card tables could also be used for a variety of other purposes. It is even likely that many of them were used primarily for activities other than card playing, much as modern-day folding card tables are used. Most Federal-period card tables are less specialized than their earlier counterparts—they generally lack the wells for counters and recessed corners for candlesticks often found on tables made in the Queen Anne and Chippendale styles (fig. 1). American Federal-period tables also rarely have the additional touch of an attached protective covering of baize or needlework, an embellishment found more frequently on earlier tables.

Conversely, one does not need a high-style table in order to play cards. A pembroke table would serve equally well, and in less affluent homes or different surroundings almost any table or horizontal surface would do (figs. 5, 6). The "card or tea table" listed in the 1813 inventory of Richard Bernard in rural Chester County, Pennsylvania, suggests the dual roles which tables must have played in many homes.[16] No doubt a wide variety of tables was pressed into use in taverns and inns, where specialization was an unnecessary luxury.

However, the conventional card table, the subject of this volume, was admirably suited to its purpose. When opened for play, a loose covering of green baize was customarily used to protect its surface; as represented in contemporary prints, the covering is either flush with the table edge or overhangs nearly to the floor. Some tables, such as the "Walnut Card Table with Drawer" owned by Dennis Whelan of West Chester, Pennsylvania, in 1819,[17] or the round Philadelphia table illustrated (cat. 50), were equipped with such "extras" as drawer or drawers for cards, counters, and other paraphernalia. Candlesticks, boxes for counters, and other specialized accouterments were all that remained to be added for the game to begin (fig. 7).

FIG. 5.
William Sidney Mount (1807–
68), *The Card Players*, ca. 1855.
Reynolda House Museum of
American Art, Winston-Salem,
North Carolina.

*Mount's painting of two men
playing cards in a ramshackle
Long Island barn is an eloquent
reminder that card playing knows
no economic or social boundaries.
For these individuals, a broken
windsor chair served as well as a
high-style card table. Although
Mount's work dates long after the
end of the Federal period, a scene
such as this was probably not un-
common in the late 18th and early
19th centuries. Morris Birkbeck
noted on a visit to Petersburg,
Virginia, in 1818, for example,
that it was "not quite two years
since half the town was destroyed
by a fire, occasioned by some
negroes playing at cards in a
stable."* [1]

1. *Notes on a Journey in America*
(London, 1818: reprint, Readex
Microprint, 1966), p. 15.

FIG. 6.
George Caleb Bingham (1811–
79), *Raftsmen Playing Cards*,
1847. The St. Louis Art Museum.

*A rude plank bench is the card
table for these boatmen floating
down the Mississippi River.
Although this painting also dates
considerably after the Federal
period, it does illustrate the fact
that card playing was (and is) a
good way to pass the time on what
otherwise would be a boring trip.
Earlier, in 1818, the boat Henry
Bradshaw Fearon took up the
Hudson River from New York to
Fishkill "was well filled with
passengers," among whom "the
general occupation was card
playing," while "one or two had a
book in their hands."* [1] *In the later
19th century, Mississippi steam-
boats became synonymous with
poker and high-stakes gambling.*

1. *Sketches of America: A Narra-
tive of a Journey of Five Thousand
Miles Through the Eastern and
Western States of America* (Lon-
don: Longman, Hurst, Rees, Orme,
& Brown, 1818), pp. 78–79.

Whist (fig. 8), loo (fig. 9), quadrille, and faro (or Pharo) are among the card games most frequently cited in contemporary references. Beginning players could learn the rules of these games and many others by consulting one of at least fourteen editions of Hoyle's *Games* published in America between 1796 (fig. 10) and 1830 (fig. 11), or one of the many English editions available at the same period. By 1830, an edition of Hoyle's rules published in New York by W. C. Borradaile included "copious directions" for the four games mentioned above and seventeen others, including piquet, quinze, vingt-un, lansquenet, rouge et noir, cribbage, matrimony, cassino, reversis, put, connexions, all fours, speculation, lottery, Pope Joan, commerce, and brag, as well as the rules for dominoes, backgammon, draughts (checkers), hazard (craps), chess, golf, cricket, billiards, tennis, horse racing, and cockfighting. Like the card tables themselves, most of these games as played in America owed much to their English background.

Different games were popular in different environments and among different sorts of people. Whist (fig. 12), a perennially popular game in which success depended on skill as well as chance, was a favorite in fashionable urban settings and in southern country houses. Loo was a favorite pastime among men and women of the upper class, who would often lose large sums of money in this fast, exciting game. The passion for loo among such individuals was satirized by George Tucker in an 1806 poem concerning "a party of ladies at loo":[18]

*Oh! then, my dear friend, what splendor was
seen,
Each dame that was there was array'd like a
queen!
The camel, the ostrich, the tortoise, the bear,
And the kid might have found, each his spoils
on the fair.*

In this English print the lady on the left appears about to take the trick in question by playing the ace of spades over the previously played three, five, and jack of the same suit, much to the chagrin of the gentleman opponent. Her horse-like grin is no doubt a result of adding this seventh trick to the book of six already gathered at her elbow. Each trick above six counted toward the game, which consisted of ten points.[1]

Whist, a forerunner of modern bridge, ordinarily required four players, the partners sitting across from each other, and is considerably more tame than games such as loo or faro. When dining in Petersburg, Virginia, in 1796, Benjamin Henry Latrobe noted that loo "made a very large party happy," while whist was only "affording a more sulky delight to a few more."[2]

1. Modern rules for the whist family of games can be found in John Scarne, *Scarne's Encyclopedia of Games* (New York: Harper and Row, 1973), pp. 118–66. This particular print by James Gillray, along with many other satirical illustrations which depict English card playing, is included in *The Works of James Gillray* (London, 1851; reprint, New York: Benjamin Blom, 1968).
2. *The Virginia Journals of Benjamin Henry Latrobe, 1795–1798*, ed. Edward C. Carter II (New Haven: Yale University Press, 1977), vol. I, p. 103.

Tho' their dresses were made of the finest of stuff,
It must be confest they were scanty enough;
Yet nought that this saving should their husbands avail,
What they take from the body they put in the tail.
When they sit, they so tighten their clothes that you can,
See a lady has legs just the same as a man.

'Ere tea was served up, they were prim as you please,
But when cards were produc'd, all was freedom and ease.
Mrs. Winloo, our hostess, each lady entreated,
To set the example, "I pray ma'am be seated—
"After you, Mrs. Clutch—Well, if you insist;
"Tom Shuffle, sit down—You prefer loo to whist."
"I'm clear for the ladies—come, Jack, take a touch,
"I'll stump Mrs. Craven, and you Mrs. Clutch."

Around the green board they now eagerly fix,
Two beaux and four ladies composing the six

"Well, Mr. Shuffle, you are dealer, begin."
"Is that the trump card? Then I can stand."
"And I must throw up"—Let me look at your hand.—

"And there's Mrs. Craven, she threw up the knave,
"I know I did, ma'am, but I don't play to save."

And thus they go on—checking, stumping and fleeting,
With much other jargon that's not worth repeating.
Till at length it struck twelve, and the winners propose,
That the loo which was "up," the sitting should close.
On a little more sport tho' the losers were bent,
They would not withhold their reluctant assent.
Mrs. Craven, who long since a word had not spoke,

FIG. 9.
Isaac Cruikshank (1756?–1811?), *Loo*, published in London, 1796. The Lewis Walpole Library.

Loo, or *pam-loo*, is a fast-paced, high-stakes game for four, five, six, or seven persons, although five, as we see here, or six is the best number. In this game, the jack of clubs is known as *pam*, and outranks every other card in the deck. Here it has just saved the player on the left from being "looed," or losing the hand. The pool in loo contains the "fish," or counters, which each player antes before the deal, and the sums forfeited by those who were looed during the preceding hand. Hands in loo move quickly, the stakes rise rapidly, and it is easy to lose a good deal of money in a very short time. Loo was perhaps the most popular game among women of society in the Federal period.[1]

1. Dolly Madison's sister Anna wrote to her of the "dash at Loo" at a Boston dinner party in 1804; see *Memoirs and Letters of Dolly Madison . . . edited by her grandniece* (Boston: Houghton, Mifflin, 1886), p. 40. Mrs. Madison herself was present when Samuel Harrison Smith first played loo (and won) in Washington in 1803; see Gaillard Hunt, ed., *The First Forty Years of Washington Society* (New York: Charles Scribner's Sons, 1906), p. 38. Loo was still popular in the highest circles in 1816 when Miss Mary Boardman Crowninshield played with Mrs. James Monroe; see *Letters of Mary Boardman Crowninshield*, ed. Francis Boardman Crowninshield (New York: Riverside Press, 1905), p. 59, quoted in Charles F. Montgomery, *American Furniture: The Federal Period* (New York: Viking Press, 1966), p. 319. The craze for loo has been noted by several later authors: see Herbert Asbury, *Sucker's Progress: An Informal History of Gambling in America from the Colonies to Canfield* (New York: Dodd, Mead, 1938), p. 50; and Henry Chafetz, *Play the Devil: A History of Gambling in the United States from 1492 to 1955* (New York: Clarkson N. Potter, 1960), pp. 35–36. "Fish" is an English corruption of the French word for counter, *fiche*.

Who scarce gave a smile to the [...?],
But, like an old mouser, sat watching her prey,
Now utter'd the ominous sound of "I play."
And swept the grand loo, thus proving the rule,
That the still sow will ever draw most from the pool.
Tho' much had been lost, yet now they had done,
The devil of one would confess she had won.
But soon I discover'd it plain could be seen,
In each lady's face what her fortune had been.

At such a game as he describes, Tucker's wife had recently lost $40, making him well qualified to judge the demeanor of winners and losers. While loo could be enjoyed by nearly anyone, the game of quadrille was probably played only by people with enough leisure to master its complicated rules.

Quicker gambling games such as faro, vingt-un (today's twenty-one or blackjack), put, and others dependent primarily on the arbitrary fall of the cards were especially popular in settings where the gambling action was more important than the niceties of card playing, as in urban taverns or rural inns. On the frontier, sedate card playing was relatively scarce. Jedediah Morse wrote of Tennessee social life, for example, that "Wrestling, jumping, running foot races, and playing at ball, are the common diversions. Dancing is coming into fashion. Card playing is a rare amusement."[19]

Benjamin Latrobe's account of an evening's entertainment in the spring of 1796 provides a good insight into the relationships between different card games.[20] La-

FIG. 10.

Title page from *Hoyle's Games Improved . . .*, by James Beaufort (Philadelphia, 1796). American Antiquarian Society.

The name of the Englishman Edmond Hoyle (1672–1769) has been inextricably linked with the rules for card playing since the appearance of his treatise on whist in 1742. Many instruction and rules manuals published after his death bear his name to the present day, even though they were written, compiled, or edited by other people (in this case, the Englishman James Beaufort). Today, "according to Hoyle" has entered the language as a reference to a higher, definitive authority.

The first three American editions of Hoyle's Games were published in 1796 in Boston, New York, and Philadelphia, the title page to which is illustrated here; the Philadelphia edition was also sold in Baltimore. Later American editions were issued in New York (1803, 1819, 1821, 1823, 1824, 1825, 1829, 1830), Philadelphia (1805, 1817), and Boston (1814).[1] The later editions tend to contain rules for more games and to be more helpful to the beginning player, while the earlier editions take much for granted and offer more in the way of strategy for the advanced player.

1. The American Antiquarian Society owns copies of the three 1796 editions and the 1805 Philadelphia edition. Copies of the 1803, 1821, 1823, 1824, and 1825 New York editions are in the Essex Institute Library. The 1829 and 1830 New York editions are in the Yale University Library. The remaining editions are listed in Frederic Jessel, comp., *A Bibliography of Works in English on Playing Cards and Gaming* (London: Longmans, Green, 1905): no. 827 (Boston, 1814); no. 829 (Philadelphia, 1817); and no. 830 (New York, 1819). Reprints of two of Hoyle's predecessors, Charles Cotton's *The Compleat Gamester* (1674) and Theophilus Lucas's *Lives of the Gamesters* (1714), can be found in *Games and Gamesters of the Restoration* (London: George Routledge and Sons, 1930).

trobe received a dinner invitation from a Dr. Stone, and when he arrived at his host's residence an hour before dinner, he found many gentlemen, "*all honorable men no doubt,*" already there and engaged in play. "They were doing no harm," Latrobe explained, "only playing at Loo." A "very sumptuous dinner" for the twenty-seven guests intervened, and after a toast to President Washington's health, "the whole party adjourned to the Drawing room." There, "Loo, the most trifling of the ingenious contrivances invented to keep folks from the vile habit of biting their nails made a very large party happy." In addition, he observed, "Whist

affording a more sulky delight to a few more." Latrobe did not join in the games, and was relieved when he could finally depart and return to the house where he was staying. Unfortunately, during his absence "A huge Mulatto more than half naked, had been left to guard the room. Overcome with sleep and toddy, he had stretched himself upon my bed, indulging the former and evacuating the latter. It was not to be remedied. The effluvia of his performance poisoned the whole chamber, and sent me back to the inn." His troubles were not over, however, for upon arriving at the inn, Latrobe found a faro game in full progress. He went upstairs anyway, determined to get some rest, "but the explosions of joy from below banished sleep till past twelve." Weariness finally overcame him, and he slept soundly until six o'clock in the morning, when a drunken colonel staggered in and collapsed on top of him.

HOYLE's GAMES

IMPROVED:

BEING

PRACTICAL TREATISES on the following FASHIONABLE GAMES, VIZ.

WHIST	CHESS
QUADRILLE	BILLIARDS
PIQUET	AND
BACK-GAMMON	TENNIS.

WITH

The eſtabliſhed RULES of GAME.

By JAMES BEAUFORT, Esq.
Of CAVENDISH-SQUARE.

PHILADELPHIA:

PRINTED FOR AND SOLD BY H. AND P. RICE, Nº. 50 MARKET STREET. SOLD ALSO BY JAMES RICE AND CO. MARKET STREET, BALTIMORE.

1796.

FIG. 10.

FIG. 11.

FIG. 12.

Although any given card table could be used for nearly any card game, certain table shapes and sizes could accommodate some games more easily than others. Two-person games, such as cribbage, required a table of only modest proportions. Loo and faro, on the other hand, were best played by more than four people, each playing independently, and thus needed relatively larger tables. The playing surface of the loo table illustrated by Thomas Sheraton in the *Cabinet Dictionary* (vol. II, pl. 58), for example, measures 4 feet 6 inches by 6 feet 9 inches. In London gaming houses, special faro tables with a recess for the banker or croupier on one side and a pattern of deep oval wells for counters around the edge were used, although no surviving American faro table is known. The triangular tripod tables used in England are not found in the Federal period, when ombre was replaced by four-handed quadrille.[21] The versatility of circular card tables no doubt largely accounts for the widespread popularity of this shape. Round tables could easily accommodate loo and faro, as well as four-handed games such as whist and quadrille. Also, tables with four legs and no flyleg or two flylegs necessitated the least amount of leg-straddling by the players, making them particularly suitable

FIG. 13.
Four playing cards made by Thomas Creswick, no. 16 Skinner Street, Snow Hill, London, ca. 1820. Cary Collection, The Beinecke Rare Book and Manuscript Library, Yale University.

Playing cards of the Federal period closely resemble those in use today, except that the court or face cards are single-headed, no indices were used, and the backs of the cards were plain. Imported English cards were generally used in the colonial period, and large quantities of them continued to be imported during the Federal period. These English cards[1] may be similar to the "quantity of real English superior Henry VIII. Playing Cards" advertised "for sale by the groce, doʒen, or single pack, at the store of T. and J. Swords, 160 Pearl-street" in the New York Evening Post, *November 5, 1802.*[2]

1. For complete details on this pack see William B. Keller, *A Catalogue of The Cary Collection of Playing Cards in the Yale University Library*, 4 vols. (New Haven: Yale University Library, 1981), entry for ENG 18, vol. 1, p. 101, and vol. 3, p. 109. General discussions of English playing cards can be found in Catherine Perry Hargrave, *A History of Playing Cards and a Bibliography of Cards and Gaming* (1930; reprint, New York: Dover Publications, 1966), pp. 169–222; Sylvia Mann, *Collecting Playing Cards* (New York: Crown Publishers, 1966), and Detlef Hoffmann, *The Playing Card: An Illustrated History* (Greenwich, Connecticut: New York Graphic Society, 1973). An extensive bibliography of playing cards from all nations is included in William Keller's catalogue of the Cary collection.
2. Rita Susswein Gottesman, comp., *The Arts and Crafts in New York: 1800–1804* (New York: The New-York Historical Society, 1965), p. 314. Many other contemporary advertisements for playing cards are reprinted in this work and in Hargrave, *A History of Playing Cards*, pp. 307–10.

for use in mixed company. Tables with essentially square tops were best suited to two- or four-handed games, in which each player sat directly across from partner or opponent.

The cards used to play these games were generally either of English (fig. 13) or American (figs. 14–16) manufacture, and differ little from those in use today. English cards had been imported into this country for many years, and they continued to move across the water in great numbers during the Federal period. Sold in book and stationery stores, they set the style for the American manufacturers who first entered the field in this period, particularly in Massachusetts and to a lesser extent in Pennsylvania. Amos Whitney, Thomas Crehore, and Jazaniah Foord were the pioneers in Massachusetts in the 1790s and, by 1814, some 400,000 packs were said to be produced annually in this country. Boston cards were imported by New York retailers as early as 1801, and by the late 1820s (or perhaps even earlier), the Foord firm was also exporting cards to

Worcester, Springfield, Providence, New Haven, Philadelphia, Baltimore, Washington, New Orleans, and elsewhere. In the Federal period, the cost of a pack of cards ranged from about 25 to 50 cents, depending on the quality of the cards. In addition to standard playing cards, educational, geographical, tarot, and other types of cards were also available.[22]

Among the necessary accouterments of the card table were small boxes (fig. 17) of varying configuration designed to hold the mother-of-pearl or ivory counters needed to play loo, quadrille, whist, Pope Joan (fig. 18), and a host of other games. Cribbage boards, sometimes with inlaid decoration, were also available for that still popular game (fig. 19).

Card playing was far from the only type of game enjoyed in the Federal period. Other table and board games, like backgammon, chess, and checkers were popular and were occasionally played on tables (fig. 20) designed specifically for them. Billiards, horse racing, hunting, fishing, ball playing, sleigh-

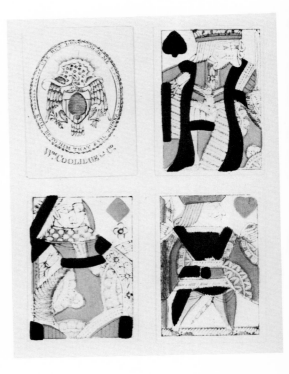

1. Charles William Janson, *The Stranger in America, 1793–1806* (London, 1807; reprint, New York: Press of the Pioneers, 1935), pp. 30–31; also see pp. 200–01.
2. William B. Keller, *A Catalogue of The Cary Collection*, entry for USA 8, vol. 2, p. 113, and vol. 4, p. 126.

ing, cockfighting, wrestling, and boxing were among the other participant and spectator sports of the time.[23]

A study of American sports from 1785 to 1835 revealed that residents of different parts of the country held different attitudes toward them: sports were played enthusiastically in the south but were regarded with skepticism in the north, while residents of the middle Atlantic states adopted a position in between.[24] This regional variation may have paralleled attitudes toward cards for even though card playing was widespread, it was still not accepted without reservation by everyone. Old objections to the custom persisted, and critics attacked card playing on several grounds (fig. 21). First, they argued, it was a waste of time in a society where attention to business and hard work were highly valued. Second, it was argued that card playing, while perhaps not necessarily evil itself, could and often did lead the player down the road to ruin. As Thomas Sheraton cautioned (*Cabinet Dictionary*, Vol. I, pp. 128–129), a card table was "a piece of furniture oftener used than to good purpose." With a logic reminiscent of the view espoused by some today that the use of marijuana is the first step toward more serious drug addiction, observers warned that "The Diversion of Cards and Dice, however Engaging, are oftner Provocatives to Avarice and Loss of Temper than mere Recreations and innocent Amusements."[25] The consequences could be much worse. As J. P. Brissot de Warville explained, probably drawing on his knowledge of the gaming houses of Europe, "the habit of them [cards] contracts the mind, prevents the acquisition of useful knowledge, leads to idleness and dissipation, and gives birth to every malignant passion."[26] Excessive gambling at cards (and other activities) was a danger to be guarded against then as now, although some modest wagering might be permitted. In Virginia, a law passed in 1792 forbade "the losing of more than twenty dollars at cards within four and twenty hours."[27] When the sums

involved became too high, blood was often shed, families were split apart, and reputations were ruined. This is what happened to "poor Tricket" in *The Gamester*. The author of this melodrama warned (p. 23): "Let each reader lay to heart the dreadful consequences of gambling: for, by first bringing a man to want, it will harden his heart even against his most beloved wife and children; and who knows whether it may not also drive him to those criminal acts, for which his very life may be justly forfeited to the laws of his country."

These caveats against card playing were essentially practical and are little different from those voiced in some quarters today, but a more deep-seated objection in Federal America was that playing at cards was a manifestation of the dreadful disease of "luxury." The symptoms of this malaise, as Kenneth Silverman has summarized, were "a passion for foreign goods, amorous trifling, ostentatious wardrobes, card playing, indifference to suffering, aristocratic longings, and preoccupation with *tone*"[28]—all of these viruses attacked the new constitution of America and threatened her republican virtue, simplicity, and independence.[29]

The role of card playing in the struggle against luxury is neatly illustrated by the controversy surrounding the founding of the Sans Souci Club, a meeting place for dancing, card playing, and socializing, in Boston. Charles Warren's study of the debate carried on in the local newspapers over this establishment[30] reveals that the battle lines were drawn largely on generational grounds: luxury (as we might expect) had greatest appeal for the young, while the older members of Boston society, raised before the Revolution, were appalled at the exchange they feared was taking place of "prudence, virtue and economy, for those glaring spectres luxury, prodigality and profligacy." Despite these warnings, many people did play cards, and several reasons for their popularity suggest themselves.

Surely many people played cards merely to

FIG. 15.
Ace of spades made by Amos Whitney and Company, Boston, 1795–1811. Cary Collection, The Beinecke Rare Book and Manuscript Library, Yale University.

Amos Whitney (1762–1804) has been identified as one of the pioneers in the American playing card industry.[1] This engraved ace of spades is one of two surviving examples bearing his label;[2] it closely resembles the ace of spades labeled by William Coolidge and Company (fig. 14).

1. Virginia and Harold Wayland, "Early American Playing-card Makers in the Boston Area, Whitney, Crehore, and Foord," *The Playing Card* (Journal of the International Playing-Card Society) 9, no. 1 (August 1980): 4–8.
2. Wayland, "Early American Playing-card Makers," p. 7. The second ace of spades, in the collection of the Society for the Preservation of New England Antiquities, Boston, was first illustrated in Catherine Perry Hargrave, "The Playing Cards of Puritan New England," *Old-Time New England* 18, no. 4 (April 1928): 176. Also see Catherine Perry Hargrave, *A History of Playing Cards*, pp. 294–95, and William B. Keller, *A Catalogue of The Cary Collection*, entry for USA 24, vol. 2, p. 116, and vol. 4, p. 130.

FIG. 16.

The twelve court cards from a deck of historical playing cards made by James Y. Humphreys (active ca. 1798–1845), Philadelphia, ca. 1828. Cary Collection, The Beinecke Rare Book and Manuscript Library, Yale University.

In this pack, American Presidents are depicted as the kings, allegorical figures as the queens, and Indians as the knaves.[1] *Based on contemporary prints,*[2] *the figures represented are: Andrew Jackson, Athena, and King Philip (spades); Thomas Jefferson, Ceres, and Joseph Brant (clubs); George Washington, Venus, and Red Jacket (hearts); John Quincy Adams, Justice, and Gy-antwachia (diamonds). James Y. Humphreys was also the publisher of* Chess Made Easy: New and Comprehensive Rules for Playing the Game of Chess (*Philadelphia, 1802*), the first book on chess to be published in this country.[3]

1. William B. Keller, *A Catalogue of The Cary Collection*, entry for USA 204, vol. 2, p. 150, and vol. 4, pp. 174–75.
2. These cards are usually dated ca. 1800; see Catherine Perry Hargrave, *A History of Playing Cards*, p. 328, and Keller, *A Catalogue of The Cary Collection*, entry for USA 204. It would appear that they were made considerably later, however, for the image of Andrew Jackson is based on a print engraved by Asher B. Durand after a portrait by John Vanderlyn and published in New York by James R. Burton in 1828; see Yale University Art Gallery, Mabel Brady Garvan Collection, acc. no. 1946.9.933. Humphreys is listed in the Philadelphia city directories from 1798 through 1845, as a printer, bookseller, and stationer and, beginning in 1814, as a playing card manufacturer.
3. Ralph K. Hagedorn, *Benjamin Franklin and Chess in Early America* (Philadelphia: University of Pennsylvania Press, 1958), pp. 48–51.

pass the time in an era that offered few diversions and lacked the modern distractions of radio, television, motion pictures, and the National Football League. As Brissot de Warville commented, "When the mind is tranquil, in the enjoyment of competence and peace, it is natural to occupy it in this way, especially in a country where there is no theatre, where men make it not a business to pay court to the women, where they read few books, and cultivate still less the sciences."[31] Many sellers of playing cards in the Federal period thus advertised that their wares would provide a "Winter Evening's Amusement."[32] Moreover, playing cards was a companionable way to fill the hours. A study of card playing in the 20th century concluded that card games allowed "families and friends to gather in the informal atmosphere of their homes in an inexpensive, relaxing, entertaining, and personally undemanding manner."[33] This conclusion is undoubtedly equally valid for a healthy percentage of Federal-period card players.

Card play also fulfilled a significant role in the relationship between the sexes. Card parties were often mixed, and the games allowed women to compete with men on equal terms, an otherwise rare occurrence. Young people in particular found card parties and other recreational events superb excuses for courting and more serious liasons.[34] Card playing was even an important part of a long-term alteration in mating customs. Lawrence Stone has detected "a slow shift from parent-directed courtship and marriage to participant-directed courtship and marriage" taking place in New England from about 1740 to 1830.[35] Frequent games of whist or quadrille were one of several key activities which allowed men and women to meet and to go about selecting their own marriage partners.

Furthermore, card playing allowed individuals to indulge their instinct for play, particularly for the types of games Roger Caillois has classified as *agón* (games based on competition) and *alea* (games based on

chance). Most card games, such as whist, combine *agón* and *alea* in a most satisfactory way that no doubt accounts for their lasting popularity. As Caillois states, in these games "chance determines the distribution of the hands dealt to each player, and the players then play the hands that blind luck has assigned to them as best they can."[36] In this respect, whist stands as an allegory for the human experience.[37]

In other games, such as faro and to a lesser extent loo, *alea* plays a larger role, and it is interesting to speculate on why these games in which the element of chance is very strong were so popular in Federal America. Faro was played by a large group of players who simply bet against the dealer and won or lost on each card turned up. These individuals, about whom the critics of card playing were worried, were probably motivated by the same complex combination of psychological factors that affect compulsive gamblers today.[38] In their frenzy, they reached the state Caillois terms *ilinx*, or vertigo (p. 73), in which "they are no longer aware of fatigue and are scarcely conscious of what is going on around them."

Gambling's appeal may have been a response to sweeping social changes taking place in America, changes which were also creating what W. J. Rorabaugh has provocatively called an "alcoholic republic."[39] In the post-Revolution years, he suggests, Americans as a whole suffered from feelings of anxiety, aggression, guilt, insecurity, and a general inability to cope with the high ideals and goals of their new society (p. 179). These conditions and others resulted in the fact that "Americans between 1790 and 1830 drank more alcoholic beverages per capita than ever before or since" (p. ix), and they may also account for the popularity of gambling at the same time. Those who sought release in the bottle may have found similar solace in the artificial stimulation of high-stakes gambling. The drunken colonels and majors who played faro all night, disturbing Latrobe's sleep,

*Small boxes such as this example,
often painted or lacquered, were
used to contain the mother-of-pearl
or ivory counters, often called fish,
used for keeping score in many
card games.*[1] *Loo, for example,
was "played with the assistance of
counters" and "two kinds of
counters are sufficient, of which the
larger may be considered as equal
to five of the smaller."*[2] *"Sets of
Loo counters," "Quadrille boxes,"
and "Quadrille pools," were
among the card-playing equipage
offered for sale in contemporary
advertisements,*[3] *and Captain
Solomon Ingraham of Norwich,
Connecticut, owned "1 card box
with Pearl Counters" valued at
$4.00 when he died in 1805.*[4]

1. A set of four red lacquered
boxes, each bearing a revolving
disk for one of the four suits of
cards, and containing ivory and
bone counters similarly marked, is
in the collection of the National
Society of the Colonial Dames of
America, Wethersfield, Connecticut; see *1776: The British Study of
the American Revolution* (London:
National Maritime Museum, 1976),
no. 77.
2. The use of counters in loo is
described in many editions of
Hoyle. A loo box in the collection
of the Henry Francis du Pont
Winterthur Museum is illustrated
in Mary Cable et al., *American
Manners and Morals* (New York:
American Heritage, 1969), p. 67.
3. Alice Morse Earle, *Customs and
Fashions in Old New England*
(1893; reprint, Rutland, Vermont:
Charles E. Tuttle Company, 1973),
p. 240, and Catherine Perry Hargrave, *A History of Playing Cards*,
pp. 309, 311.
4. Nina Fletcher Little, *Neat and
Tidy: Boxes and Their Contents
Used in Early American Households*
(New York: E. P. Dutton, 1980),
p. 175.

were combining the two methods of release
from the tensions and insecurities of every-
day life.

And, although the answers to such questions are beyond the scope of this essay, it is
tempting to dive into the murky waters of
association and suggest what some of the
deeper levels of meaning might have been
for card playing in Federal America. Perhaps
reckless gambling at loo was a subconscious
allegory for the risky speculations endemic
in the economic life of the time. New England
merchants and sea captains may have enjoyed

whist because it involved the same combination of luck and skill, the same ability to
calculate what was in other people's hands or
minds, and the same need to work independently and yet cooperatively, as were required
to complete a successful trading voyage to
the Orient. Did newly independent Americans relish in whist, quadrille, and other
games the democratic thrill of gaining victory
by vanquishing an opponent's king with a
lowly two of trumps? Certainly, cards were a
safe diversion, a means of comfortably socializing, while avoiding disruptive and poten-

FIG. 18.
Charles Williams, *Pope-Joan*, published in London, 1805. The Lewis Walpole Library.

Candlesticks, a snuffer and tray, and a round box for counters rest on this circular card table which is protected by a removable green cover. The game of Pope Joan is in progress here. The nine of diamonds was called Pope, and when it was turned up as trump, a relatively rare occurrence, the dealer won the hand and the game, as well as a sum for every card dealt to each player. This good fortune has apparently just been bestowed on the player on the right.

FIG. 19.
Thomas Rowlandson (1756–1827), *Twopenny Cribbage*, published in London, 1799. The Lewis Walpole Library.

Still popular today, cribbage is ordinarily played by two people, as in this view, using a standard deck and a board with holes and pegs for keeping score.[1] "New In Laid Cribbage Boxes" were advertised in the Salem *Gazette in 1784 and may have resembled the one in use here.[2]*

1. John Scarne, *Scarne's Encyclopedia of Games*, pp. 221–27.
2. Alice Morse Earle, *Customs and Fashions in Old New England*, p. 240. An illustration of an inlaid cribbage board dated 1735 can be found in Jane Carson, *Colonial Virginians at Play* (Williamsburg, Virginia: Colonial Williamsburg, 1965), opposite p. 70, and an English or American mahogany cribbage board, with a box in the center to hold the cards, dated 1790–1830, in the collection of the Henry Francis du Pont Winterthur Museum, is illustrated in Nina Fletcher Little, *Neat and Tidy*, p. 175, fig. 175.

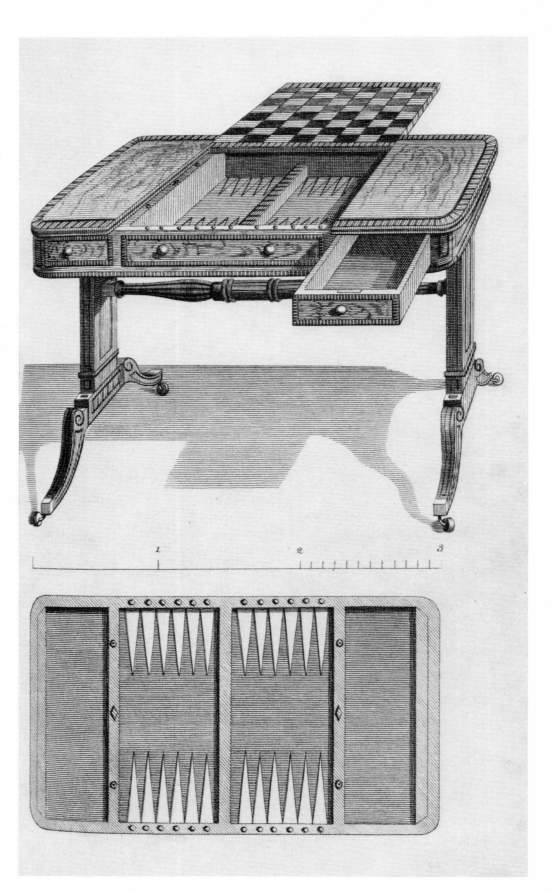

FIG. 20.
Design for an "Occasional Table," from Thomas Sheraton, *The Cabinet Dictionary* (London, 1803), vol. 2, plate 59. Yale University Art Gallery.

English and American gaming tables of this general type, designed specifically for backgammon and chess, were also used in Federal America, although made on a much smaller scale than regular card tables.[1] *Such specialized examples were probably custom-made and found only in the homes of the more well-to-do; portable folding backgammon and chess boards much like those in use today were less expensive substitutes.*

1. American Federal-period gaming tables are rare. Among those from various regions and in varying designs which have been published are a Boston table in the collection of Mr. and Mrs. George M. Kaufman (see *Paul Revere's Boston, 1735–1818* [Boston: Museum of Fine Arts, 1975], pp. 194–95); a New York example by Charles Honore Lannuier now in the Museum of the City of New York (see Nancy McClelland, *Duncan Phyfe and the English Regency, 1795–1830* [New York: William R. Scott, 1939], pl. 173); a table attributed to Baltimore in a private collection (see Helen Comstock, "Baltimore Furniture in the Collection of Mr. and Mrs. Sifford Pearre," *Antiques* 82, no. 6 [December 1962]: 633); and two Massachusetts tables in the Bayou Bend collection (see David B. Warren, *Bayou Bend: American Furniture, Paintings and Silver from the Bayou Bend Collection* [Houston: The Museum of Fine Arts, Houston, 1975], nos. 156, 157).

tially dangerous arguments in an era of virulent political controversy. Women may have especially enjoyed trouncing their male opponents. Was gambling in frontier taverns a means of attaining an intense state of consciousness which reinforced the vigor of the self in the face of the rigors of living on the edge of the wilderness?

It may be possible to formulate answers to these types of questions, and to test their validity as hypotheses, by examining a specific game in detail. A close look at the symbolic content of the rules and strategy of loo suggests several reasons why this game may have been so popular in upwardly mobile, fashionable circles of Federal America, and how a particular game might mirror the attitudes and values of its time.[40] Loo (called lanterloo in earlier times and pam-loo later on) resembles poker in some respects, but whereas poker is generally played by men, loo was played by both sexes, and was especially popular with women. This aspect of the game alone—the idea of women gambling in public—was sufficiently novel to guarantee a large share of loo's success.[41] The fact that the term for losing a hand, "looed," is pronounced the same as lewd, lent the game a mildly risqué tone, and was no doubt the source of many puns. It was recorded that the ladies, "when they were looed, pronounced the word in a very mincing manner,"[42] and in George Tucker's poem on loo, Tom Shuffle remarks meaningfully to Mrs. Crutch:

"*No indeed: But I've notic'd whenever you* stood,
"*If I was before you I always was* loo'd.

While such remarks are hardly titillating, they added a little spice to the game that made it attractive to people who considered themselves to be smart and *au courant*. Such badinage also played a role in the new rituals of courtship in which card playing was an important part.

The game can be played by four, five, six, or seven players, although it is best played by five or six.[43] To begin the game, the dealer puts five counters in the pool, and then deals five cards to each player. After the players have evaluated their cards, each has the option to play (or stand, as they called it), or to fold (throw up). A player choosing to participate is allowed to hold or to discard all or part of his hand, in an attempt to strengthen it by drawing to a "flush" or "blaze,"[44] or by increasing his number of trumps. If no one has a flush or blaze, in which instance the player wins the hand immediately, the cards are played one at a time in turn, each player having to follow suit if possible; the high card or the highest trump takes the trick.

If a player fails to win at least one of the five tricks in each hand, he is "looed" and must forfeit a sum to the pool. In limited loo, the amount (called the loo) is a standard, predetermined figure, perhaps 20 or 25 counters. But in unlimited loo, the player is liable for the entire sum contained in the pool, the pool consisting of the five counters entered by the dealer of the hand and the loos from previous hands. The winners of tricks divide the pool proportionately. In unlimited loo, the pool can rise to a considerable sum after only a few hands and losses could therefore be very high. Winnings were generally distributed somewhat equally, unless a player was dealt or drew to a flush or blaze and won the entire pool himself.

Part of loo's appeal may have been derived from its combination of elements that looked back toward the early 18th century with others that looked forward to the later 19th century. One of the most interesting features of the standard five-card version of loo is the fact that the knave (or jack) of clubs, referred to as pam, has extraordinary powers. This card "ranks above every other card in the pack . . . is subject to no laws, but may be played on any suit, at any time, even though you have in your hand the suit which is led." Moreover, and most significantly, "if you hold pam, you cannot be looed." Pam's prowess, determined arbitrarily by the rules of the game, is reminiscent of the type of

*A strong moral undercurrent
against gambling at cards and
dice exists in American literature
and legislation from the 17th
century to the present. Parson
Weems's windy diatribe about
gambling was only one of a series
of tracts he penned that were directed against various sins and idle
practices.*

*Weems would have been proud of
Lyman Beecher (1775–1863).
When Beecher entered Yale in
1793 the "college was in a most
ungodly state. The college church
was almost extinct. Most of the
students were skeptical, and row-
dies were plenty. Wine and liquors
were kept in many rooms; intem-
perance, profanity, gambling, and
licentiousness were common."
Beecher, by his own account,
narrowly escaped these temptations.
He "was invited to play [cards],
once, in a classmate's room. I did
so, and won. Next day I won
again, then lost, and ended in
debt. I saw immediately where-
unto that would grow; obtained
leave of absence, went home for a
week, till cured of that mania,
and never touched a card afterward."[1]*

*The portrait painter Chester
Harding (1792–1866) had a
similar educational experience
while traveling along the Mohawk
River in upstate New York about
1815. Harding (who should have
known better, since he "had been
taught to believe by my father
that cards and novels were the
chief instruments of the Devil in
seducing mortals from the paths of
virtue"), was fleeced of a few
dollars by three strangers who
played a simple card trick on the
unsuspecting painter. Harding
"bore the loss of the money better
than I did the way in which it was
lost," and the "lesson has never
been forgotten."[2] Unlike Beecher*

hereditary authority taken for granted in the
17th and 18th centuries, and would seem to
have had little appeal for republican Americans. However, in the symbolic card family,
the jack represents the younger son or heir,
while the suit of clubs has the emotional
connotation of fear and the state of being
exploited.[45] The importance of pam in loo,
therefore, might be seen as an elevation of
the previously oppressed younger son over
traditional, established authority, a leitmotif
the significance of which would presumably
not have been lost on American patriots.

Loo also places a great deal of responsibility on individuals. They must choose
whether or not to play each hand, to stand
or to throw up. If the decision is made to
play, they then can choose which cards to
hold or to discard. Partnerships of any kind

were not allowed. The first goal of each
player was to protect himself by "getting
safe"—winning a trick—and thereby avoid
the possibility of being looed. This aspect of
the game may have been one reason why loo
had such appeal among women. Women
could play independently; all players, men and
women alike, were equal (unless someone
held pam).

The decision to play or not to play, made
after examining the cards, was regarded as a
particularly important facet of the game, and
one which distinguishes loo from other card
games. "From this peculiarity in the game, a
coolness and command of temper is of the
utmost importance. It is of less consequence
to know how to play the cards well, than it is
to know when to stand, and when to throw
up." This allows the individual a remarkable
amount of personal freedom and autonomy.
If the player is dealt a bad hand (in loo or in
life, by the conditions of his or her birth), he
can simply stand his ground, wait, and ven-
ture forth again under different circumstances.
There is a freedom of choice not present in
whist, for example, where one must simply
cope with the hand that is dealt. Acceptance
of one's position in loo is not required; the
potential for improvement is always there. A
servant need not always be a servant, or a
woman must not always accept inferior stat-
us, might be two of the lessons implied. This
is perfectly in harmony with the egalitarian,
individualistic atmosphere of the era.

In each hand, the immediate goal after
winning a trick, was to try to stop as many
other players as possible from winning any
tricks. This technique, "to play for the good
of the loo," required the player "to loo as
many as possible, without any regard to
making tricks," even though one's eventual
share of the pool was determined by the
number of tricks won. This was considered
the honorable thing to do, even though it
meant personal disaster for the player who
was looed. For without the possibility of a
loo, there could be no advantage to all. The
greatest good for the greatest number is the

34

and Harding, however, many Americans continued card playing and gambling, as do the two men in the background of this illustration.

1. *The Autobiography of Lyman Beecher*, ed. Barbara M. Cross (Cambridge, Massachusetts: The Belknap Press of Harvard University Press, 1961), vol. I, p. 27.
2. *A Sketch of Chester Harding, Artist, Drawn by His Own Hand*, ed. Margaret E. White (1929; reprint, New York: Kennedy Galleries / Da Capo Press, 1970), pp. 11–13, 21. Harding's reminiscences were originally written in 1865.

principal underlying this strategy, a principle that is in harmony with Federal beliefs.

A significant aspect of loo is its combination of fluidity and stability, of innovation and tradition. The game lacks rigidity in several ways, and pam is an additional variable that preserves its holder's options. But once a hand has started, play moves along in an ordered, controlled way. Trump is arbitrarily determined by turning up a card, and the cards rank as in whist (ace is high, again indicating much regard for the individual). Players must follow suit, and are governed by standard card-playing rules and etiquette. Thus while there is a great deal of variability inherent in the game, there is a solid and reassuring foundation of traditional values underneath. The old order has not been overthrown entirely.

Loo thus emphasized the importance of individual autonomy, of caution, and of working for the common good once the individual's security was achieved. It rewarded those who took a middle course: "A person who has the command of his temper, and is governed solely by judgment and prudence; who is not too much elated by good fortune, nor too much depressed by bad, possesses a great advantage." The virtues required in loo might well be those required to cope with the fluctuating economic fortunes of the time, or the Federalist–Republican debates over the nature of the new government. Pursuing a cautious, steady course was a way for a person to navigate the hazards of loo, and also to maintain his equilibrium amid the insecurities of life in a new nation uncertain yet optimistic about its future. The loo player who threw caution to the wind and repeatedly stood on poor hands, thus inevitably going down gloriously, had his parallel in the speculators of the time, such as Robert Morris, who "financed" the Revolution but then lost his fortune in land speculations during the 1790s and ended his career in debtor's prison.

It is important to remember that it would be all too easy to overstate the significance of card playing in Federal life. There is very little evidence that it possessed for society at large the same deep symbolism that the cockfight held for the natives of Bali[46] or that horse racing held for the gentry in late 17th- and early 18th-century Virginia.[47] Cards were popular both before and after the Federal era, and it is important to see Federal card games as a relative high point in card-playing in American history, rather than as an isolated phenomenon. It might be instructive to search for characteristics common to eras when card playing was at one of its periodic high points of popularity, or when other types of games were extraordinarily popular. Are there any parallels, for example, in the national temperament during the Federal period and during the early 1920s, when the craze for Mah-Jongg reached epic proportions, or during the early 1950s when the canasta fad swept the country, nearly doubling the number of playing cards sold each year?[48] Are these types of games, for example, particularly popular during post war periods? Although much has been written about the causes and effects of gambling, as yet there has been little research into the seemingly fruitful question of the significance of card playing and similar amusements in American social history.[49]

Notes

Most of the sources used are cited below. The reader is also directed to the references cited in the figure captions. The writer is grateful for the assistance of Barbara McLean Ward, Edward S. Cooke Jr., Edgar de N. Mayhew, Joan H. Sussler, and Kevin M. Sweeney.

1. See *Publications of the Colonial Society of Massachusetts* 31 (1935): 338; also see the 1767 rules on p. 357. The early Massachusetts laws on gaming are reproduced in *The Colonial Laws of Massachusetts, Reprinted from the Edition of 1672, with the Supplements Through 1686* (Boston, 1887), pp. 57–58. Prosecutions under this law are recorded in several places; see for example *Records and Files of the Quarterly Courts of Essex County, Massachusetts* (Salem: Essex Institute, 1974), vol. IX (1683–86), p. 24. For other comments on card playing in the 17th century, see Edwin Powers, *Crime and Punishment in Early Massachusetts, 1620–1692: A Documentary History* (Boston: Beacon Press, 1966), pp. 205–06, and Foster Rhea Dulles, *A History of Recreation: America Learns to Play*, 2nd ed. (New York: Appleton-Century-Crofts, 1965), pp. 5–6, 19.

2. See Joseph Downs, *American Furniture: Queen Anne and Chippendale Periods in The Henry Francis du Pont Winterthur Museum* (New York: Macmillan, 1952), nos. 335–49, and Morrison H. Heckscher, "The New York serpentine card table," *Antiques* 103, no. 5 (May 1973): 974–83.

3. Quoted in Dulles, *History of Recreation*, p. 44. An excellent discussion of card playing in the pre-Revolutionary south can be found in Jane Carson, *Colonial Virginians at Play* (Williamsburg, Virginia: Colonial Williamsburg, 1965), pp. 49–72.

4. The social history of the Federal period is discussed in John Allen Krout and Dixon Ryan Fox, *The Completion of Independence, 1790–1830* (1944; reprint, New York: The Macmillan Company, 1958); and Russel Blaine Nye, *The Cultural Life of the New Nation, 1776–1830* (New York: Harper & Row, 1960). Documents pertaining to the culture of the era are excerpted in Gordon S. Wood, ed., *The Rising Glory of America, 1760–1820* (New York: George Braziller, 1971).

5. *The United States in 1800* (Ithaca, New York: Cornell University Press, 1963), p. 64.

6. Mrs. Anne N. Royall, *Sketches of History, Life, and Manners in the United States* (New Haven: printed for the author, 1826), p. 359.

7. Washington card parties are mentioned in Gaillard Hunt, ed., *The First Forty Years of Washington Society, Portrayed by the Family Letters of Mrs. Samuel Harrison Smith* (New York: Charles Scribner's Sons, 1906), pp. 38, 45, 55–56. The Penrise incident is described in Charles William Janson, *The Stranger in America, 1793–1806* (London, 1807; reprint, New York: Press of the Pioneers, 1935), p. 309. An even bloodier conflict over cards is also discussed on the same page.

8. "Letters of Rebecca Franks," *The Pennsylvania Magazine of History and Biography* 23, no. 3 (1899): 304, quoted in Susan Burrows Swan, *Plain & Fancy: American Women and Their Needlework, 1700–1850* (New York: Holt, Rinehart and Winston, 1977), p. 151. Sally Otis, quoted in Samuel Eliot Morison, *Harrison Gray Otis, 1765–1848: The Urbane Federalist* (Boston: Houghton Mifflin, 1969), p. 146. Jane Louise Mesick, *The English Traveller in America, 1785–1835* (New York: Columbia University Press, 1922), p. 105. This work and Allan Nevins, ed., *American Social History As Recorded by British Travellers* (1923; reprint, New York: Henry Holt, 1934), are invaluable guides to the very useful travel literature of the period.

9. *The New Democracy in America: Travels of Francisco de Miranda in the United States, 1783–84*, trans. Judson P. Wood; ed. John S. Ezell (Norman, Oklahoma: University of Oklahoma Press, 1963), p. 54.

10. Latrobe's plan, now in the Library of Congress, is illustrated and discussed in Talbot Hamlin, *Benjamin Henry Latrobe* (New York: Oxford University Press, 1955), pp. 117–19, pl. 9.

11. Charles Warren, "Samuel Adams and the Sans Souci Club in 1785," Massachusetts Historical Society *Proceedings* 60 (1927): 318–44; Thomas Pemberton's 1794 description of the Boston theater is quoted in Harold Kirker, *The Architecture of Charles Bulfinch* (Cambridge, Massachusetts: Harvard University Press, 1969), p. 68.

12. Page 11; *The Gamester*, by an unknown author, was probably first published in England. It was printed here by B. & J. Johnson, no. 147 High-Street, Philadelphia, and bears an illustration of Tricket and his companion Betsworth playing cards on a roof they should have been repairing.

13. "The Furnishings of Richmond Hill in 1797: The Home of Aaron Burr in New York City," *The New-York Historical Society Quarterly Bulletin* 11, no. 1 (April 1927): 17–18.

14. Gerald W. R. Ward, *The Peirce-Nichols House* (Salem: Essex Institute, 1976), p. 19. Robert C. Alberts, *The Golden Voyage: The Life and Times of William Bingham, 1752–1804* (Boston: Houghton Mifflin, 1969), pp. 470–71; lottery was a card game of the period for a large number of players. Marie G. Kimball, "The Original Furnishings of the White House, Part I," *Antiques* 15, no. 6 (June 1929): 485–86. Garrett, "The Furnishing of Newport Houses, 1780–1800," *Rhode Island History* 18, no. 1 (January

1959): 15. Cooke, "Domestic Space in the Federal Period: Inventories of Salem Merchants," *Essex Institute Historical Collections* 116, no. 4 (October 1980): 248–64; quotation p. 251.

15. Charles F. Montgomery, *American Furniture: The Federal Period, 1788–1825* (New York: Viking Press, 1966), pp. 319–20, 360. Also see Ralph Fastnedge, *Sheraton Furniture* (London: Faber & Faber, 1962), p. 55, n. 1, which refers to a 1782 advertisement in the Dublin *Evening Post* offering for sale "Card Tables on a new construction (both ornamented and plain) which appear like small Pier Tables." Berry B. Tracy has gone so far as to state that the "primary function" of card tables "was as ornament," while "only secondarily" were they used for card playing; see his *Federal Furniture and Decorative Arts at Boscobel* (New York: Boscobel Restoration, and Harry N. Abrams, 1981), p. 51. For a general discussion of the Federal interior see Edgar deN. Mayhew and Minor Myers Jr., *A Documentary History of American Interiors from the Colonial Era to 1915* (New York: Charles Scribner's Sons, 1980), pp. 78–99.

16. Margaret Schiffer, *Chester County, Pennsylvania, Inventories, 1682–1850* (Exton, Pennsylvania: Schiffer Publishing, 1974), p. 126.

17. Schiffer, p. 126.

18. Tucker's poem, entitled "*A letter from Hickory Cornhill Esq. to his friend in the country,*" was originally published in the Richmond, Virginia, *Enquirer*, January 9, 1806. The excerpt included here is based on the text as originally published; a slightly different text is reprinted in Henry Chafetz, *Play the Devil: A History of Gambling in the United States from 1492 to 1955* (New York: Clarkson N. Potter, 1960), pp. 35–36. For information on Tucker (1775–1861) see Robert Colin McLean, *George Tucker: Moral Philosopher and Man of Letters* (Chapel Hill, North Carolina: The University of North Carolina Press, 1961), pp. 55–57.

19. *The American Geography; or, A View of the Present Situation of the United States of America* (London: John Stockdale, 1794), p. 532.

20. *The Virginia Journals of Benjamin Henry Latrobe, 1795–1798*, ed. Edward C. Carter II (New Haven: Yale University Press, 1977), vol. 1, pp. 103–04. Later, a fight broke out at his inn, and "in the fray the Faro table was overset"; see p. 106.

21. For a discussion of the evolution and varieties of English card tables see Ralph Edwards, *The Shorter Dictionary of English Furniture* (London: Country Life, 1964), pp. 517–27.

22. The information in the paragraph is based upon Catherine Perry Hargrave, *A History of Playing Cards and a Bibliography of Cards and Gaming* (1930; reprint, New York: Dover Publications, 1966), pp. 291–96, 301, 302, 327; Virginia and Harold Wayland, "Early American Playing-card Makers in the Boston Area, Whitney, Crehore and Foord," *The Playing Card* (Journal of the International Playing-card Society) 9, no. 1 (August 1980): 3–22; and William B. Keller, *A Catalogue of the Cary Collection of Playing Cards in the Yale University Library*, 4 vols. (New Haven: Yale University Library, 1981), entries for English and American cards.

23. Jennie Holliman, *American Sports, 1785–1835* (Durham, North Carolina: Seeman Press, 1931), and Louise C. Belden, "Billiards in America before 1830," *Antiques* 87, no. 1 (January 1965): 99–101.

24. Holliman, pp. 178–92.

25. *The Universal Penman, Engraved by George Bickham, London, 1743* (New York: Dover Publications, 1941), p. 87.

26. *New Travels in the United States of America Performed in 1788* (London: J. S. Jordan, 1792), vol. I, p. 103.

27. Duc de Liancourt La Rochefoucault, *Travels Through the United States of North America* (London: T. Davison, 1799), vol. II, p. 39.

28. *A Cultural History of the American Revolution* (New York: Thomas Y. Crowell, 1976), p. 506 and passim.

29. For a discussion of the threat of luxury to the new republic and its consequences, see Silverman, *A Cultural History*, pp. 504–36; Howard Mumford Jones, *O Strange New World* (New York: Viking Press, 1967), chap. IX; and Neil Harris, *The Artist in American Society* (New York: George Braziller, 1966), chap. 2.

30. "Samuel Adams and the Sans Souci Club," p. 322.

31. *New Travels*, vol. I, p. 102–03.

32. See, for example, the advertisement of T. and J. Swords in the New-York *Evening Post* for November 5, 1802, cited in Rita Susswein Gottesman, comp., *The Arts and Crafts in New York, 1800–1804* (New York: The New-York Historical Society, 1965), p. 314, and the 1794 ad cited in Hargrave, *A History of Playing Cards*, p. 307.

33. Irving Crespi, "The Social Significance of Card Playing As a Leisure Time Activity," *American Sociological Review* 21 (1956): 717–21; quotation p. 720.

34. Robert W. Malcolmson, *Popular Recreations in English Society, 1700–1850* (Cambridge: Cambridge University Press, 1973), p. 54.

35. *The Family, Sex and Marriage in England, 1500–1800* (New York: Harper & Row, 1977), pp. 320–21; also pp. 316, 402.

36. *Man, Play, and Games*, trans. Meyer Borash (New York: Free Press of Glencoe, 1961), pp. 14–19, 36, 54.

37. The wider social implications of changes in the game of whist during the mid-18th century are sug-

gested in Ronald Paulson, *Popular and Polite Art in the Age of Hogarth and Fielding* (Notre Dame, Indiana: University of Notre Dame Press, 1979), chap. 7, "Card Games and Hoyle's Whist."

38. There is a vast theoretical literature on gambling. Those works consulted by the writer include David D. Allen, *The Nature of Gambling* (New York: Coward-McCann, 1952); Edmund Bergler, *The Psychology of Gambling* (New York: Hill and Wang, 1957); Jay Livingston, *Compulsive Gamblers: Observations on Action and Abstinence* (New York: Harper & Row, 1974); Robert O. Herman, *Gamblers and Gambling: Motives, Institutions, and Controls* (Lexington, Massachusetts: D. C. Heath, 1976); and William R. Eadington, ed., *Gambling and Society: Interdisciplinary Studies on the Subject of Gambling* (Springfield, Illinois: Charles C. Thomas, 1976). Additional references can be found in Stephen Powell, comp., *A Gambling Bibliography Based on the Collection, University of Nevada, Las Vegas* (Las Vegas: University of Nevada, 1972).

39. Rorabaugh, *The Alcoholic Republic: An American Tradition* (New York: Oxford University Press, 1979).

40. The analysis offered here is based on the methods used in Charlotte Olmsted, *Heads I Win, Tails You Lose* (New York: Macmillan, 1962), chap. 4, and Paulson, "Card Games and Hoyle's Whist." The quotations concerning the rules of loo are derived from *Hoyle's Improved Edition of the Rules for Playing Fashionable Games* (New York: W. C. Borradaile, 1830), pp. 138–53. Modern rules for several varieties of loo can be found in John Scarne, *Scarne's Encyclopedia of Games* (New York: Harper & Row, 1973), pp. 249–50.

41. Women had played cards for money in the colonial era, but the sums involved were generally small, and significant gambling by women, even in the south, was rare. See Julia Cherry Spruill, *Women's Life and Work in the Southern Colonies* (1938; reprint, New York: W. W. Norton, 1972), p. 108. The novelty of playing cards for money was mentioned in a letter of January 17, 1801, from Maria Trumbull to her mother; see *A Season in New York: Letters of Harriet and Maria Trumbull*, ed. Helen M. Morgan (Pittsburgh: University of Pittsburgh Press, 1969), pp. 92–95.

42. Sir Augustus Foster, Secretary of the British Legation in Washington, 1801–05, quoted in Herbert Asbury, *Sucker's Progress: An Informal History of Gambling in America from the Colonies to Canfield* (New York: Dodd, Mead, 1938), p. 50.

43. "If there be less than five, a loo will seldom happen, and if more than six, the pack will frequently be insufficient."

44. "*Flush* is five cards, all of one suit. *Pam flush* is four flush cards and pam. *Blaze* is five face or court cards. *Pam blaze* is four blaze cards and pam. . . . They rank in the following order: 1st, a *pam-flush*, or *pam-blaze*; —2d, a *flush of trumps*; —3d, any *other flush*; —4th, a *blaze*; —and if there be two or more equal flushes or blazes out, the eldest is the best."

45. Olmsted, *Heads I Win, Tails You Lose*, pp. 37–38. The exact date when pam was introduced as a standard part of loo is unclear. It was not part of lanterloo as decribed by John Cotton in *The Compleat Gamester* (1674 and 1734 editions), but does appear in early 19th-century rules for the game.

46. Clifford Geertz, *The Interpretation of Cultures: Selected Essays* (New York: Basic Books, 1973), chap. 15, "Deep Play: Notes on the Balinese Cockfight."

47. T. H. Breen, "Horses and Gentlemen: The Cultural Significance of Gambling Among the Gentry of Virginia," *William and Mary Quarterly*, 3rd ser., 34, no. 2 (April 1977): 239–57.

48. Frederick Lewis Allen, *Only Yesterday* (1931; reprint, New York: Harper & Row, 1957), p. 82; Crespi, "Social Significance," p. 717.

49. In addition to Caillois, *Man, Play, and Games*, and the brief article by Crespi, little else has been written on card games in this regard, although Johan Huizinga's well-known work *Homo Ludens: A Study of the Play Element in Culture* (London: Temple Smith, 1970), originally published in 1938, is helpful. Louis A. Zurcher Jr., "The 'Friendly' Poker Game: A Study of an Ephemeral Role," *Social Forces* 49 (1970): 173–86, is an interesting look at the various relationships and forces at work during card playing. Many references to research on all types of games in all cultures can be found in Elliott M. Avedon and Brian Sutton-Smith, *The Study of Games* (New York: John Wiley & Sons, 1971).

Design Books and Price Books for American Federal-Period Card Tables

Patricia E. Kane

The card tables included in Hewitt's study reflect the stylistic movement called neoclassicism, which spread through Europe and America in the second half of the 18th century. In America, furniture of this era is generally referred to as Federal since it came into fashion following the Revolution, when the federal government was formed. The new style rejected the asymmetrical and curvilinear forms and the naturalistic and Chinese ornament of the rococo, which in English and American furniture is customarily identified as the Chippendale style. Instead, it relied upon geometry, strict axial symmetry, and classical motifs. The overall appearance of Federal furniture is angular, light, and fragile, with ornament held within the confines of form.

A stylistic analysis of Federal-period card tables is not the aim of this essay. Rather, as a complement to Hewitt's systematic analysis, it examines the design books and price books of the 1790–1820 period to find what they reveal about card tables of that era. This traditional approach explores the nature of the ideas coming from England, the ways in which those ideas were interpreted in America, the contemporary terminology that was used to describe forms and details of card tables, the costs involved in producing them, and the advent of price books at a time when cabinetmaking was undergoing a transformation from craft to industry in this country.

The pertinent English design books are *The Cabinet-Maker and Upholsterer's Guide* (1788; 1789; 1794) by George Hepplewhite (d. 1786), *The Cabinet-Maker and Upholsterer's Drawing-Book* (published serially 1791–93; 1794; 1802), and *The Cabinet Dictionary* (1803) by Thomas Sheraton (1751–1806). Price books were a new phenomenon in this period. Although they are thought to have existed in manuscript form as early as the mid-18th century, the first published example, *The London Cabinet Book of Prices*, appeared in 1788. Price books are of two types—retail price agreements compiled by masters, and prices of piecework drawn up by journeymen, by masters, or by masters and journeymen in cooperation. As such they are valuable sources for detailed information on the shapes and ornament of a wide assortment of furniture forms. The first London price book was followed by a second edition in 1793 and a third in 1803. Also emanating from London in the period of Hewitt's study were *The Prices of Cabinet Work* (1797) and *The London Cabinet-Makers' Union Book of Prices* (1811). The London price books spawned American counterparts in the largest and most highly organized centers of cabinetmaking. Those considered here pertain to wage agreements between masters and journeymen: *The Journeymen Cabinet and Chair-Makers Philadelphia Book of Prices* (1795), *The Cabinet-Makers' Philadelphia and London Book of Prices* (1796), *The Journeymen Cabinet and Chair Makers' New-York Book of Prices* (1796), *The New-York Book of Prices for Cabinet and Chair Work Agreed*

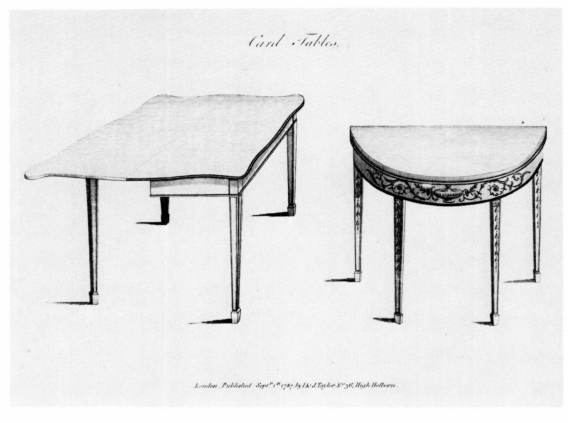

Upon by the Employers (1802), *The New-York Revised Prices for Manufacturing Cabinet and Chair Work* (1810), *The Journeymen Cabinet and Chairmakers' Pennsylvania Book of Prices* (1811), and *The New-York Book of Prices for Manufacturing Cabinet and Chair Work* (1817).[1]

There is ample evidence both from surviving furniture and documentary sources that design and price books were widely owned and used in America. Numerous examples of American furniture have a close affinity to British designs.[2] The Boston cabinetmaker Thomas Seymour (1771–1848) owned a first edition of Thomas Sheraton's *Drawing-Book*.[3] Advertisements like this one of the New York cabinetmaker Charles Watts appeared in American newspapers: "wanted from 8 to 15 Journeymen Cabinet and Chair-Makers, to go to Charleston, South Carolina. . . . I hereby oblige myself to pay to any good workman, who is capable of doing the general run of Cabinet-

work seventy-five percent advance on the New London book of Cabinet prices, published in 1793."[4] Duncan Phyfe owned a copy of the *New-York Revised Prices for Manufacturing Cabinet and Chair Work* (1810), and at the time of his death in 1854 his estate included "1 lot of Cabinet Makers' Books and Drawings."[5]

The purposes of the various design books and price books were quite distinct, and they appealed to different audiences. George Hepplewhite's posthumously published *Guide* was in the tradition of earlier 18th-century furniture pattern books such as Thomas Chippendale's *The Gentleman and Cabinet-Maker's Director* (1754, 1755, 1762), William Ince and John Mayhew's *The Universal System of Household Furniture* (1759–62), and Robert Manwaring's *The Cabinet and Chair Maker's Real Friend and Companion* (1765), all of which reported on the latest London fashions.

Hepplewhite's book addressed the broad-

FIG. 23.
George Hepplewhite, *The Cabinet-Maker and Upholsterer's Guide* (London, 1794). Plate 61. The Beinecke Rare Book and Manuscript Library, Yale University.

est possible audience, including both the "mechanic" and the "gentleman" as well as "Countrymen and Artizans whose distance from the metropolis [London] makes even an imperfect knowledge of its improvements acquired with much trouble and expence."[6] Certainly Americans could be counted among this group. Hepplewhite devotes two plates to card tables (figs. 22, 23) and in a brief explanation states (p. 12): "*Card tables* may be either square, circular or oval: the inner part is lined with green cloth; the fronts may be enriched with inlaid or painted ornaments; the tops also admit of great elegance in the same styles. Plate 61 shews four designs proper for inlaid or painted *tops* for Card Tables." Of the two tables shown, one is square with serpentine front and serpentine ends, the other is circular. These two shapes were very popular in America; however, no American tables are known with the elaborate painted or inlaid tops shown in his Plate 61. While it is not possible to say that American craftsmen copied card table designs directly from Hepplewhite, his book nevertheless communicated the latest London styles and provided a visual vocabulary of forms and appropriate ornamentation.

Thomas Sheraton's *Drawing-Book*, on the other hand, was intended for the more specialized use of cabinetmaker and upholsterer. It offered instruction for making perspective drawings and guidelines for understanding the principles of geometry, for craftsmen seeking to improve their skills, "especially [for] such of them as have a number of men under their directions."[7] Sheraton was convinced that a knowledge of the five orders of architecture and the rules of proportion had lasting value that transcended fashion which accordingly was of secondary importance, although Part III of the *Drawing-Book* does contain designs for contemporary furniture. Sheraton was apparently a trained cabinetmaker, but after arriving in London from Stockton-on-Tees in 1791, he made his career in teaching perspective drawing and

producing designs for cabinetmakers. He was also an ardent Baptist, and the Baptists' opposition to card playing may account in part for the absence of card-table designs in the first edition of the *Drawing-Book* and for Sheraton's cryptic opening statement about the card table in the *Cabinet Dictionary*, "A piece of furniture oftener used than to good purpose."[8] In the 1802 edition of the *Drawing-Book* two plates are devoted to card tables. One shows two tables with construction plans for the frames (fig. 24); the other (fig. 25) shows designs for pier and card table legs. The commentary on card tables in the *Drawing-Book* is practical;[9] it discusses the construction of the core of card table tops and suggests they be made from four-inch pieces of deal or mahogany, joined together, a production technique taken up again by Sheraton in the *Cabinet Dictionary*.

The price books, published by practicing cabinetmakers, contain detailed lists of the individual components for an assortment of furniture, which were expressed in the jargon of the day. For each part a price was given as the amount a journeyman was to be paid for making it (fig. 26). The basic form is described in a heading with options listed below as "Extras." Cost tables at the back, for computing such details as banding, stringing, and moldings, are a key section in all editions.

The first scholar to use cabinetmakers' price books as an interpretive tool was Charles Montgomery in *American Furniture: The Federal Period*, which presents much basic information about them. In addition to the specific data the price books contain about Federal-period card tables, they are helpful in providing evidence about the costs of producing the tables, the contemporary terminology for the forms, and their stylistic development.

The majority of Federal card tables feature the work of many hands—specialists such as turners, carvers, and inlayers—and, since these skills were outside the compe-

FIG. 24.
Thomas Sheraton, *The Cabinet-Maker and Upholsterer's Drawing-Book* (London, 1802). Plate 11. The Beinecke Rare Book and Manuscript Library, Yale University.

tence of the journeyman cabinetmaker, the costs for them are not included in the price books. Consequently, we can establish a cost only for a card table that is exclusively the product of journeyman skills. For instance, the Philadelphia card table (cat. 45) listed in the 1811 Philadelphia price book as a kidney-end table with serpentine middle, cost $4.68 to make the basic form, which was "three feet long with three fast and one flyleg, solid top, the rails veneered." When one consults the cost tables at the back of the book, however, for the inlaid ornament on the cuffs, the plain stringing on the legs and edge of the tops, the treble stringing at the skirt, and the panels on the pilasters, an additional $2.31 can be tallied. This is almost half again the amount for the basic table.[10] Similar computations can be made for the table with the label of Charles

Courtright (cat. 39) from the 1802 New York price book. For £1.19.0 one could purchase a circular table three feet long with four fast and one flyleg, veneered rails, an astragal or five strings on the frame, and a veneered top with three joints, clamped, and the edges cross- or long-banded. An examination of the table, however, reveals that it has these additional features: treble stringing inlaid around the perimeter of the top leaf, plain stringing on the corners of the top, three ovals with treble stringing on the aprons, cuffs, and stringing on three sides of the front legs and on two sides of the fixed legs. When the costs of these ornamental features are calculated an additional 13s, 8d is added, or a third the amount of the basic cost.[11] In other words, the price books do not contain costs of work that would be done by specialists.[12] The only types of

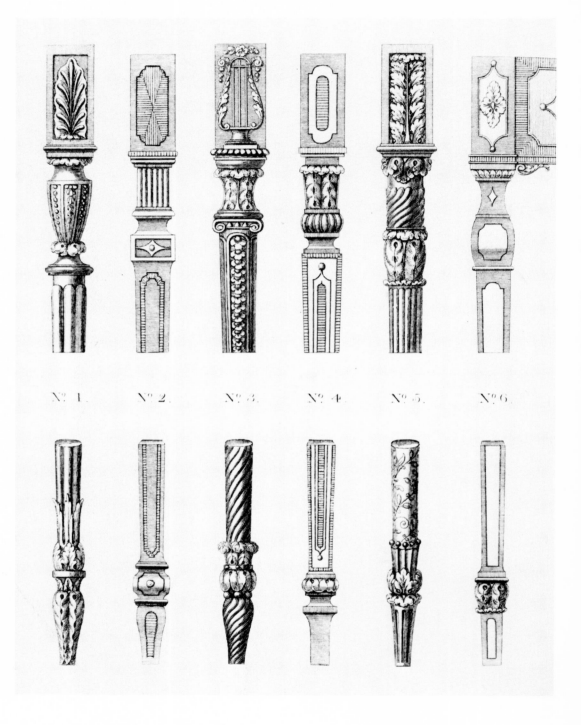

No. 1.   No. 2.   No. 3.   No. 4.   No. 5.   No. 6.

£. s. d.

For the price of crofs-banding, extra work in legs, &c.—
See Tables of ditto.
Oiling and polifhing, when lin'd - - - - - - - - - - - - 0 0 6
Ditto, when folid or veneer'd - - - - - - - - - - - - - 0 0 8

A CIRCULAR CARD TABLE,

THREE feet long, one fly foot, fquare edge to the tops,
plain Marlbro' legs - - - - - - - - - - - - - - 0 10 6

EXTRAS.

Each inch, more or lefs, in length - - - - - - - - - - 0 0 3
An extra fly foot - - - - - - - - - - - - - - - - - 0 0 8
An aftragal round the bottom of the rail, when the legs
are flufh - 0 0 9
If continued on the back rail, extra - - - - - - - - - - 0 0 3
Each extra miter, when the legs project - - - - - - - - 0 0 0½
Rounding the edge of the top - - - - - - - - - - - - 0 0 6
An aftragal, or hollow and two beads on the edge of ditto 0 1 9
Glueing up the top, either folid or to veneer on, at per joint 0 0 1
Cutting down ftuff for ditto, each cut - - - - - - - - 0 0 0½
Clamping the top to appear as folid, each clamp - - - - 0 0 4
Veneering the tops, each fide - - - - - - - - - - - - 0 0 9
Each joint in the veneer - - - - - - - - - - - - - - 0 0 6
Veneering the edge of the top crofs-way, at per foot - - - 0 0 1½
Each corner ftring in the fweep part, per foot - - - - - 0 0 1¼
Ditto on the back, per foot - - - - - - - - - - - - - 0 0 1
Lipping the top for cloth fet againft cleaning up.
Sinking a folid top for cloth - - - - - - - - - - - - 0 1 2
Lining ditto with cloth - - - - - - - - - - - - - - 0 0 10

When

£. s. d.

When the workman does not lay the cloth, but is required
to clean the band after - - - - - - - - - - - - - - 0 0 3
A ftring between the band and cloth - - - - - - - - - 0 0 9
Working a hollow on the edge of the under top - - - - - 0 0 4
Staining ditto - - - - - - - - - - - - - - - - - - 0 0 4
Veneering the rail long-way - - - - - - - - - - - - - 0 0 10
Ditto the back rail - - - - - - - - - - - - - - - - 0 0 5
If crofs-way, each joint extra - - - - - - - - - - - - 0 0 1
A drawer in front - - - - - - - - - - - - - - - - - 0 5 0
Sawing out each leg - - - - - - - - - - - - - - - - 0 0 0½
Ditto the joint rail - - - - - - - - - - - - - - - - 0 0 0½
Tapering legs, each fide - - - - - - - - - - - - - - 0 0 0½
If made eliptic, extra - - - - - - - - - - - - - - - 0 1 0
For the price of crofs-banding, &c.—*See Tables of ditto.*
Oiling and polifhing, when lin'd - - - - - - - - - - - 0 0 6
Ditto, when folid or veneer'd - - - - - - - - - - - - 0 0 8

A CARD TABLE, WITH CANTED CORNER, folid,
fquare edge to the tops, one fly foot, plain Marlbro' legs 0 10 6
A plain drawer in front - - - - - - - - - - - - - - 0 3 3
Veneering the front and end rails - - - - - - - - - - 0 1 2
A ftring betwixt the band and cloth - - - - - - - - - 0 1 0
An aftragal on the bottom of the frame - - - - - - - - 0 1 0
For the price of banding—*See Table of ditto.*
All other extras to be paid for as Circular Card Table.

A CARD TABLE, WITH ROUND CORNER, folid, the
front legs placed in the center of the corner, fquare edge
to the tops, one fly foot, plain Marlbro' legs - - - - - 0 11 0

O 2   A plain

FIG. 26.
The Cabinet-Makers' London Book of Prices and Designs of Cabinet Work, London, 1793. Pages 98 and 99. Yale University Art Gallery.

pictorial inlay discussed in the price books are fluting and patera.[13]

The stylistic progression of shapes can also be determined from the price books. The 1788 London book describes two basic shapes for card tables: "square with plain Marlbro' feet," and "circular with plain Marlbro' legs." For the square shape (shape 3 in Hewitt's essay) there were two extras that could be chosen to vary the form. A square table could be made with serpentine front and straight ends (a shape not found by Hewitt, and hence probably quite rare in America) or with serpentine front and serpentine ends. The latter was illustrated by Hepplewhite (fig. 22) and was made in America with canted corners (shapes 7, 13) and with pointed corners (shape 14). The choice of shapes in the first London price book was quite limited, but with the 1793 edition four had been added—card tables with canted corners, round corners, quarter-round corners, and ovolo corners. Sheraton used the term "sash corner" to describe the ovolo corner.[14] In America the first two forms—canted corners and round corners—achieved only limited popularity (shapes 17, 15), the third was not found on any tables that could be reasonably assigned to a particular region, but the fourth, card tables with ovolo corners (shape 2), attained wide popularity. The 1793 London book also listed an additional option under circular tables, elliptical. This form, essentially oval, has not been found among American tables. The six shapes of card tables in the 1793 London book continued to be standard in subsequent editions of the London books published during the period of Hewitt's study.[15]

Philadelphia journeymen were the first in America to follow the lead of their London counterparts by publishing a price book. No copy of *The Philadelphia Cabinet and Chair Makers' Book of Prices Instituted April 14, 1794* is known to survive despite the fact that Thomas Timmings, Christopher Appleton, and John Gregory deposited one in the office of the Clerk of the District of Pennsylvania on April 13, 1794, on behalf of the Federal Society of Chair-Makers.[16] In 1795 the same journeymen published a second "corrected and enlarged" edition called *The Journeymen Cabinet and Chair-Makers Philadelphia Book of Prices* in which four shapes for card tables—square, circular, ovolo corner, and hollow corner—are listed.[17] Despite fewer headings for card tables, the close kinship in phraseology of this book with the 1793 London book gives clear evidence that the Philadelphia journeymen used the London book as their model. The 1795 Philadelphia price book was used in turn as a model by the New York journeymen for their first price book published in 1796. The 1795 Philadelphia price book was quickly followed (as a result of a journeymen's strike) by a new price book in 1796 which follows much more exactly the London price book of 1793.

With the publication of a second New York book in 1802, American cabinetmakers placed less reliance on London books and began to state and codify their own practices. For instances, the six card-table headings in the 1802 New York book differed from the six standard headings in the London books. The New York headings are for square, circular, and ovolo-corner card tables, with each listed as solid or veneered.

Tables with ovolo corners have options for serpentine fronts and/or serpentine end rails, a particularly lively form that appears on cat. 40. A table with canted corners is listed under "solid Circular Card Table." The standard London headings for tables with quarter-round corners or with round corners do not appear. Another option never found in the London price books, a square table with elliptic front (shape 4), is found for the first time in this New York edition. This shape, though found by Hewitt to be "popular" elsewhere in America, was not used often in New York.

The division of the tables into three kinds of shapes that were either solid or veneered corresponds with New York's predilection for more extensive use of veneer than any other center, particularly for table leaves. Another New York regional characteristic incorporated into the 1802 price book was the additional flyleg construction. Four fixed legs and an additional fifth leg on card tables was common construction in New York during the Chippendale period and obviously was continued in the Federal period. The 1802 edition of the price book thus documents New York's attention to two technical aspects of construction— veneered tops and additional flylegs. The veneer was not merely ornamental but served as the finished surface for a joined core intended to overcome the warpage inherent in a solid top. However, among surviving card tables solid tops have actually warped less.

By 1810 when the third price book was published in New York, the London books served even less as a model. The major headings for card tables in the 1810 book are square, circular, and elliptic. The absence of tables with canted or ovolo corners suggests that by 1810 they were no longer commonly made in New York. Also indicative of New York regional style preference is a separate heading for the elliptic card table, the predominant shape of New York turned-leg tables. In the London price books, instructions are given for making circular tables elliptic, but never for making them double or treble elliptic. Both of the latter are forms that New York cabinetmakers produced with considerable finesse (cats. 42, 43) and the double elliptic shape also occurs on a few Philadelphia tables. The New York tables usually have dark, richly figured mahogany veneer on their rails and are supported on finely turned and reeded legs. They are eloquent pieces revealing the high degree of skill and individuality New York cabinetmakers attained in the first decade of the 19th century.

Philadelphia published its fourth book of prices in 1811 and, like the New York books of 1802 and 1810, it also shifts away from the English model and reflects particular Philadelphia style preferences. The shift, however, was not so dramatic in Philadelphia as in New York. Philadelphia cabinetmakers retained five of the basic London shapes: square, circular, canted corners, round corners, and ovolo corners. They introduced two innovative forms, however—tables with serpentine corners and straight front and end rails, and the kidney-end card table with serpentine middle (shape 5), the latter one of the most popular forms of Philadelphia tables. Each of these two shapes allowed options for a round front (curving inward) or an elliptic front (bowing outward). And of these options, card tables with serpentine corners and elliptic fronts (shape 12) were the most popular form on turned-leg tables from this area. Kidney-end tables with a round front (shape 21), however, were produced only occasionally.

The last of the American price books to fall within the date range of Hewitt's study is *The New-York Book of Prices for Manufacturing Cabinet and Chair Work* (1817). The headings for card tables in that volume did not change appreciably from the 1810 edition, although there are more options under square tables.

Perhaps the most important revelation from this comparison of English and American price books is that the American cabinetmakers' dependency on London books continued only for the first decade after the styles were published; by the beginning of the 19th century New York and Philadelphia cabinetmakers went their own way. The London books published during the period of the study (1788, 1793, 1797, 1803, 1811) give information for a total of nine table shapes, whereas Hewitt recorded a total of twenty-six in America. A random survey of approximately fifty English tables from this period reveals little variation in their shapes; most are circular, elliptic, or square with round corners. If the sample of English tables were enlarged, many more variations would probably come to light. In general, it seems that American cabinetmakers found many more solutions to the problem of shape than their English counterparts did. Few, if any, American tables, however, can boast the wealth of ornament that Hepplewhite recommended in his *Guide* (figs. 22, 23).

The introduction of innovative shapes in the American price books indicates that imitation within a center was certainly a force at work in the development of regional styles. Individual craftsmen, whose identities are not known, must have been responsible for creating the double and treble elliptic forms in New York and the kidney-end and serpentine-cornered tables in Philadelphia, which their competitors then copied. There is some documentary evidence to suggest how this process worked. Marilynn Johnson, in her study of New York cabinetmaker John Hewitt's account book, found that he was aware and made note of furniture details produced by two of New York's leading cabinetmakers, Duncan Phyfe and Charles Honoré Lannuier.[18] Regional characteristics frequently come about through such imitation.

Useful as price books are for understanding the contemporary terminology of forms, for plotting stylistic progression, for providing evidence about the costs of production, and for assessing American departures from English models, more important are the questions about the changes taking place in the cabinetmaking industry both in England and America beginning in the late 1780s raised by the very existence of these books. Why do the published price books appear in the late 18th century? Why was there a need for wage agreements between journeymen and master cabinetmakers? Answers to these questions must be pondered in light of a larger social and economic context including the general economy, markets, technology, apprenticeship, labor, business methods, shop practices, volume, and means of production. As we explore these areas we find that a 150-year tradition in the creation of American furniture was in a state of transformation from craft to industry.

From manuscripts and contemporary publications, there is ample evidence to document small 18th-century workshops being replaced by larger enterprises that required greater amounts of capital to establish and maintain.[19] In these larger establishments, the master of the shop assumed a managerial role, rarely working side by side with his journeymen. Most advertisements of cabinetmakers that appeared in colonial newspapers correspond with what the economic historian John Commons describes as the "retail-order phase" of American economic development.[20] A master with one or two journeymen and apprentices made and kept on hand a small stock of ready-made furniture, and also made furniture on order, that is "bespoke work." Such is the advertisement of Willet and Pearsee, of New York.

Cabinet and Chair-makers . . . Continues to make in the very best manner Cabinet and Chair-Work of every kind. As they are determined by being punctual in performing, and in finishing their work with the greatest neatness and care, to aim at giving general satisfaction. They humbly embrace this way of offering their service, and will with gratitude acknowl-edge the kindness of all such as please to favour them with their commands. They have on hand at present made of the best Mahogany, and in the neatest Manner,
A very handsome Desk and Book-Case,
A chest upon Chest,
A Lady's Dressing-Chest and Book-Case,
Three Desks, Three Sets of Chairs,
A Pair of Card-Tables, and several Tea-Tables, Stands,
Breakfast and China Tables, Bureaus &c. &c.
N.B. *Two Apprentices are wanting at the above place.*[21]

"Wareroom," "warehouse," and "manufactory" imply larger capital investments for display space, in the stock itself, and a larger number of employees. The phenomenon of a warehouse to display furniture which had been produced by workmen under the supervision of a master craftsman can be documented in England as early as 1723, when the London cabinetmaker Robert Hodson advertised "At Hodsons Looking Glass and Cabinet Warehouse in Frith Street Soho is ready made great variety of all sorts of Furniture . . . by choice and experienced Workmen employ'd in his own house."[22] By the mid-18th century, advertisements of furniture warerooms or warehouses in London were fairly commonplace.[23] In America, on the other hand, the terms wareroom or warehouse by cabinetmaking firms in newspaper advertisements can rarely be documented until after the Revolution, by which time they occur in most of the major urban centers. Among the earliest is the Baltimore Cabinet Warehouse of Gordon and Bankson advertised in 1784.[24] "Manufactory" does not appear until the last quarter of the 18th century, even in England.[25] In America the word appears in advertisements just after the Revolution, for instance the 1785 advertisement of Samuel Claphamson, "Cabinet and Chair Maker, In Market street . . . Manufactory back of the Old Gaol."[26] A critical factor that goes hand in hand with cabinet warerooms or manufactories is that the furniture in them was not only for sale to the retail trade, but also to fill wholesale orders. Although the availability of Windsor chairs as wholesale merchandise can be found before the Revolution, advertisements for other furniture at wholesale are rarely found in America until afterward.[27]

The growth of the furniture industry in the late 18th and early 19th centuries depended upon the expansion of the domestic market. Without wider and larger markets for their goods there would have been no reason for American cabinetmakers to increase the scale of their operations. Although the American economy had been expanding throughout colonial times, in the early national period the rate of expansion accelerated and changed the manner in which goods were produced and distributed. The ratification of the Constitution laid the legal foundations for a national market and aided its emergence.[28] But two factors played an especially significant role in the United States' economic development at this time. One was the outbreak of the Napoleonic wars in 1793, which led to what has been called "the golden age of American shipping," the period between 1793 and 1808 when America supplied foodstuffs and raw materials to Europe, and, as a neutral power, took over a large part of the carrying trade previously conducted by England and France. The second development, a growing cotton trade, spurred by Eli Whitney's invention of the cotton gin in 1793, fostered a period of extraordinary profits for southern cotton growers and had profound effects throughout the American economy.[29]

To meet the demands of widening markets, manufacturers adopted more efficient means to produce more goods, which usually involved division of labor, specialization, and often the increased use of power-driven machinery. In the furniture industry there is no evidence of the use of power-driven machinery prior to the establishment of Lambert Hitchcock's chair factory in Barkhamsted, Connecticut, in 1818. Self-employment, hand tools, and small workshops continued to dominate the scene, but the foundations of a new order were being laid. Dynamic forces were at work, such as the spirit of entrepreneurship defined by Stuart Bruchey as "the desire for efficiency in the use of economic resources" which increasingly permeated American business life.[30]

As the expanding American economy stimulated the growth of cabinetmaking, the effects on journeymen were manifold. The possibility of becoming a master was not so easy, since establishing such a business now required the command of greater amounts of capital. In other words, more individuals were being relegated to lifelong roles as wage earners. Journeymen's relationships with masters were less harmonious, too. With what Commons defines (p. 61) as the "wholesale-order phase" that emerged after the Revolution, the masters of shops adjusted their methods of doing business. To meet the new competition, masters were likely to reduce wages, to seek more efficient means of production, to find added and larger sources of financing, and to enter new and distant markets. It becomes evident that the added costs of credit, warehousing, and transport would compel the master to produce at less cost in order to be competitive. The threat of compromise both to earnings and job integrity would take on great importance to the journeymen in shops practicing under the new business methods.

By publishing price books the journeymen attempted to exert pressure on their employers to pay a just price for their work. The most marketable item a journeyman possessed was his skill, the ability to make a piece of furniture from start to finish. The publication of price books by the journeymen cabinetmakers in the late 18th century can be interpreted then as a struggle on their part to forestall the erosion of the value of their craft skill. There is evidence that the publication of price books was undertaken in a spirit of harmony with masters rather than in a spirit of conflict. In the introduction to the first London price book, for instance, the journeymen addressed themselves to the master cabinetmakers of London and Westminster "desirous of showing every possible degree of respect to their employers." Their stated aims were to rid the trade of certain disadvantages "that one man shall get double the money *per* week that another gets, though of equal or superiour abilities, from the mere circumstances of his work being better paid for, and, which is frequently the case, requiring less merit in the execution. . . . We only wish to obtain a comfortable subsistence, so justly due to every ingenious mechanic."[31] Despite the tone of harmony, the need to publish the books underscores the existence of journeymen's grievances, and the efforts of the master cabinetmakers to compromise their role.

Although the events surrounding the publication of the first American price book in Philadelphia in 1794 cannot be clearly understood as the result of the masters' attempt to reduce wages, the 1796 price book does contain in its "Introduction" essentially an escalator clause geared to inflation. This suggests that the masters may not actually have reduced wages but on the other hand may also not have advanced them in an inflationary time, which for the journeyman would have the same effect as actually cutting pay.

The journeymen who struck in 1802 against the master cabinetmakers in New York claimed they did so because masters had attempted to reduce wages. Their grievances were addressed to the public in the *American Advertiser:*

With a view to prevent disputes between the employers and their journeymen, there has existed in this city, for many years past, a Book of Prices, in which is specified the precise sum to be paid by the master cabinet-maker to his journeymen, for every particular piece of

workmanship in that line. Since the first establishment of this book, the rates have, at different times, varied according to circumstances. On former occasions, however, no alteration was ever attempted with respect to the prices, except at a meeting of a joint committee from the employers and journeymen, by whom, after the matter in dispute had been fully discussed, it was at least settled by the mutual consent of both parties.

In the present instance, however, the conduct of the employers has been exceedingly different: —They have associated by themselves, and, without deigning to have any consultation with us, have presented to us a New Book of Prices, which, on an average, will deduct at least 15 per cent. from our former wages—and they have bound themselves under a considerable penalty to each other, that they will not employ any workmen except according to the prices which they themselves have laid down in their new fashioned book.

In retaliation the New York journeymen opened their own wareroom in competition with the masters. In their rebuttal the masters did not claim not to have cut wages:

the new book of prices which they have spoken of had become absolutely necessary, for the old one had undergone so many alterations that it became difficult to understand it; in consequence of which frequent mistakes were made in the settlement of Journeymen's wages. It was of course no less to the interest of the journeyman than to that of the employer, that a new set of regulations should be made by which each could without any difficulty adjust their accounts. A new book of prices was therefore agreed upon by the Master Cabinet Makers, in which they have endeavored to fix the prices of labour at an equitable rate, and according to which an industrious man may earn from twelve to fourteen shillings a day. A very large majority of the Journeymen expressed themselves satisfied with the prices lately established, and continue to work for their employers on those terms.[32]

While it was probably true that a new book of prices was in order since, as shown above, there was a considerable change in specifications from the 1796 to the 1802 edition, the decline in economic conditions following the treaty of Amiens in 1802 may also have motivated masters to change their journeymen's pay scale.[33]

The second consequence of the emerging wholesale-order phase Commons observed was that masters of shops were likely to find better methods of production, or exercise what Bruchey calls entrepreneurship. To survive in the more highly charged competitive atmosphere of the late 18th and early 19th centuries, the edge went to those who devised efficient use of economic resources.

Mabel Munson Swan amply documented the large network of cabinetmakers and the specialists traditionally allied with them—turners, carvers, upholsterers—that developed in Salem. She quoted from instructions given by Elijah Sanderson to Jeremiah Briggs, supercargo of a brig on which a quantity of furniture was being shipped:[34]

It often happens that furniture shipt by different people on board the same vessel is invoiced at different prices some higher and some lower of the same kind and quality and sometimes there is a difference in the goodness of the work and stock and when the whole is sold together at a particular rate for the invoice and all the different invoices sold together, it is a disadvantage to those whose furniture put at a lower rate is of a quality to have it sold together—therefore I wish you to sell mine by itself—not to mix it in a bargain with others and let me have the benefit of the sale of my own—you will find that my furniture is all marked with a brand E S on the back of each piece besides the mark on the case.

Sanderson's instructions reveal the disadvantages faced by craftsmen competing in a market of eroding product standards that today would be called quality inflation. Since supercargoes often had difficulty in disposing of cargoes at all, it is quite easy to see how cabinetmakers would be compelled to cut costs to price their work competitively and thereby ensure a profit. Elijah Sanderson's maintenance of quality standards and his desire to receive a just price for his work put him at a disadvantage.

One of the conclusions Hewitt reached in his analysis of 400 card tables was that those made north of Providence were consistently more economically produced than tables made south of Massachusetts. Although it cannot be proved that the motivation behind the construction choices of Massachusetts and New Hampshire cabinetmakers versus cabinetmakers in the eight regions to the south were made in response to market competition, the obvious advantages the differences would provide in a competitive market makes such an interpretation compelling. Of these areas it is known that Massachusetts tables often competed in the same market as tables from New York.[35] Perhaps Massachusetts cabinetmakers economized on production methods to keep their prices lower, due to higher freight costs to reach markets farther south.

Hewitt has also suggested that parts of tables such as hinged rails and sets of legs may have been made by specialists. Certainly given the master cabinetmakers' need to find more expeditious methods of production, it is likely that subdivision of tasks was becoming a trade practice. From the merchant-employer's point of view it was economical to utilize a less skilled worker who could be hired to do routine work for a lower wage than that demanded by a journeyman who had served a traditional apprenticeship. Other studies have documented that as the 18th century drew to a close, apprenticeships became shorter.[36] That the value of skill was being eroded in the cabinetmaking trade can be inferred from one of the stated aims of journeymen's societies—to ensure that those who practiced in the trade had adequate training. For instance, the bylaws of the Mutual Society of Journeymen Cabinet Makers of the City of

New-York states "That no person shall be admitted a member of this Society without producing his indenture, or otherwise satisfying the Society that he has served four years to the business."[37]

Finally, Commons' third generalization about aspects of the emerging wholesale-order phase was that merchant-employers would find larger sources of marketing and financing. Although furniture had been exported during colonial times, the size of the potential market never supported production on the scale it assumed during the Federal period. It is clear that, with the growth of both the economy and of population in the post-Revolutionary period, new and distant markets opened and local markets expanded, which cabinetmakers among others sought to exploit. As Hewitt has shown, the vast majority of card tables conform to standard regional norms, which suggests that they were produced for sale ready-made rather than to the specifications of individual customers. In other words, furniture increasingly became a commodity manufactured through more efficient production methods rather than an object crafted to individual preferences.

The price books then reflect a transition in the cabinetmaking trade from "bespoke work" to "order work." The very process of preparing the price books for publication meant that a group of craftsman in a region had to arrive at a consensus, a conscious setting to paper of standards they would follow. While it is clear that price books did not preclude creativity and innovation, they nonetheless must have fostered standard practice. They signal a change in business methods and a consequent stratification of journeymen and master cabinetmakers as their goals were less in harmony.

1. These price books are hereafter referred to by the place and date of publication.

2. Many pieces of American furniture were inspired by the plates in Hepplewhite's *Guide* and Sheraton's *Drawing-Book*. Among the outstanding examples from Hepplewhite are shield-back chairs with carving attributed to Samuel McIntire of Salem for the Derby family, derived from Plate 2 of the 1794 edition (see Montgomery, *American Furniture: The Federal Period* [New York: Viking Press, 1966], p. 75, no. 14). A square-back sofa with carving of the type attributed to Samuel McIntire of Salem is derived from plate 35 of Sheraton's *Drawing-Book* (see Montgomery, pp. 304–05, nos. 269–70).

3. Cited by Charles F. Montgomery, "Bibliographical Note," in Thomas Sheraton, *The Cabinet-Maker and Upholsterer's Drawing-Book* (1802; reprint, New York: Praeger Publishers, 1970), p. xx. Seymour's copy is now owned by the Museum of Fine Arts, Boston.

4. Rita Susswein Gottesman, comp., *The Arts and Crafts in New York 1777–1799* (New York: The New-York Historical Society, 1954), pp. 130–31.

5. Michael Brown, "Duncan Phyfe" (unpublished Master's Thesis, University of Delaware, 1978), pp. 42–43. Phyfe's 1810 New York price book is now in the Winterthur Museum Libraries.

6. *The Cabinet-Maker and Upholsterer's Guide* (1794; reprint, New York: Dover Publications, 1969), Preface, n.p.

7. Sheraton, *Drawing-Book*, pp. 5–6.

8. *Cabinet Dictionary* (1803; reprint, New York: Praeger Publishers, 1970), vol. I, pp. 128–29.

9. "Appendix" in Sheraton, *Drawing-Book*, p. 17.

10. Cat. 45 is made of walnut rather than mahogany and the basic cost may therefore have been slightly less than $4.68 (p. 36 of the 1811 price book). The costs for additional ornament were tallied in the following way. The cuffs were computed from "A Table of Banding," p. 83: "When band is grooved in from straight edge, half an inch wide or straight part per foot; Ditto with a single string on each side, at per foot $.11." Since each cuff is approximately 1 inch in length and there are four on each leg, there is 16 inches of banding or 1 foot 4 inches or $.15 worth of banding. The stringing was calculated from "A table of paneling with strings" (p. 95). Under "Pilasters, legs, stump feet etc.": the four pilaster panels with "astragal top and hollow bottom" were $.14 each or $.56 total. Stringing per foot on serpentine or hollow work as single string such as leaves was $.04 per foot; the 120 inches on each leaf came to $.80. The 60 inches of treble string at $.06 per foot came to $.30. The 240 inches of plain string on the legs came to $.50.

11. The basic cost of the table was found on p. 21 of the 1802 price book. The additional ornament was calculated from cost tables at the back of the book. The approximately 53 inches of treble stringing on the perimeter of the top was calculated from Table No. I (p. 57) "stringing in straight or sweep'd work, let in from a straight edge per foot 2d per foot," totals 9d. The 19 inches of stringing on each of the corners of the top was calculated from the same table. The total amount of stringing was 6 feet 4 inches; at 2 1/2d per foot it totals 1 shilling, 2 pence. The second part of Table No. I concerns plinthing legs: "For a plinth with a string on each edge, on four sides of legs, including two mitres" cost d5. The table has plinths on three sides of each leg, for a total of 2s, 1d. The stringing on the legs was calculated from Table No. II (p. 57): "Pannelling with Strings or Pillasters, Legs, Stump Feet, Table Claws, Etc." Two lines in the charts were consulted: "Forming a square panel, with a single string 6 inches long and under" 4d, plus "Every 4 inches extra length of pannel 1/2d." The legs have ten panels, each approximately 20 inches long for a total cost of 4 shillings. The ovals on the aprons were calculated from Table No. III (p. 58) "A Table of Pannelling with Strings on Doors, Drawer Fronts, Table Rails, etc." Each oval is approximately 18 inches long and is surrounded by treble string. The cost of an oval from 1 foot to 2 feet long was 1 shilling 6 pence with treble string, but because it was let in on round work the price was increased by one-quarter for a total of 5s, 8d.

12. William MacPherson Hornor Jr., *Blue Book: Philadelphia Furniture* (1935; reprint, Washington, D.C.: Highland House Publishers, 1977), p. 242. Hornor says that Christopher Appleton, who appeared as a member of the Federal Society in 1794, set himself up as a professional inlayer at least by the year 1799.

13. In the 1795 Philadelphia price book, No. XII is "A Table of Fluting" as it is in the 1796 New York price book; it is No. VII in the 1802 New York price book (p. 60). The 1796 New York price book also lists "for an oval patrie, two and a half inches long, with twelve strait points, fill'd up at the ends with different wood, and a single string round ditto £0.1.3" and "making a half circular shade eight inches long and under £0.2.6" (pp. 76–77).

14. "Descriptive Index; Tables of Various Kinds," in Sheraton, *Drawing-Book*, n.p.

15. The lack of any appreciable changes from the 1793 to the 1803 edition suggests that, by 1803, card tables supported on a center pedestal with pillars and claws had not become a standard style in the London cabinet industry. Not until the 1811 *London*

Cabinet-Makers' Union Book of Prices, were pillar and claw tables listed along with the earlier Marlborough-leg forms.

16. Alfred Coxe Prime, comp., *The Arts and Crafts in Philadelphia, Maryland, and South Carolina 1786–1800*, ser. 2 (1932; reprint, New York: Da Capo Press, 1969), pp. 204–05.

17. What Philadelphia called a hollow-corner card table was probably called a card table with quarter-round corners in London.

18. Marilynn A. Johnson, "John Hewitt, Cabinetmaker," *Winterthur Portfolio 4* (Charlottesville: University Press of Virginia, 1968): 199.

19. J. Stewart Johnson, "New York Cabinetmaking Prior to the Revolution" (unpublished Masters' Thesis, University of Delaware, 1964), pp. 46–47. Johnson's study of the account books of Joshua Delaplaine, the most important body of documents for a pre-Revolutionary New York cabinetmaker, suggests that Delaplaine probably never had more than one or two journeymen in his employ at any one time. See Morrison H. Heckscher, "The Organization and Practice of Philadelphia Cabinetmaking Establishments 1790 to 1820" (unpublished Masters' Thesis, University of Delaware, 1963), p. 22. Heckscher's study of the Samuel Ashton papers for the years 1795–1803, the most important known accounts for Philadelphia cabinetmaking in the Federal period in terms of what they reveal about master–employee relations, shows that eight men were working for Ashton at any one time. In 1798 George Shipley, cabinetmaker, advertised the availability for sale of his cabinetmaking establishment in the New York *Daily Advertiser*; he described it as always having employment for about ten men (Gottesman, *1777–1799*, p. 127). Marilynn A. Johnson's study of the New York City cabinetmaker John Hewitt's account book reveals that in the period 1809 to 1812, Hewitt employed sixteen men in the production of his furniture (pp. 199–200).

20. John R. Commons et al., *History of Labor in the United States*, 4 vols. (New York: Macmillan, 1918–35), vol. 1, p. 56.

21. *Rivington's New York Gazetteer*, April 22, 1773, quoted in Rita Susswein Gottesman, comp., *The Arts and Crafts in New York: 1726–1776* (1936; reprint, New York: Da Capo Press, 1970), p. 119.

22. Sir Ambrose Heal, *The London Furniture Makers* (1953; reprint, New York: Dover Publications, 1972), pp. 80, 85.

23. Heal documents numerous instances of cabinet warehouses being advertised. Among the more outstanding examples is the firm of George Seddon which had a disastrous fire in 1768. Newspaper accounts reported that he employed eighty cabinetmakers (p. 161). The firm of Peter Burcham advertised wholesale and retail furniture in the mid-1750s (pp. 17, 29).

24. Alfred Coxe Prime, comp., *The Arts and Crafts in Philadelphia, Maryland, and South Carolina: Part I, 1721–1785* (1929; reprint, New York: Da Capo Press, 1969), pp. 168–69. Although Ethel Hall Bjerkoe, *The Cabinetmakers of America* (Garden City, New York: Doubleday, 1957), p. 37, cites a typescript in the Maryland Historical Society indicating that Gordon and Bankson advertised a cabinet warehouse in the *Maryland Gazette*, July 18, 1750, a search of that newspaper does not show such an advertisement at that time. A possible exception to the post-Revolutionary appearance of warehouses is the advertisement of Robert Moore in the *Pennsylvania Chronicle* in 1769 in which he mentions a "show–shop" (Prime, *Part I*, pp. 177–78).

25. The earliest use of the term cited by Heal is the trade card for the firm of Vickers and Rutledge "Upholders [Upholsterers]/Cabinet-Makers/& Undertakers/Successors to Mr. Bailey/at their Manufactory, Conduit Street,/Hanover-Square/London" which Heal places in the 1775–80 period (pp. 182, 189).

26. Prime, *Part I*, p. 162.

27. A possible exception is the advertisement of the New York cabinetmaker Samuel Prince in 1775: "Orders for the West Indies, and elsewhere, compleated on the shortest notice." Gottesman, *1726–1776*, p. 116.

28. Stuart Bruchey, *The Roots of American Economic Growth, 1607–1861* (New York: Harper & Row, 1965), p. 192.

29. Curtis Nettels, *The Emergence of a National Economy 1775–1815* (New York: Holt, Rinehart and Winston, 1962), p. 192.

30. Bruchey, p. 209.

31. *The London Cabinet Book of Prices*, 1788, pp. iv–v.

32. Rita Susswein Gottesman, comp., *The Arts and Crafts in New York 1800–1804* (New York: The New-York Historical Society, 1965), pp. 145, 147.

33. Donald R. Adams Jr., "Wage Rates in the Early National Period: Philadelphia 1785–1830," *Journal of Economic History* 28 (1968): 405–06. Although Adams' research, which indicates that wage rates declined in 1802–03 because the Peace of Amiens substantially reduced U.S. income from foreign trade and shipping, was based on Philadelphia, the same phenomenon may have pertained to New York.

34. Swan, *Samuel McIntire, Carver, and the Sandersons, Early Salem Cabinet Makers* (Salem: Essex Institute, 1934), p. 9.

35. Swan, p. 11.

36. Montgomery, p. 11.

37. *Constitution and Byelaws of the Mutual Society of Journeymen Cabinet Makers* (New York: D. Denniston, 1800), p. 8.

Regional Characteristics of American Federal-Period Card Tables

Benjamin A. Hewitt

The aim of this study is to establish verifiable data about the regional characteristics of one form of American furniture—Federal-period card tables. One hundred and seventy-six characteristics of a large homogeneous sample of objects—four hundred card tables produced in the United States between 1790 and 1820—were studied by quantitative research methods to identify the ways craftsmen in various regions designed and ornamented them and constructed their parts. Comprehensive information about these card tables are here shown to provide reliable data for making attributions. Interpretation of the data has revealed ways in which Federal cabinetmakers utilized specialists and geared their production principally for customers of ready-made tables, which they sometimes customized with extra features, rather than for those who wanted custom work.

The identification of regional schools of cabinetmaking has been a concern of American furniture scholars for the last half-century. Among the early pioneers in that effort was William MacPherson Hornor Jr., whose *Blue Book: Philadelphia Furniture* (1935) was the first major work to discuss in depth the furniture from a major American furniture-producing center. Since that time numerous exhibitions and publications have been devoted to various geographical areas. Some works have addressed the question on an interregional basis, usually with the aim of defining those characteristics that differentiate furniture of one region from another.

Such was the goal of Joseph Downs in his remarks on "Regional Characteristics" in the introduction to *American Furniture: Queen Anne and Chippendale* (1952). The object of William R. Johnson's article, "Anatomy of the Chair," in the Metropolitan Museum of Art *Bulletin* (November 1962) was much the same. Later, John T. Kirk's *American Chairs: Queen Anne and Chippendale* (1972) studied the same form in greater depth. Kirk's principal concern is the correct regional identification of chairs from these two stylistic periods, although he does raise some of the more elusive issues of why objects produced in particular regions come to be the way they are.

Most recently, Charles F. Montgomery, in his essay "Regional Preferences and Characteristics in American Decorative Arts: 1750–1800," *American Art 1750–1800: Towards Independence* (1976), was interested not so much in defining what various characteristics were as in grappling with the question of what caused them to arise in the first place. He came to the conclusion that, in large part, regional characteristics were the result of specialization and craft organization.

Craft practices and organization have been the subject of study for some time, but regional characteristics have been studied only comparatively recently. Such documents as account books, which recorded financial transactions, and newspaper advertisements, which informed the public of available goods or services, have provided information concerning the sizes of shops, the kinds of furniture produced, and the breadth of activities from which cabinet-makers earned their living. These have shown that most pre-Revolutionary cabinet-makers had small shops with one or two apprentices and gave personal attention to individual orders. Seemingly rarely did shops have many employees and large work units.

Documentary research of Federal cabinet-makers presents a different picture. In urban centers the industry was geared to meet markets which were no longer predominant-ly local. Scholars have established that craftsmen in urban areas increased their scale of operations and employed specialists —carvers, turners, gilders, and inlay makers —in increasing numbers. They have identi-fied many of these craftsmen and their roles. From advertisements they have inferred that stocks of ready-made furniture were kept on hand to satisfy the expanded retail and wholesale demand that followed on the growth of domestic markets after the Revo-lution.[1] With the ratification of the Constitu-tion in 1789, the United States government encouraged the development of "manufac-turing" in America by providing a sound uniform currency, protective tariffs, and free trade over state boundaries. These new ad-vantages to the producer-merchant, coupled with postwar economic prosperity and the expansion of the urban population, created a large market for well-made furniture of sophisticated design. The end of English dominance also allowed Americans to ex-pand their trade and increased the market for American-made goods. Furniture made by shopwork production methods was suited to this widening retail and wholesale market because it could be produced quickly and in-expensively. Many cabinetmakers were stim-ulated to enlarge their shops and to develop efficient manufacturing methods that in-creased their productivity. Some forsook cabinetmaking and expanded into mercantile businesses to become entrepreneurs of com-modities, often including furniture not of their own manufacture.

However, specific information on the day-to-day operations of cabinet shops is elusive because most extant documents do not detail them. An exception are the bills, re-ceipts, letters, and contracts of the Salem cabinetmakers Elijah (1751–1825) and Jacob (1757–1810) Sanderson, at the Essex Insti-tute. Mabel Munson Swan's research in these documents (*Samuel McIntire, Carver, and the Sandersons, Early Salem Cabinetmakers* [1934]) revealed not only that enormous quantities of furniture were manufactured by many Salem shops but also that the Sander-son shop in particular achieved a high level of production by employing a manager and a superintendent as well as the traditional journeymen and apprentices, and by util-izing the piecework system under which many shops employed the same specialists (chiefly carvers, upholsterers, and turners).

The present quantitative study, which has focused on objects rather than on docu-ments, has both reinforced the conclusions drawn by previous scholars and identified a number of ways in which cabinetmakers in the Federal period utilized specialists and standardized their production for largely re-tail and wholesale markets. It has developed regional norms for the characteristics of one form of furniture, by means of which we can make reliable attributions and can specu-late about the reasons craftsmen in various regions produced one form of furniture in different ways.

The findings are presented through a dis-cussion of the methodology and an analysis of the regional characteristics of the form, ornament, and construction of Federal-period card tables. Data from these analyses have led to hypotheses about cabinetmakers' use of sets of legs and hinged rails produced by specialists, their economical use of labor and materials to increase productivity, and the standardized practices of cabinet shops. These findings have generated distinctions between furniture produced for a retail and wholesale market and that made on custom order for patrons with particular preferences.

The Methodology

The study of regionalism would be simplified if numerous examples of documented furniture from various regions existed. Their characteristics could then be tallied and compared; but most furniture is not documented and therefore representative samples must be compiled by relying on the documented examples that do exist. Federal card tables were ideal candidates for this study because hundreds are known to exist, and the origins of many are documented by a label, brand, or inscription. At the outset it was assumed that by finding as many documented tables as possible, one could identify their characteristics and use those characteristics to identify the origin of undocumented tables and thus build sizable representative samples.

Card tables in the study were limited to those which (1) were believed to have been produced within the thirty-year period, 1790–1820; (2) have four, five, or six legs, directly fastened into the table rails; (3) are decorated with ornament such as veneer, inlay, or relief; and (4) have no significant replaced parts, such as rails, legs, and tops. To prevent the analysis from becoming more complex, painted, pedestal-base, and lyre-support tables were excluded from the study.

For the sake of uniformity, the author in person collected all data about the four hundred card tables, most of which were owned by museums, collectors, and dealers on the East Coast between Maine and South Carolina, but a few of which were housed in the Midwest, West, and Hawaii. Vigorous efforts were made to locate all documented tables known to exist.

Quantitative and qualitative information (176 items) was assembled for each table, and this in turn was transmuted into numerical codes for computer analysis. Quantitative information included such dimensions as the table's overall height, width, depth, and apron height; the thickness of each of its rails and braces; and the height and width by which the angle of the dovetails could be computed. Specific parts were counted: dovetails, flylegs, fast legs, and tenons; the horizontal and vertical laminations of each curved rail; the reeds in turned legs; and the sides of straight legs which were tapered, inlaid, or carved.

Some of the qualitative information described construction materials and methods, such as the kinds of primary and secondary woods and veneers, the types of fasteners used to attach the top to the frame and the hinged rails to the rear, and the methods by which the flyleg, flying rail, and each curved rail were constructed. Other qualitative information pertained to decoration: the specific kinds of ornament at each place on the table; the shapes of inlaid panels on aprons, pilasters, and legs; the particular patterned and pictorial inlays and where each was placed on the table.

Statistical Analyses

Preliminary inspection of the data collected from 75 documented tables, organized according to regional origin, revealed the importance of dividing the sample in two: tables with straight legs (278), and tables with turned legs (122). This division was necessary because the construction, style, and ornament of straight- and of turned-leg tables of the same origin were so distinctive that the two groups appeared to be of different origin. Some characteristics which redundantly described almost all of the documented tables were identified and eliminated.

In order to attribute the origin of undocumented straight-leg tables, the data about them and about documented tables were analyzed to bring together regional groups, or clusters, of tables sharing groups, or clusters, of statistically significant regional characteristics.[2] The same procedure was then followed for turned-leg tables.

The documented tables in the clusters (but in the case of Baltimore, tables attributed to or with an early provenance in that city) identified twelve regions where straight-leg tables were produced: urban New Hampshire, rural Massachusetts–New Hampshire, Newburyport, Salem, the Boston area, Newport, Providence, Connecticut, New York, the Philadelphia area, Baltimore, and Annapolis; and six regions where turned-leg tables were produced: rural Massachusetts–New Hampshire, Newburyport, Salem, the Boston area, New York, and the Philadelphia area.[3] Most regions had more than one cluster. There were also clusters with sizable numbers of tables which could be identified with no region because they included no documented example, and there were some tables that fell into no cluster.[4]

Because it was found that regional groups could not be refined further through block clustering, another statistical technique was used to reveal in which, if any, of the twelve regions the unidentified tables originated.[5] To accomplish this, data from identified tables were analyzed to determine the characteristics that differentiate each regional group from all the other regional groups.

This step entailed the development of quantitative formulae which were then applied to the unidentified tables.

The accuracy of these statistical attributions of tables to their regional origins was found to be close to 100 percent for tables that originated in Newport, Providence, Connecticut, New York, the Philadelphia area, Baltimore, and Annapolis. It was between 87 and 93 percent for tables that originated in urban New Hampshire, rural Massachusetts–New Hampshire, Newburyport, Salem, and the Boston area. However, the probability of accurate classification was close to 100 percent for tables that originated in all of the Massachusetts and New Hampshire centers if they are considered as one. Thus it was possible to develop regional groups of tables whose comprehensive characteristics could be studied. The total number of tables was reduced to 265 straight-leg and 109 turned-leg tables because some tables had repairs, replacements, and damage and tables with characteristics atypical of any region or typical of more than one region were classified with a probability of origin too low to be reliable.

Recognizable regional styles of Federal card tables were developed in nine urban centers and three broader geographical areas. The number of straight-leg and turned-leg

	Straight-leg tables	Turned-leg tables	Total
Urban New Hampshire	8		8
Rural Massachusetts–New Hampshire	23	13	36
Newburyport	22	11	33
Salem	24	24	48
Boston area	69	32	101
Newport	11		11
Providence	16		16
Connecticut	10		10
New York	15	12	27
Philadelphia area	19	17	36
Baltimore	43		43
Annapolis	5		5
Total	265	109	374

tables produced in each center is shown on the accompanying tabulation.

A small but distinctive sample which includes documented examples from Concord and Keene was called urban New Hampshire. Rural Massachusetts–New Hampshire includes documented tables originating between Hingham, Massachusetts, in the east, Greenfield, Massachusetts, in the west, Springfield, Massachusetts, in the south, and Bedford, New Hampshire, in the north. This area overlapped urban New Hampshire. All of the documented tables in the region called Salem came from that town except one, which was produced in nearby Lynn. The designation "area" is used with Boston because tables in this regional group were produced in Boston and the neighboring towns of Charlestown, East Sudbury, and Dorchester. Connecticut includes documented tables from Hartford and New London. And "area" is also used for Philadelphia since the sample includes tables from West Chester and Trenton.

After the goups were defined, regional frequencies of characteristics that seemed useful in making comparisons among regions were tabulated. These tabulations appear in charts I–XIV (at end of text). It should be borne in mind, however, that these charted frequencies have a probability of error because the probabilities that tables are assigned to the region where they originated are high but not perfect.

Regional Characteristics in Form, Ornament, and Construction

Tabulations produced by the computer of the regional frequencies characterizing Federal-period card tables are discussed below under three major headings: form, ornament, and construction. Analysis of form includes straight legs, turned legs, and shapes of the leaves and frames of the tables. The discussion of ornament considers relief (which includes carving), veneer, stringing and banding (which include plain and patterned inlay), pictorial inlay, and facade designs. Construction explores the internal elements of the tables—secondary woods, the curved and hinged rails, the back of the tables, the construction of flylegs, and the use of leaf-edge tenons and medial braces.

FORM

Card tables made within the Federal period have certain features in common. With few exceptions they were designed with a hinged leaf overlying a fixed leaf, whose shapes conform to a supporting frame which is in turn supported by four, five, or six legs. The lower leaf is attached to the table frame generally by means of screws running through the frame into the underside of the leaf. It is attached to the upper leaf by hinges set into the outside edge of the leaves' rear corners. In the closed position the tables were designed to be placed against a wall with their leaves closed. For card playing, or other purpose, the table was placed in a free-standing position with its upper leaf opened and supported by one or two rear legs which were hinged and movable for this purpose.

The legs supporting the frame were arranged in three basic ways (the two front legs were always fixed, and at the rear one or two movable legs, called flylegs, supported the top in open position): (1) a fixed left rear leg and a movable right rear leg; (2) two movable rear legs; (3) two or three fixed rear legs with a movable additional leg adjacent to the fixed right leg.[6] None of the three basic arrangements was unique to a particular region. Preferences were found for the first arrangement in urban New Hampshire, rural Masschusetts–New Hampshire, Newburyport, Salem, the Boston area, Providence, the Philadelphia area, Baltimore, and Annapolis; for the second in Salem, Newport, and Baltimore; and for the third in Newport, Connecticut, and New

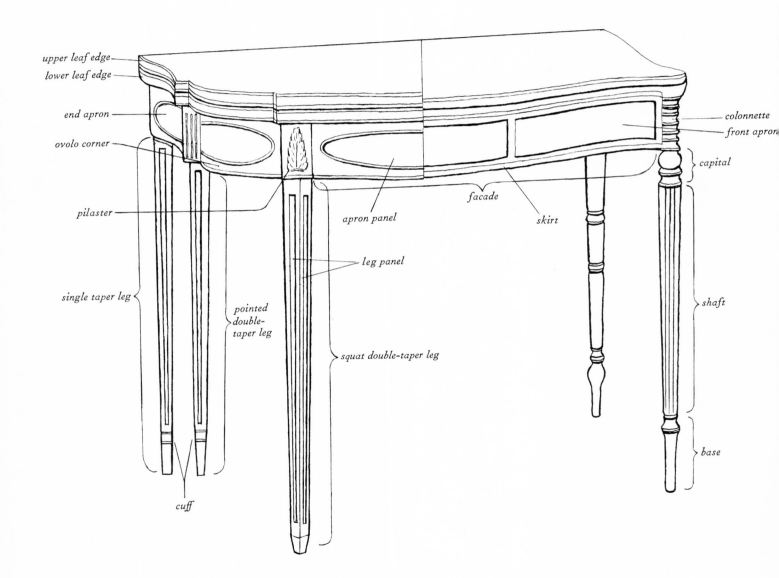

upper leaf edge

lower leaf edge

end apron

ovolo corner

pilaster

single taper leg

pointed
double-
taper leg

cuff

leg panel

squat double-taper leg

apron panel

facade

skirt

colonnette

front apron

capital

shaft

base

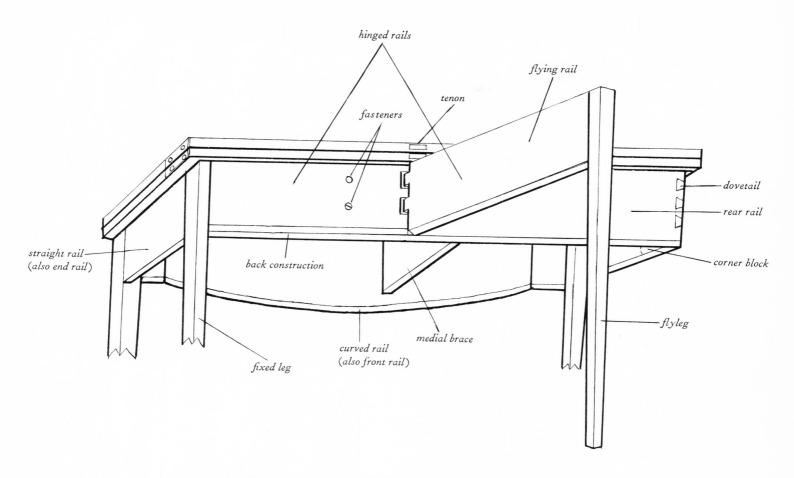

hinged rails

flying rail

tenon

fasteners

dovetail

rear rail

straight rail (also end rail)

corner block

back construction

flyleg

fixed leg

medial brace

curved rail (also front rail)

York. The legs were either straight or turned.

STRAIGHT LEGS

On Federal furniture, straight legs came into fashion earlier than turned legs. Six shapes of straight legs were identified in the study. The single taper, which narrows regularly from the line of the skirt to the floor, was used everywhere and its frequencies are consistently high (fig. 27). A closely related form, the pointed double taper, narrows regularly from the line of the skirt to about four inches above the floor, and then tapers a second time more sharply and pointedly (fig. 28). It was found only in urban New Hampshire, rural Massachusetts–New Hampshire, Salem, and the Boston area. Closely related to the latter is the squat double taper which narrows regularly from

the skirt to about two inches above the floor, where it tapers a second time to end in a stubby point (fig.29). This leg was found only on tables from the Boston area. A pentagon-shaped leg, or single taper, five-sided, was found on one table by Holmes Weaver of Newport (no. 228). Sometimes the base of the leg was shaped to form a foot, such as the single taper with spade foot, called a therm foot in the period (cat. 17). The tapering sides of this foot were either cut from the solid or applied. It was found on tables from Salem, Providence, Baltimore, and Annapolis. A variation of this is the single taper with knopped foot, found on a table by John and Thomas Seymour of Boston (fig. 30).

The data (chart I) reveal that only the squat double taper, found exclusively in the Boston area, is a reliable indicator of regional origin. Although the pointed double taper narrows the possibility of origin to one of the four Massachusetts and New Hampshire centers, the single taper with knopped foot and the single taper five-sided are rare occurrences undoubtedly made on special order. The wide geographic distribution and variations in the shape of the spade on the single-taper leg with spade foot suggest that they were made in many areas by different craftsmen.

TURNED LEGS

On the other hand, turned legs, made by specialists who traditionally served the furniture industry (turners), are highly reliable indicators of regional origin. From the days of the earliest settlers in America, turners had made such wooden-wares as plates and chairs, which they sold directly to the public, and also had made turned parts to the

 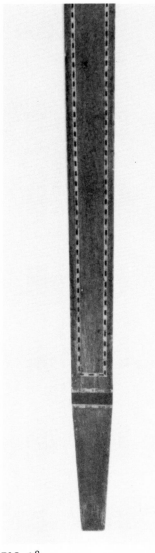 

FIG. 27.
Single taper leg. Detail of cat. 1.

FIG. 28.
Pointed double-taper leg. Detail of cat. 2.

FIG. 29.
Squat double-taper leg. Detail of cat. 24.

specifications of craftsmen in many trades. Many cabinetmakers were also skilled in the craft of turning, but some patronized turners, particularly in urban areas where greater degrees of specialization occurred earlier.[7] This piecework system was advantageous to both the turner and the cabinetmaker: by supplying many customers, the turner might earn a good living; by utilizing turners as they were needed, cabinetmakers reduced their overhead of full-time employees. Furniture historians have long hypothesized that piecework contributed to the phenomenon of regional characteristics, since the few turners that cabinetmakers drew upon in a particular locale produced the same or similar parts for many shops.

This study has analyzed the capital and base turnings (the areas at the top and bottom of the leg) and the shafts (the tapering section between the capital and base) to determine the interregional differences and intraregional similarities of these parts, and thus to identify those that are reliable indicators of regional origin.

The data reveal that eleven capital or base turnings can be regarded as reliable indicators of regional origin because they are unique to a center (chart II). In New York, capital 1 and base 1 (fig.31) were found with very little variation; 92 percent had these turnings. Nine New York card tables, of which one is by Charles Honoré Lannuier (cat. 41) and two by John Dolan (cat. 43),

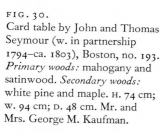

FIG. 30.
Card table by John and Thomas Seymour (w. in partnership 1794–ca. 1803), Boston, no. 193. *Primary woods:* mahogany and satinwood. *Secondary woods:* white pine and maple. H. 74 cm; W. 94 cm; D. 48 cm. Mr. and Mrs. George M. Kaufman.

For a customer who wanted a uniquely ornamented table, John Seymour and Son of Boston created a facade with festoons of bellflowers attached to delicate bowknots with pendant bellflowers. They embellished the perimeter of the top with ovals and circles and the legs with satinwood veneer inset with bellflowers. To enhance its singularity they specially constructed single-taper legs with knopped feet. This table has seven construction points, three more than the sturdiest of the local ready-made output, perhaps to ensure its durability.

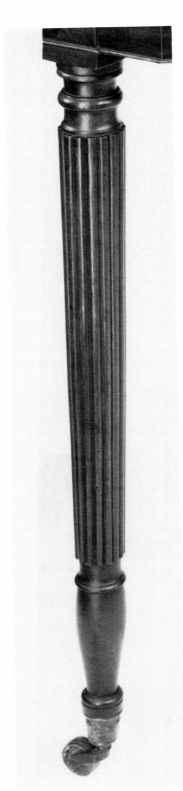

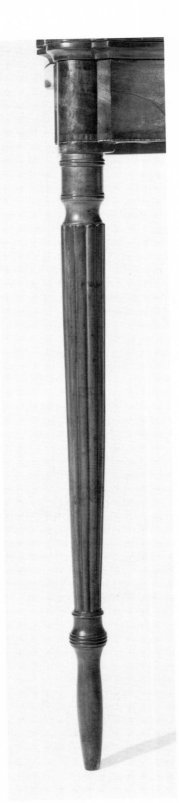

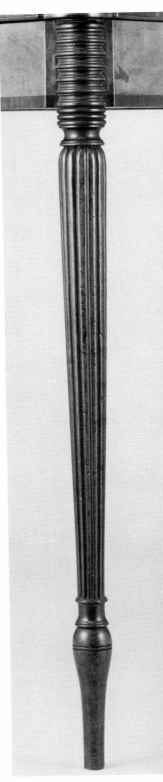

FIG. 31.
Capital 1, base 1, shaft 1. Detail
of cat. 41.

FIG. 32.
Capital 2, base 2a, shaft 1. Detail
of cat. 18.

FIG. 33.
Capital 2, base 2b, shaft 1. Detail
of no. 109.

FIG. 34.
Capital 3, base 3, shaft 2.
Detail of cat. 27.

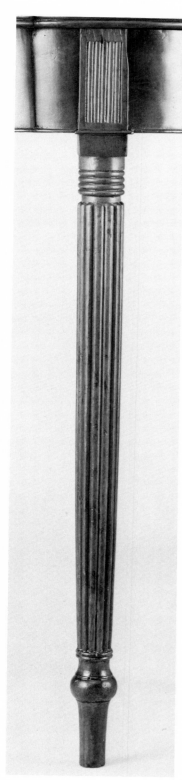

FIG. 35.
Capital 4a, base 4, shaft 1. Detail of cat. 46.

have capital 1 and base 1 on their legs and each of their shafts (shaft 1) has 15 reeds. The legs of three other New York tables have the same turnings, but the shafts of two have 14 reeds and the shafts on one have 16 reeds.

All the tables with base 2a turnings (attenuated bulbous foot), a unique Salem turning, also have capital 2 turnings (fig. 32). Capital 2 is also found on 22 percent of the Boston tables in combination with base 2b (short bulbous foot), which has a frequency of 28 percent for Salem as opposed to only 6 percent for Boston, it is a fairly strong indicator of Salem regional origin (fig. 33). Joseph True (1785–1873), the Salem carver, turner, and cabinetmaker, may well be the craftsman who created these turnings. Base 2a appears on a card table by William Hook (cat. 18) and a number of other pieces of Salem furniture by various cabinetmakers, just at the period when documents show that True was working for them.[8] Thus, half the Salem tables (those that combine capital 2 with either base 2a or 2b) may have been turned by the same specialist. Legs with capital 3 and base 3 were found on tables made in Salem, but these turnings are also found in Boston (fig. 34).

Eighty-one percent of the Philadelphia tables have either capital 4a (fig. 35) or capital 4b (fig. 36) with base 4. Capitals 4a and 4b are closely related, but both can be found with variations. The turnings are always comprised of three parts: a square above a plain turning over a ring. Below this, the form varies. It may have as many as five more shallowly grooved rings (capital 4a), or may be comprised of combinations of half-round, half-hollow, ogee, or plain turnings (capital 4b). All end in a ring. The hiatus between the capital and the shaft is likely to be evident because the turner rarely smoothed the tops of the reeds or carved them as if to disappear under the final ring. Variations were also found in base 4 (hollow, bulb, and taper). It begins with a deep hollow that swells into a bulb that may be grooved

or ringed, and then recedes into a plain taper that may terminate plainly or in a ball or spade. Another turner in Philadelphia was probably responsible for 13 percent of the tables from the region which have capital 5 and base 5 (fig. 37). Invariably these turnings are accompanied by shaft 3, a plain taper.

Base 6 was a turning unique to the Boston area, but capital 6, although popular in Boston (fig. 38), was found occasionally in rural Massachusetts–New Hampshire. In the latter area many cabinetmakers turned their own legs, but one specialist appears to have turned the legs with either capital 7 or base 7 found on a few tables by different makers (fig. 39). Examples are the table by I. Wilder (cat. 7), a painted table also by him,[9] and a table stamped T. Greene.[10] Figure 39 shows shaft 4, ringed, curving taper, which was also found only in rural Massachusetts-New Hampshire.

Capital 8 is comprised of miscellaneous capital turnings that show significant variation from those listed above; however, base 8 is unique to the Boston area where it is found on a few tables (fig. 40).

This survey of turnings shows that in eleven instances a capital or base turning in itself can be regarded as a reliable indicator of regional origin. These are capital 1 for New York, capitals 4a, 4b, and 5 for the Philadelphia area, and capital 7 for rural Massachusetts–New Hamphire; base 1 for New York, base 2a for Salem, bases 4 and 5 for the Philadelphia area, bases 6 and 8 for the Boston area, and base 7 for rural Massachusetts–New Hampshire. One of the most striking facts revealed by chart II is that in Newburyport there was probably no specialist turner of card-table legs. This fact is shown by the percentage of 100 for the miscellaneous capital 8 and base 9 turnings. These data underscore that in some areas there was a high degree of specialization in the tightly knit local furniture industries where cabinetmakers found it more economical to purchase the turner's components; in

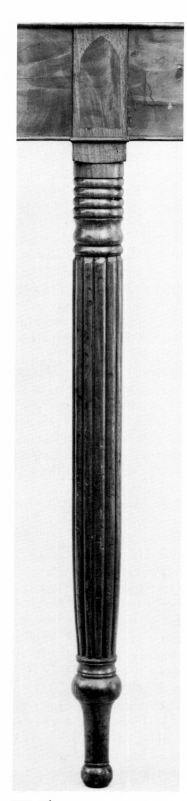

FIG. 36.
Capital 4b, base 4, shaft 2. Detail
of cat. 47.

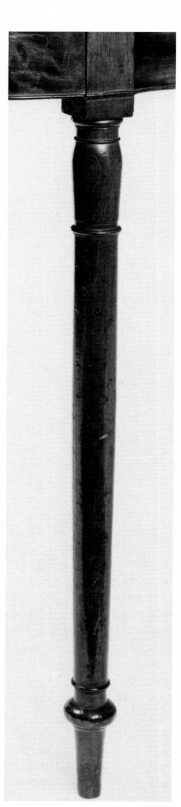

FIG. 37.
Capital 5, base 5, shaft 3. Detail
of cat. 48.

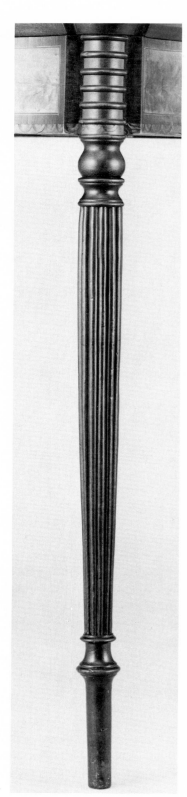

FIG. 38.
Capital 6, base 6, shaft 2. Detail
of cat. 27.

FIG. 39.
Capital 7, base 7, shaft 4. Detail
of cat. 7.

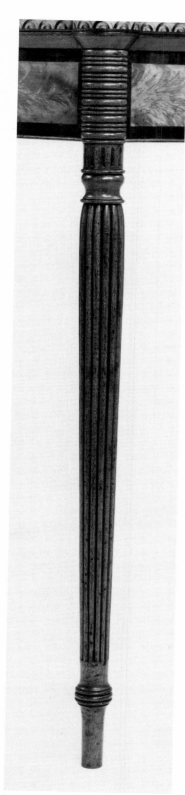

FIG. 40.
Capital 8, base 8, shaft 2. Detail
of cat. 25.

other areas, such as Newburyport, very little specialization in turning existed.

SHAPES OF FEDERAL CARD TABLES

The "shape" refers to the outline of a table's leaves and their supporting frame as they would appear from directly above with the table in the closed position. Twenty-six shapes were found among the tables in the study, and there are undoubtedly others. The nomenclature used here to describe the shapes was either taken directly or derived from that found in price books published between 1788 and 1817 in London, New York, and Philadelphia.[11] Three shapes (1, 10, 11) come under the broad category of circular tables and were constructed with arced rear corners. The other twenty-three shapes come under the broad category of square tables and were constructed with rear corners of 90 degrees. The exact shapes of square tables were specified by qualifying phrases that defined the shape of the front and end rails if they were not straight, and of the front corners if they were not square. A "square card table with elliptic front" (shape 4), for instance, had straight end rails, square corners, and an elliptic front rail. Some shapes are termed popular because they were produced in two or more regions, in at least one of which the frequency was high. Some were termed rare because their frequency in relation to all tables was less than 4 percent. A shape could be popular on straight-leg tables and rare on turned-leg tables, or vice versa. Chart III refers to straight-leg tables and chart IV to turned-leg tables.

Twelve popular shapes were identified (fig. 41). Of these, six (1–6) were used for straight-leg tables. Only one shape (6) was used on both types of tables.

The most popular table shape, circular (shape 1), accounts for one-third of the straight-leg tables in the study and was produced in every center (chart III, 1). The popularity of circular tables may relate to

their compact dimensions and appearance in the closed position, the equidistant placement of the legs across their width, and the many illustrations of this shape in English design books, which could have made it seem fashionable. In addition, some buyers may have preferred circular tables because they easily accommodated more than four card players.

Square with ovolo corners (shape 2) was found everywhere except Annapolis and was the shape used most often on New York straight-leg tables (chart III, 2). The form was also "rare" on turned-leg tables (chart IV, 8). On the other hand, square (shape 3) was most popular in Connecticut and Annapolis. The four straight rails, four square corners, and the alignment of the front and rear legs did not create a visually appealing form.[12]

Comprising only 6.8 percent of the total straight-leg sample, square with elliptic front (shape 4) has much the same appearance as square tables because the front and rear legs of the table are equidistant (chart III, 4). The form was most popular in urban New Hampshire and rural Massachusetts–New Hampshire, but was used rarely on turned-leg tables (chart IV, 10). This shape was not described in the London price books, but it was listed in the New York and Philadelphia price books.[13] Also distinctively American are kidney-end card tables with serpentine middle (shape 5). Although this shape was found on a Boston table and a Baltimore table it was used principally in Philadelphia (chart III, 5) where it was listed in the 1811 price book.[14] On turned-leg tables the shape was rare but was used in Philadelphia (chart IV, 11).

Square with elliptic front and serpentine ends (shape 6) was the only one found to be popular for both straight-leg and turned-leg tables; it has a curvate form with the front legs closer together than the rear legs (chart III, 6; chart IV, 3). This shape may be an American adaptation of the form described in the London price books as "square table

FIG. 41.
Twenty-six shapes of Federal
period card tables:

1. *Circular*

2. *Square with ovolo corners*

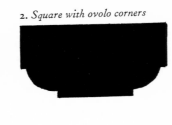

3. *Square*

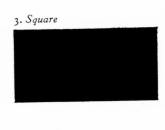

4. *Square with elliptic front*

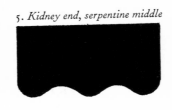

5. *Kidney end, serpentine middle*

6. *Square with elliptic front,
serpentine ends*

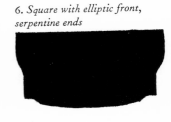

7. *Square with serpentine front,
serpentine ends, ovolo corners over
colonnettes*

8. *Square with elliptic front,
half-elliptic ends, ovolo corners*

9. *Square with elliptic and hollow
front, half-elliptic and hollow ends
ovolo corners*

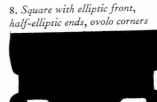

10. *Double elliptic*

11. *Treble elliptic*

12. *Square with elliptic front,
serpentine corners*

13. *Square with serpentine front,
serpentine ends, canted corners*

14. *Square with serpentine front,
serpentine ends*

15. *Square with round corners*

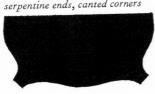

16. Square with round corners, three-quarter colonnettes

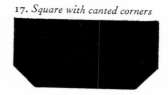

17. Square with canted corners

18. Square with canted corners, eight equal sides

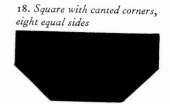

19. Square with serpentine front, ovolo corners

20. Square with serpentine front, serpentine ends, ovolo corners

21. Kidney end with round middle

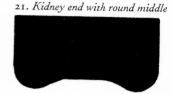

22. Square with serpentine and round middle front, serpentine ends, ovolo corners, three-quarter colonnettes

23. Kidney end with elliptic front

24. Square with elliptic front, half-elliptic ends

25. Square with canted and ovolo corners

26. Square with elliptic front, canted corners

with serpentine front and half serpentine ends."[15] It was the most popular shape used on Salem straight-leg tables.

Of the popular shapes on turned-leg tables, 7, 8, and 9 were found only in Massachusetts and New Hampshire (chart IV, 1, 2, 4). Shapes 7 and 8 were used in all four centers and shape 9 was found only in rural Massachusetts–New Hampshire and Newburyport. On all of these the inward curve of the end rails places the legs slightly closer together at the front corners, where the tops of the legs, or colonnettes, are engaged to the apron.

The popular shapes on New York turned-leg tables were 10, double elliptic, and 11, treble elliptic (chart IV, 5, 6). Not surprisingly, these distinctly American forms are listed in the New York price books.[16] The double elliptic form also was found on a few Philadelphia tables (cat. 46). Philadelphia-area cabinetmakers, however, developed another

FIG. 42.
One of a set of four card tables by John Townsend (1732–1809), Newport, Rhode Island, ca. 1800, no. 229. *Primary woods:* mahogany inlaid with holly. *Secondary woods*: chestnut, tulip, white pine. H. 69 cm; w. 86 cm; D. 34 cm. Mr. and Mrs. Stanley Stone.

The rare shape of this table, with serpentine front and serpentine ends, was probably inspired by London styles. It is closely related to shape 7, with ovolo corners, which was so popular in Massachusetts and New Hampshire. For three reasons this table is readily identified as custommade: its shape is rare, its rails are solid mahogany, and it has a drawer in the end, all of which required Townsend to individually fashion the tops and rails instead of using ready-made components.

highly curvate form, shape 12, for their turned-leg tables (chart IV, 7). This is described in the 1811 Philadelphia price book as "card table with serpentine corners, elliptic front, and straight end rails."[17]

The remaining fourteen shapes are "rare." They account for only 11 percent of the straight-leg tables in the study and 13.7 percent of the turned-leg tables. Cabinetmakers derived some of the rare shapes from price books. Shapes 13–18 are comparable to forms found in the London price books.[18] Shapes 19 and 20 relate to the New York[19] and Philadelphia books, and shapes 21–23 are described exclusively in the 1811 Philadelphia price book.[20] Shape 24 appears to be a variation of the popular shape 8, and shapes 25 and 26 are quite individual interpretations.

Shapes 13 and 14 are basically similar. Shape 13, with its canted corners, is very like the English model and was found on tables from Newburyport, the Boston area, and Annapolis (chart III, 7 and chart IV, 12).[21] Shape 14 is somewhat more atypical since its front corners are rather pointed. It was found on tables from Newport (fig. 42)[22] and Connecticut (chart III, 8).[23] Shapes 13 and 14 are variations of shape 7, the most popular form of turned-leg tables from Massachusetts and New Hampshire.

Shapes 15 and 16 are also closely related. The former, first described in the London book of prices for 1793 as a "square card table with round corners"[24] and sometimes called a D-shaped card table today, was infrequently used in America and was found only in Newburyport, Salem, and Providence (chart III, 9). Shape 16 was found only in Boston (chart IV, 13).

Both shape 17, found on one New York table (chart IV, 14), and shape 18, on one Newport table (chart III, 10), are square with canted corners,[25] although the latter has eight equal sides when open. In the New York price books of 1802 and 1811 under the heading "an ovolo corner card table" there were options for having the serpentine

front (shape 19) or for having both front and ends serpentine (shape 20), which would suggest that these forms were particularly popular in New York.[26] However, no tables of shape 19 were found from New York and only one of shape 20 was seen (chart III, 11, 12; cat. 40). Shape 19 does occur on tables from Newburyport, the Philadelphia area, and Baltimore.[27] Cabinetmakers in these centers may have combined the options listed in the price books for ovolo corner and square tables to arrive at this form.

The penchant of the Philadelphia area for card tables of curvate form is reflected in their price book of 1811 which describes a "kidney end card table with round middle" (shape 21) and a "kidney end card table with elliptic front" (shape 23).[28] Tables of the former shape were found in Philadelphia and Baltimore (chart III, 13), and the latter in the Philadelphia area (chart IV, 16), Newburyport, and Boston (chart III, 14). Shape 22, called here square with serpentine and round middle front, serpentine ends, ovolo corners, and three-quarter colonnettes, was found on one Philadelphia table and may be an adaptation of shape 21 (chart III, 15).

The last three shapes (24–26) are very unusual and cannot be directly related to price-book descriptions. Shape 24, with elliptic front and half-elliptic ends, found in rural Massachusetts–New Hampshire and Salem (chart III, 15 and chart IV, 17), is related to shape 8, one of the popular forms of turned-leg tables in Massachusetts–New Hampshire. Shape 25, with canted and ovolo corners, found in the Boston area, suggests that a cabinetmaker derived the form from square tables (shape 1) to accommodate a turned-leg table (chart IV, 18). To produce shape 26, found in urban New Hampshire, a cabinetmaker probably combined shape 4, square with elliptic front, and shape 17, square with canted corners (chart III, 16).

There are seven documented instances of two or more ready-made tables produced by the same maker. In four instances the tables are the only shape known to have been made by those craftsmen. This is true of the three circular tables (shape 1) by Jacob Forster of Charlestown, Massachusetts (cat. 24), the two tables by Elisha Tucker of Boston (nos. 136, 165) that are square with elliptic fronts and serpentine ends (shape 6), the two tables by John Dolan of New York (cat. 43) which are treble elliptic (shape 11), and two tables by Rogers and Atwood of Newburyport (cat. 10) which are kidney end with elliptic front (shape 23). In two remaining instances, the majority of the makers' documented examples were of one shape. Of six tables by Joseph Short of Newburyport (cat. 9), five were square with ovolo corners (shape 2), and three of four tables of cabinetmaker John Dunlap II of Antrim (cat. 4) were square with elliptic front (shape 4). Only in the case of John Shaw of Annapolis can it be documented that a maker produced three or more shapes (cat. 55, 56). This evidence suggests that cabinetmakers were able to standardize their production by specializing in tables of a certain shape. In this way, cabinetmakers, particularly those in urban areas, were able to employ relatively unskilled craftsmen who could be easily taught to perform such a standard operation as sawing out tops and rails from the same patterns to be stockpiled for later assembly.

The statistics suggest that the tables classified as "popular" were the ones that shops manufactured in large quantities for sale in warehouses to retail customers or to wholesale merchants for export. Such tables were part of a cabinetmaker's regular ready-made output. But production of tables of rare shapes was a different matter; because the data suggest that these were produced in small quantity, they are more likely to have been made on special order and the customer paid extra for the individualized craftsmanship they required.

The data also suggest that as the period progressed, cabinetmakers within regions specialized increasingly. Turned-leg tables were produced later than straight-leg tables, and it is significant that fewer shapes of turned- than straight-leg tables were produced in the regions under study. For example, in rural Massachusetts–New Hampshire, Salem, and Boston about 60 percent of the tables were square with serpentine front and serpentine ends (shape 7), whereas earlier in the period, cabinetmakers in those regions had made a greater variety of shapes of straight-leg tables (charts III, IV).

CONCLUSION. The foregoing analysis of the aspects of tables that contribute to their form—straight legs, turned legs, and shapes—has revealed that only a few characteristics emerge as highly significant indicators of regional origin. For straight legs, the squat double taper is found *only* in the Boston area. For turned legs, capital 1 and base 1 indicate a New York origin; capitals 4a, 4b, 5 and bases 4 and 5 indicate the Philadelphia area; capital 7 and base 7 indicate rural Massachusetts–New Hampshire; base 2a indicates Salem; and bases 6 and 8 indicate the Boston area. Shape 11 indicates a New York origin; shapes 5 and 12, with very high probability, indicate a Philadelphia origin; and shape 9, with very high probability, indicates Newburyport.

ORNAMENT

Ornament in furniture of the Federal period relied on the definition of geometric shapes and a vocabulary of neoclassical motifs. The former were often achieved through the use of veneer, stringing, and banding, and the latter was created by carving and pictorial inlay.

Cabinetmakers traditionally used specialists to produce ornament for them, if specialists were available. The degree of specialization, in any economy, depends upon the size of the population and the size of the potential market. Therefore it usually occurs first in urban settings. Among the specialists who traditionally served cabinetmakers were carvers, gilders, japanners, inlay makers, and turners. Carvers were much in demand in the Chippendale period to produce elaborate asymmetrical ornament. Carving continued to be important in America in the Federal period, but is less evident on card tables than on other furniture forms. In general, Federal-period card tables did not utilize the skills of gilders and japanners, but those of the inlay, maker were in great demand. Inlay, fashionable in the Queen Anne period (1730–60) but eclipsed in the Chippendale period, became widely used in the Federal period. The increased demand for it encouraged some craftsmen to specialize in its production.

Four broad classifications of ornament are found on Federal card tables—relief (which includes carving), veneer, stringing and banding (which include plain and patterned inlay), and pictorial inlay. Regional frequencies for each type (charts V–VII) and for placement (charts VIII, IX), discussed in the sections that follow, yield conclusions about the regional production of ornament by specialists, the reliability of the various types as indicators of regional origin, and the preferences of regional cabinetmakers in utilizing ornament for the facade designs of their tables.

RELIEF ORNAMENT

Relief on Federal card tables consists of carving and molding. Most of this was probably made by carvers to the specifications of cabinetmakers and includes drapery, cornucopias, baskets of fruit, and reeded and fluted panels. Shop employees produced such simpler types of relief ornament as hollowed, reeded, or rounded leaf edges, molded straight legs, and beading that was sometimes nailed or glued to the bottom of the rails. In addition they made the raised molding to divide aprons into rectangular units, to frame the perimeter of pilasters, and to mark the cuffs.[29] The highest frequencies for relief ornament were found in Annapolis and Connecticut for straight-leg tables and in the Philadelphia area, New-

buryport, and New York for turned-leg tables (chart V, 1).

VENEER

Federal cabinetmakers used veneer to create a variety of ornamental effects. By using one sheet of veneer across a table's facade they could create the look of solid wood. By slicing a sheet and butting the ends they could make symmetrical patterns. By carefully choosing a highly figured veneer, they could produce more richly textured surfaces than are customarily found on furniture of solid wood. By selecting different species of wood they could arrange contrasts in color and texture, especially to create a play of geometric shapes characteristic of the neoclassical style.

Veneer was found on the aprons of almost all Federal card tables, but the number of different pieces used varied among regions.[30] For straight- and turned-leg tables, the average number of veneers was greatest in Salem and the Boston area; somewhat less in urban New Hampshire, rural Massachusetts–New Hampshire, and New York; and least in the Philadelphia area and in Annapolis (chart V, 2).

STRINGING AND BANDING

The most widely used types of inlaid ornament on Federal furniture were stringing and banding. Stringing, thin lines of light or dark wood, was often inset directly into furniture in that form or cut into small pieces to create patterned strips of light and dark woods. Banding refers to slightly wider strips of wood in which the grain was arranged in the direction of the strip, at a diagonal angle to the strip, or crosswise to the strip. The demand for inlays, which were an important element in creating the characteristic emphasis on geometric forms in neoclassical-style furniture, encouraged some craftsmen to become specialists in the production and sale of stringing and banding.[31]

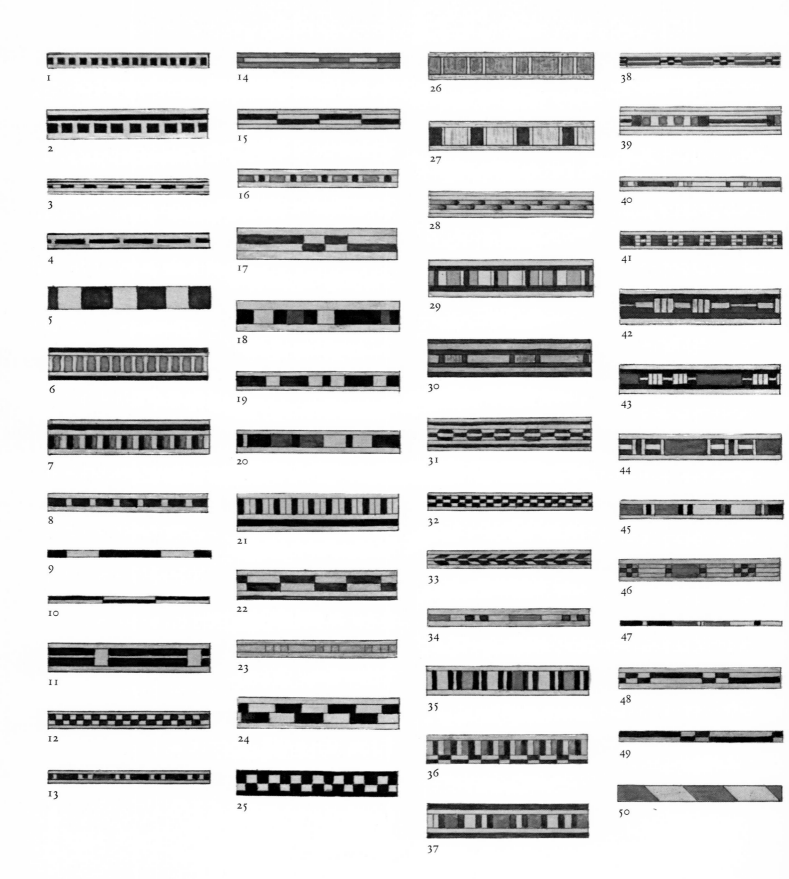

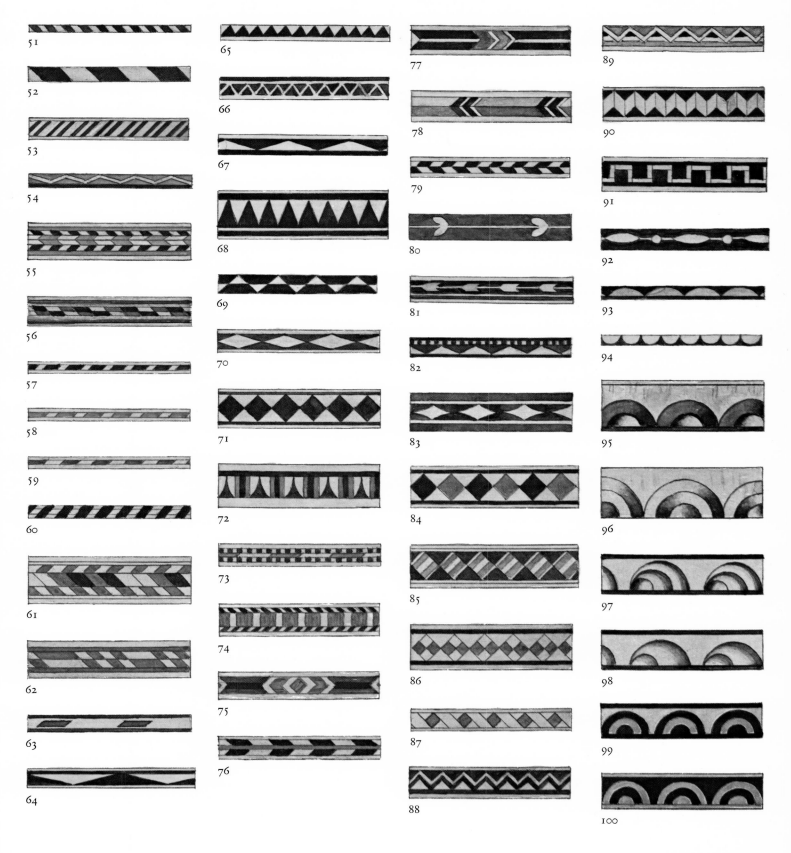

51

52

53

54

55

56

57

58

59

60

61

62

63

64

65

66

67

68

69

70

71

72

73

74

75

76

77

78

79

80

81

82

83

84

85

86

87

88

89

90

91

92

93

94

95

96

97

98

99

100

101

102

103

104

105

106

107

108

109

110

111

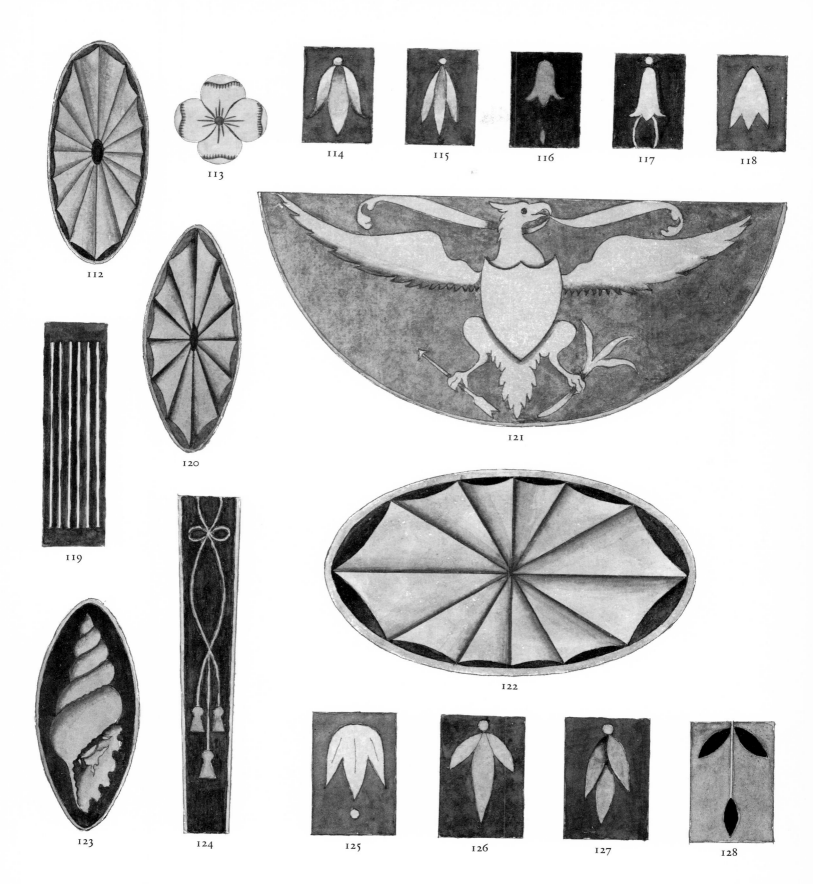

112

113

114

115

116

117

118

119

120

121

122

123

124

125

126

127

128

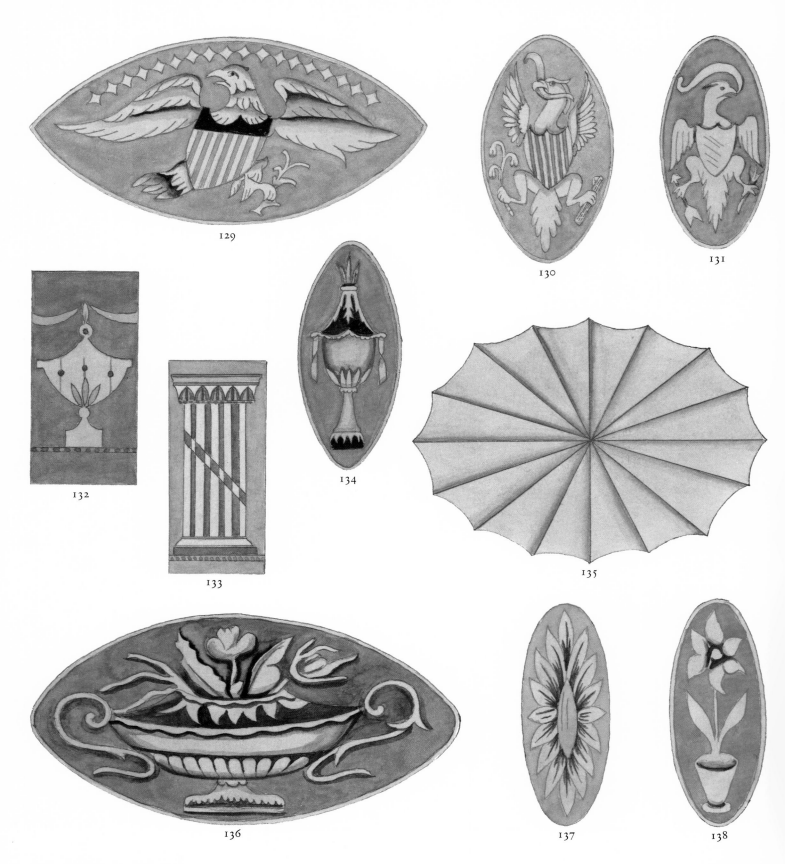

129

130

131

132

133

134

135

136

137

138

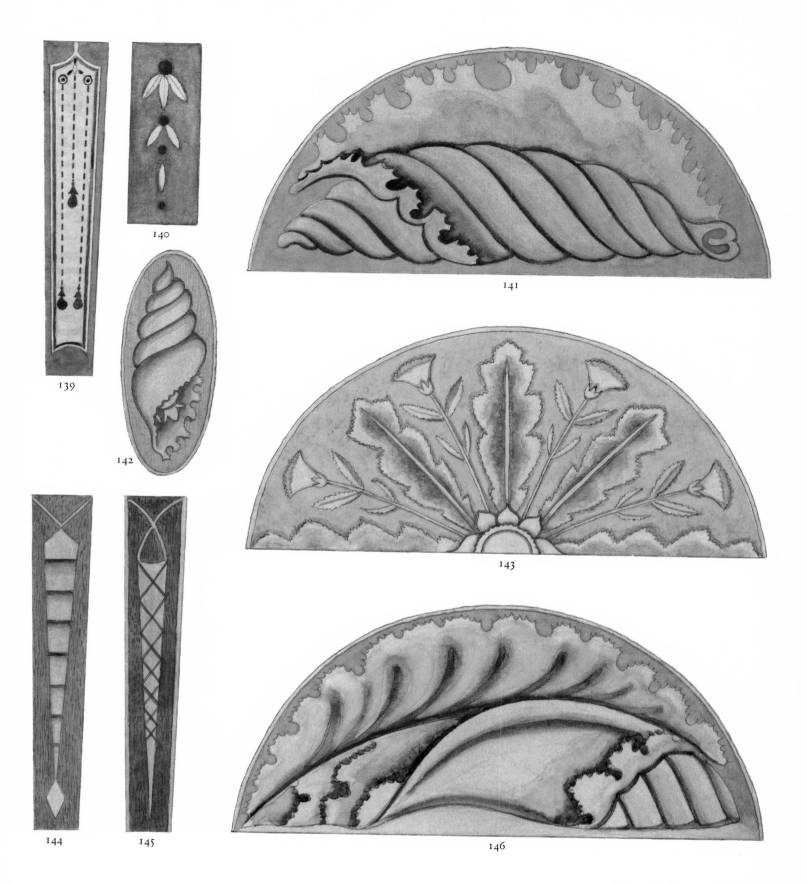

139　140　141　142　143　144　145　146

147

148

149

150

151

PLAIN INLAY

For the purposes of this study, plain stringing used by itself or in combination with banding is called plain inlay. It could appear as (1) single thin lines of light or dark wood; (2) two to five thin lines of light and dark wood combined to create a thicker and more noticeable contrast of colors; and (3) a combination of (1) or (2) with crossbanding or banding which results in a contrast of textures and colors (patterned inlays are illustrated on pp. 74–75 and listed on pp. 184–85).

Plain inlay is a versatile ornament. It accents the straight lines of leaf edges and skirts, borders the tops of tables, or creates round, oval, or other shaped panels in legs, pilasters, and aprons.[32] Plain inlay was used most on straight-leg tables made in New York and on turned-leg tables made in Boston and Salem (chart V, 3).

PATTERNED INLAY

Patterned inlays create a more colorful, and usually a stronger, visual appeal than plain inlay. Patterned inlays are composed of from two to twenty-four small pieces of wood usually of different shapes, such as square, rectangular, triangular, oval, and circular. The woods are natural, dyed, or scorched. After a pattern was composed, it was repeated to form a strip from which the amount desired could be cut and inset singly or in combination with any of the three types of plain inlay described above.

Patterned inlay was used interchangeably with but less extensively than plain inlay at all places on card tables where the latter was found. It may have been used less because craftsmen had to spend more time fashioning it themselves or had to purchase it from specialists, and hence it was more expensive. Of the one hundred different patterned inlays found on tables in the study, some appeared only once and some appeared as many as twenty times. These data suggest that patterns were available in uneven quantities and that the more frequently seen ones may have been made by specialists.

The highest frequencies for patterned inlay were found in urban New Hampshire, rural Massachusetts–New Hampshire, Salem, the Boston area, and Baltimore (chart V, 4). These regional preferences correspond with the numbers of individual patterns recorded for each center, with the exception of urban New Hampshire where only seven individual patterns were found. In rural Massachusetts–New Hampshire, Salem, the Boston area, and Baltimore, however, from 29 to 47 different patterned inlays were found, a number significantly greater than the 2 to 17 inlays found in each of the other eight centers (chart VI, 1A).

Furniture historians have long speculated on the validity of patterned inlays as a factor in determining regional origin. The data in chart VI (1B, 1C) show that in all the centers except Baltimore, cabinetmakers used more patterned inlays that were shared by two or more centers than were unique to their center. This is reinforced by data in chart VI, 2, which reveal the large numbers of patterns used commonly among the twelve centers. The availability of many patterns in more than one region demonstrates the unreliability of using specific patterns as factors to hypothesize regional origin. Subsequent researchers of patterned inlay who increase the sample of furniture forms they investigate will probably find that many more of the fifty-four inlays found to be unique were in fact shared by several centers. Because patterned inlay was readily adaptable for use on different furniture forms, inlay makers could and apparently did find a market for it in other centers.

PICTORIAL INLAY

Pictorial inlays create focal points on card tables in carefully detailed portraits or light-wood silhouettes of buds, leafage, flowers, and architectural and abstract forms. In this study the inlays are classified into two kinds according to their complexity: single-unit inlays, made of one piece of wood; and integrated inlays, made of two or more pieces.

Single-unit inlays were of two types, plain and engraved; and integrated inlays were also of two types, simply integrated and inset and integrated (illustrated on pp. 76–80 and listed on p. 186).

Single-unit inlay. Single-unit inlay was produced by cutting thin slices from a block of wood shaped to a three-dimensional form. Sometimes individual pieces of single-unit inlay were used to form a composite picture, such as the crossed branches (inlay 151) on a Providence table. In this process each piece was still cut out and inlaid individually.

To enhance the appearance or representational quality of single-unit inlays, craftsmen sometimes engraved or scratched the surface of the wood with dark lines. If the surface was left plain, they have been designated as *plain single-unit inlays*, for example the bellflower (inlay 118) on a Boston table. If the surface was engraved they are called *engraved single-unit inlays*, like the bellflower (inlay 125) on a table by Stephen and Thomas Goddard (cat. 28).

A few single-unit inlays were probably made by specialists, such as the carefully executed bellflower (inlay 116) found on the legs of five New York tables (cats. 37, 38) believed to have been manufactured in different cabinet shops. However, because of the modest degree of skill needed, single-unit inlays are presumed to have been made by craftsmen in the shops that used them. Hence they are unique to their areas and are therefore reliable indicators of origin.

Other examples of single-unit inlays are: a blossom (inlay 113) on a Baltimore table; a bellflower (inlay 128) on four tables by John Dunlap of Antrim, New Hampshire (cat. 4); an urn (inlay 101) and tassel motifs (inlay 124) on tables attributed to Holmes Weaver of Newport (cat. 29); and an urn (inlay 132) on a table attributed to Thomas Howard of Providence (cat. 33).

Integrated inlay. In integrated inlay, on the other hand, the form of the object represented is made of at least two pieces of wood (but more often of many pieces) which had been cut by patterns in jig-saw fashion and were then glued to one another. Before being glued together, the parts were often stained to change their color or scorched in hot sand to shade the edges.

If the pieces that make up the inlay were inset directly into a piece of furniture without being surrounded by a framing element, they are designated as *simple-integrated inlay*, like the diamond (inlay 103) on a table by John Dunlap II. A simple-integrated inlay popular on New York ovolo-corner tables are flutes (inlay 119). There is one group of flute inlays, however, whose correct classification is ambiguous (they are similar to flute inlay 110). The ambiguity lies in knowing whether they were made by individual cabinetmakers who inlaid them piece by piece, or whether they were purchased as prefabricated units from a specialist, as the definition of simple-integrated inlay implies.[33]

In the second group of integrated inlays, the pieces of wood that make up the inlay are surrounded by a plain, contrasting wood of geometric shape usually framed by string inlay. These are called *inset-integrated inlay*, such as the urn (inlay 134) found on tables from Boston (cats. 21, 22) and in similar form on tables from urban New Hampshire (cat. 1). As with single-unit inlay, integrated inlays could be combined by the inlayer to form a larger composite design, as is seen in the bellflowers (inlay 115) on the legs of a Baltimore table (cat. 51).

The more complicated fashioning necessary to produce integrated inlays suggests that they were made by specialists who worked either in America or abroad. Thus integrated inlays are reliable indicators of regional origin only if those unique to a center were produced there. Four steps were used to determine which pictorial inlays unique to centers could reasonably be presumed to have been made there.

The first step entailed determining regional preferences for pictorial inlay by counting its occurrence at specific places on tables.[34] The greatest amounts of pictorial inlay were used in New York, Newport, and Baltimore (chart V, 5).

The second step used the same data to compute regional preferences for pictorial inlay at specific places on tables. Pilasters, shafts, and apron centers, in that order, were most commonly inlaid. The center of the top was ornamented with pictorial inlay infrequently, but the practice was most common in Baltimore. The apron adjacent to the ovolo corners was inlaid only in New York. Rarer than all the above was pictorial inlay on the corners of the top, cuffs, and the four corners of the front apron (chart VIII, 1).

The third step entailed computing the regional preferences for the types of pictorial inlays. Single-unit inlays, those believed to be made in cabinet shops, were not used at all in Newburyport, the Philadelphia area, or Annapolis, and were used very infrequently in urban New Hampshire, Salem, and Baltimore (chart VIII, 2). Thus, one can conclude that cabinetmakers in these six centers did not gear their shops to produce pictorial inlay but relied on specialists for most of what they used. However, since the amounts of pictorial inlay used in the Philadelphia area, Annapolis, Salem, and Newburyport were less than in other regions (chart V, 5), it can be further concluded that specialist inlay makers did not work in those centers. Hence the probability is high that most of the specialist-made, or integrated inlays, unique to those four centers or shared only by those centers, were imported from other American centers or from Europe.

The fourth step involved tallying the occurrence of each inlay by region to determine which were unique and which were shared by centers. Newburyport, Salem, the Philadelphia area, and Annapolis yield a combined total of fourteen unique inlays (chart VII, 1B). Eleven of these were integrated inlays. Because it is very unlikely that specialists worked in these centers, it can be concluded that these inlays were imported.

Additionally, any inlays shared by these four centers must also have been imported. Those illustrated here are a shell (inlay 142) and a thistle (cat. 11) shared by Newburyport and Salem;[35] an eagle (inlay 105) on one Philadelphia table;[36] a large shell used to ornament the top of a Newburyport table (inlay 146), a second on the top of a Salem table (cat. 17) and a third on the front of a Philadelphia table (cat 44).[37]

Eagle inlay 105 is similar in design to Baltimore eagles (inlays 131, 149) and may have been imported from there. The shells, with their high degree of elaboration, are unlike shell inlays found elsewhere in America and may therefore have come from Europe. Imported shells are one form of inlay known to have been sold in America, as an advertisement in the New York *Argus* in 1796 demonstrates, "Shells for Cabinet Work—to Cabinet Makers. A gentleman has just arrived from London with an Assortment of Shells for cabinetwork, which he will dispose of on reasonable terms, for cash. Enquire of C. Brenneyson No. 263 Broadway."[38]

The mean number of places on urban New Hampshire and Baltimore tables where pictorial inlay was used was high (chart V, 5). Therefore it is likely that most of the integrated inlays unique to those two centers were made by specialists there and hence are reliable indicators of origin. Four integrated inlays were unique to urban New Hampshire. They are blossoms on a stem and a column (inlay 133) found in three different, but very similar, variations (cat. 2).[39]

In Baltimore, however, the story is quite different, because such a large number of integrated inlays was unique to that center (chart VII, 1B). Since a specialist inlay maker, Thomas Barrett, is known to have worked there, this is not surprising. They may have been made there by Barrett and others, but some are known to have been imported.[40] Those illustrated here include two types of bellflowers (inlays 114,

115); two types of eagles (inlays 106, 121); two shells (inlays 102, 141); two forms of paterae (inlays 111, 112); various complex demilune inlays of acorns, thistles, buds, and leaves, like inlay 143; and finally tassels (inlay 139).

Since the cabinetmakers in the remaining centers—rural Massachusetts–New Hampshire, the Boston area, Providence, Newport, Connecticut, and New York—employed in approximately equal amounts either specialist-made inlay or inlay produced in their own shops (chart VIII, 2), the statistics cannot be used to show conclusively that the integrated inlays unique to those areas were produced there. If inlays are unique to those areas, however, the probabilities are high that they were made there. Those illustrated here are: for rural Massachusetts–New Hampshire segmented icicles (inlay 144); for Boston an eagle in a wide oval (inlay 129) and an eagle in springing position (inlay 109); for Providence, eagles (inlays 104, 150) similar to the Boston eagle (inlay 129), and a segmented icicle (cat. 32); for New York, an eagle (inlay 130), two forms of paterae (inlays 120, 148), and vertical lines of light and dark banding (inlay 119).

The integrated inlays shared by two or more centers where specialist inlay makers worked are not reliable indicators of regional origin. Included in this group are a 12-point patera (inlay 122); an urn with flowers and leaves (inlay 136); a long oval shell (similar to inlay 123); a covered urn (inlay 134); and finally, a sprig of buds, leaves, and flowers (inlay 107).

Of the 162 pictorial inlays found in the study, 138 were unique to a particular center (chart VII, 1). However, 11 of those were shown above to have been imported, leaving 127 (78 percent) that have a high probability of having been made in the center where they were used. Many of these are single-unit inlays.

The production of integrated inlay for export was limited by a number of factors.

Unlike patterned inlay, which by its nature was adaptable for use in many places on many different types of furniture, pictorial inlay was bound by its shape and size for use on a limited range of places on specific pieces of furniture. For example, an eagle in a wide oval (inlay 129), used to ornament the center of an apron, would not also be suitable to ornament pilasters. The varied regional preferences for the amount of pictorial inlay used, for the places where it was employed on tables, and for its details and motifs also argue against a ready market for pictorial inlays outside a local area. Because most pictorial inlays are closely bound to local markets, they are a reliable indicator for establishing the regional origins of card tables.

FACADE DESIGNS

The principal area on Federal-period card tables to be ornamented was the facade, which is the area bounded by the front pilasters or colonettes, the lower leaf edge, and the skirt. For this study, fifteen facade designs were classified into one unit, two units, and three units (fig. 43). One-unit designs (1–7) encompass the entire facade with ornament, sometimes continuing uninterrupted from one side to the other. Two-unit designs (8, 9) are divided at the center by a vertical line of ornament to create two identically ornamented parts. Three-unit designs (10–15) are vertically divided into three parts—the two outer of equal width and the central one of varying width and with identical or different ornament. The regional frequencies of these facade designs, and those of thirteen others called miscellaneous (because each occurred only once), are detailed in chart X.

Since a one-unit design has one kind of veneer, its color is usually uniform; it may be made up of one or more pieces of one kind of unornamented veneer (facade 1), or it may be a single veneer inlaid with a panel of stringing (facade 2). The former was the

FIG. 43.
Facade designs. One-unit facades 1–7; two-unit facades 8, 9; three-unit facades 10–15.

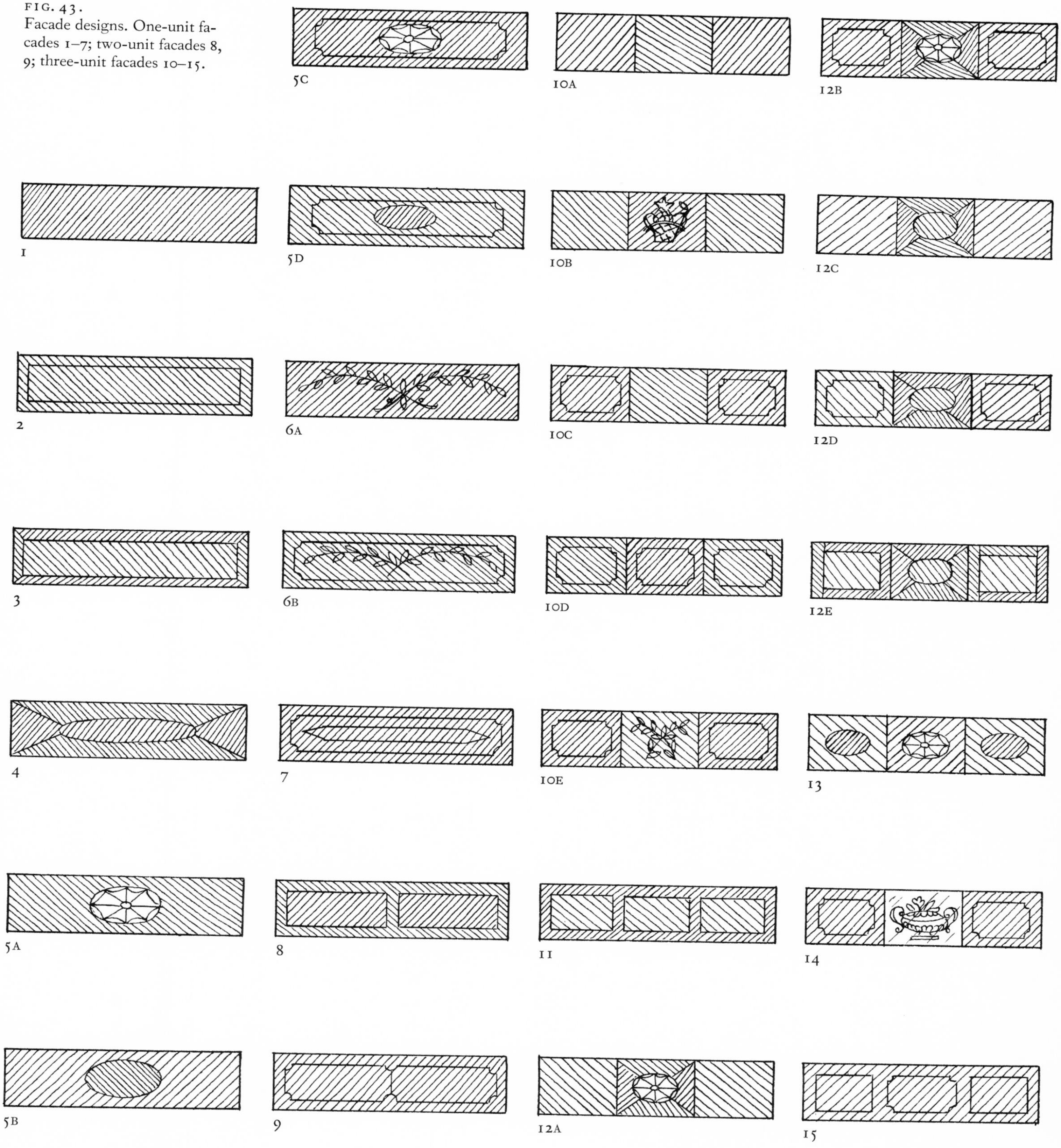

5C

10A

12B

1

5D

10B

12C

2

6A

10C

12D

3

6B

10D

12E

4

7

10E

13

5A

8

11

14

5B

9

12A

15

one most widely used on straight- and turned-leg tables; the latter was widely used only on straight-leg tables. A variation of facades 1 and 2 was facade 3, a rare design composed of a narrow perimetral panel of crossbanding or banding, sometimes combined with string inlay, surrounding a rectangular panel of veneer.

The four remaining one-unit facade designs were found only on straight-leg tables. Used in a number of centers, but favored in New York, facade 4 is composed of a central oval veneer surrounded by plain inlay and flanked by triangles created by mitering pieces of cross-grain veneer at the four corners. Facade 5 (found mostly in New England) is varied by having at its center an inset-integrated pictorial inlay (5A), a geometric panel of veneer (5B), an inset-integrated pictorial inlay surrounded by a panel of stringing at the perimeter (5C), or a geometric panel of veneer surrounded by a panel of stringing at the perimeter (5D).

Facade 6 differs only in the type of its pictorial inlay. Instead of being inset-integrated, facade 6 has either a simple-integrated pictorial inlay or a single-unit inlay at the center of the apron (6A), which is sometimes surrounded by a panel of stringing (6B). Facade 7, composed of a single sheet of veneer inlaid with two panels of stringing, one within the other, was very infrequently found.

Two-unit facades (8, 9) appear on small numbers of straight- and turned-leg tables from three centers each. These designs are composed of one kind of veneer divided at the center either by crossbanding and inlay, which continues around the entire perimeter of both units (facade 8), or by a thin line of inlay at the end of the two panels (facade 9).

Three-unit facades (10–15) have a design made up of three rectangular forms of matching or contrasting veneer enclosing a panel of stringing, a veneer of geometric form, or a pictorial inlay. Three-unit facades, then, are often lively plays of shapes within shapes, accented by contrasts in texture and color. Facade designs 10, 11, and 12 were particularly favored on straight- and turned-leg tables from New England, and designs 13, 14, and 15 were used predominantly on straight-leg tables from New York, the Philadelphia area, and Baltimore.

On facade 10 the units are treated with either plain veneer (10A), carving applied to the center unit (10B), panels of string inlay in the two outer units (10C), panels of string inlay in all three units (10D), or panels of string inlay in the two outer units and a simple-integrated pictorial inlay or single-unit inlay in the central unit (10E).

An outstanding example of the rare facade 11 is on the table by Adams and Todd of Boston (cat. 25), in which three units of the same veneer are surrounded by crossbanding or patterned inlay which provides contrast in texture or color.

Higher in frequency in the Boston area and Salem than in other centers, facade 12 has a distinctive oval panel in the central rectangular unit. The variations within this general pattern are plain outer units and a pictorial inlay within the central oval (12A), panels of stringing in the outer units and a pictorial inlay within the central oval (12B), plain outer units with a veneered central oval (12C), panels of stringing in the outer units and a veneered central oval (12D), and perimetral crossbanding in the outer units and a veneered central oval (12E). The resulting apron design is complex and can be rendered with either subtle or bold variations in texture and color.

Few New York, Philadelphia area, and Baltimore tables have three-unit facades. These include facade 13, similar to but more colorful than 12A and 12B because it has veneer within the side units; facade 14 with an eglomise rectangle at the center; and facade 15 with identical panels of string inlay in the single veneer spanning the apron.

Specific facade designs suggest but do not define where tables originated. High frequencies of facade 1 on turned-leg tables suggest origin in Newburyport or the Philadelphia area; of facade 4 on straight-leg tables, an origin in New York; and of facade 12, origin in Salem or the Boston area.

Facade designs are related to the shapes of tables. All circular tables have the plainer one-unit designs (facades 1–7) which are usually repeated in each of the three apron sections. Two-unit and the more complex composition of three-unit facades (8–15) were used only on square tables.

Individual shops repeatedly used the same facade design.[41] This practice and a preference for tables of one shape underscore the standardized production methods employed by Federal-period shops. Cabinetmakers saved themselves time by using a basic design and varying its details, for instance by using plain inlay on one table and patterned inlay on another. This practice standardized the work of the inlayer and limited the kinds of ornament a shop had to keep on hand. It also obviated the need for many templates. These savings in time and materials promoted efficiency and economy.

CONCLUSION. Cabinetmakers in various regions combined the five kinds of ornament and facade designs to create tables with recognizable regional styles. For example, tables from Newport (cats. 28, 29) and Baltimore (cats. 51–53) and straight-leg tables from New York (cat. 38) have a strong vertical thrust because cabinetmakers in those areas preferred to ornament the pilaster and shafts with pictorial inlay and to use one-unit facade designs with little contrast in the color of the veneers. On the other hand, on square tables with both straight and turned legs from Salem (cats. 14, 18, 19) and the Boston area (cats. 21, 22, 25, 27), cabinetmakers made the center of the facade their focal point by using complex three-unit designs which they veneered with various woods outlined by string inlay; on straight-leg tables they restrained their use of inlays on the legs. The horizontal lines of tables from urban New Hampshire (cat. 1) and straight-leg tables from rural Massachusetts–

New Hampshire (cat. 6) were emphasized by the makers' preferences for patterned inlay on the leaf edges and skirts and single-unit facades. On turned-leg tables from Newburyport (cat. 12), the uniformly dark color of mahogany was subtly ornamented with relief on the leaf edges, skirts, and sometimes on the facades.

The data reveal that patterned inlays are not reliable indicators of regional origin because they were traded extensively among centers, but that single-unit inlays are reliable indicators because most were produced within the shops that used them. Some integrated pictorial inlays are reliable indicators of region when their origin can be established. Facade designs in general are only suggestive of regional origin; they are closely related to table shapes, and data about them on documented tables suggest that, like table shapes, they were used repeatedly by individual shops. Hence they are an example of how cabinet shops standardized their production.

CONSTRUCTION

Both aesthetic and practical considerations—shape and use—affected the construction of Federal-period card tables. Because the shapes of the tables reflected the aesthetic of the neoclassical style, which often combined straight and curved lines, cabinetmakers had to devise ways of constructing rails that curved. The tables were also designed to be used either closed against a wall or freestanding with the upper leaf unfolded; the cabinetmakers had therefore to construct the rear rail to accommodate a movable leg (called the flyleg) which supported the upper leaf when it was unfolded. Five aspects of interior construction affected by these aesthetic and practical considerations—secondary woods, rails, flyleg construction, leaf-edge tenons, and medial braces—are examined, and the regional preferences for the use of each are here discussed.

Woods, and secondary woods in particular, have long been recognized as a valuable tool in determining the origin of American furniture. An innovative compilation of information on them was the chart developed by Charles Montgomery which appears in the introduction to his *American Furniture: The Federal Period* (p. 37). The chart is organized into primary and secondary woods, with indications of the relative frequencies with which the woods were found in broad geographic regions. Although Montgomery's presentation is different from that in this study, and his chart is based on an analysis of 491 assorted pieces of furniture as compared with the single form analyzed here, much comparable information about the regional use of secondary woods is revealed.

In the present study the species of secondary woods were identified by eye and tabulated in chart XI. Secondary woods in card tables were characteristically combined in different areas, and the frequencies of their use can provide evidence for regional attributions. For example, in Massachusetts and New Hampshire, white pine is to be found on almost every table. However, while cherry was used more than birch or maple in urban New Hampshire and rural Massachusetts–New Hampshire, the converse was true in the other three centers of Massachusetts and New Hampshire. On most Newport, Providence, Connecticut, and New York tables, white pine is combined with birch, maple, or cherry. The presence of chestnut adds weight to an attribution to the first three regions, but tulip poplar does likewise for New York. The combined use of oak and white pine suggests that a table originated in the Philadelphia area. On the other hand, oak combined with taeda pine is characteristic of many Baltimore tables and of the Annapolis tables in the study.

RAILS

On Federal-period card tables the frames are comprised of four, five, or six rails, and hinged rails. The front and end rails may be straight or curved, but the two rear rails are always straight. If a table has curved rails it

FIG. 44.
Single-board construction of curved front and end rails.

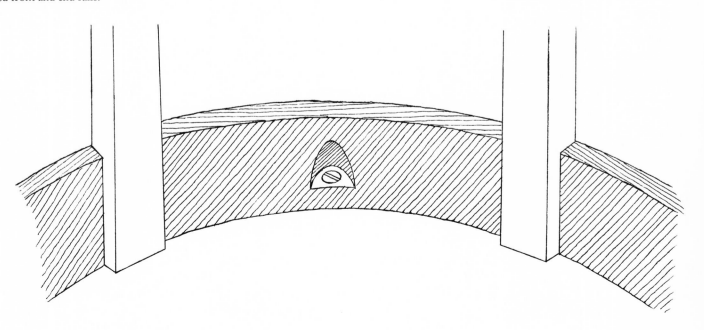

may have as few as one or as many as five. The analysis of the rails is divided into three major categories: curved-rail construction pertains to the shape and appearance of the table; hinged-rail construction relates to the provision of either one or two flying rails to which a flyleg is mortised; back construction refers to the method by which the hinged rails are fastened to the rear rail so that the flying rail is movable.

Curved rails. Ninety-six percent of the tables in the study have at least one curved, or shaped, rail, and a few have as many as five. Although straight rails were always sawn from a single board, curved rails were constructed according to one of the following four methods (chart XII, 1).[42] (1) In single-board construction, the rails were sawn as a single board to the required shape, length, and height (fig. 44). (2) In horizontal-lamination construction, two to six strips of wood, usually of alternating grain, were sawn to the required shape and glued together to form the rails (fig. 45). (3) The kerf rail, always quarter-round in shape and used only at the front corners, was produced by slitting a thin board of appropriate length and height at approximately quarter-inch

intervals, filling the slits with glue, bending the board to shape, and pressing coarse muslin against the glue (fig. 46). (4) In vertical-lamination construction, four or five very thin slices of wood, usually of alternating grain, were cut to the desired length and height, bent to shape, and glued together. Like the kerf, it is found only in quarter-round shape and at the front corners (fig. 47).

Single-board construction of curved rails was found predominantly in rural Massachusetts–New Hampshire, Newburyport, Salem, and the Boston area. Preferences for the number of laminations on horizontally laminated rails were regional. In urban New Hampshire, Newburyport, Salem, the Boston area, and Providence, one or two laminations predominated. From Newport south, greater numbers of laminations were found. With one exception, the kerf rail was used on straight-leg tables with ovolo corners and occurred with greatest frequency in rural Massachusetts–New Hampshire. Vertically laminated rail construction was found only on New York straight-leg tables with ovolo corners. Although kerf and vertically laminated rails are useful indi-

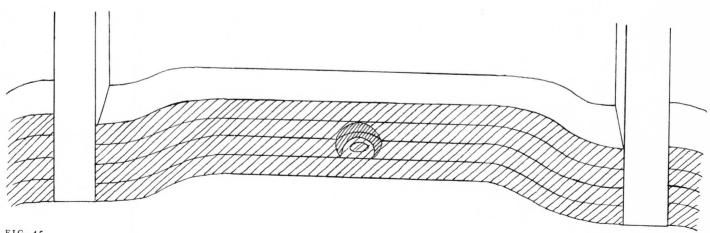

FIG. 45.
Horizontal-lamination construction of curved front and end rails.

FIG. 46.
Kerf construction of an ovolo
rail.

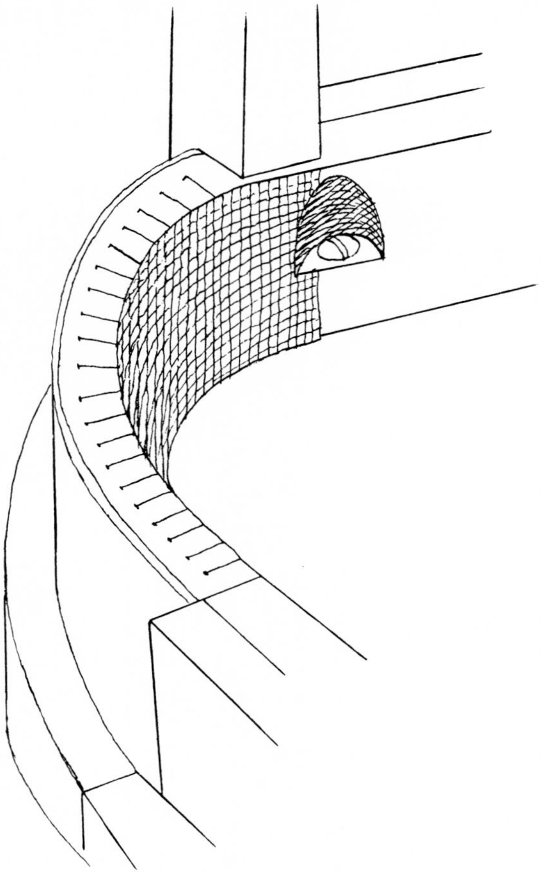

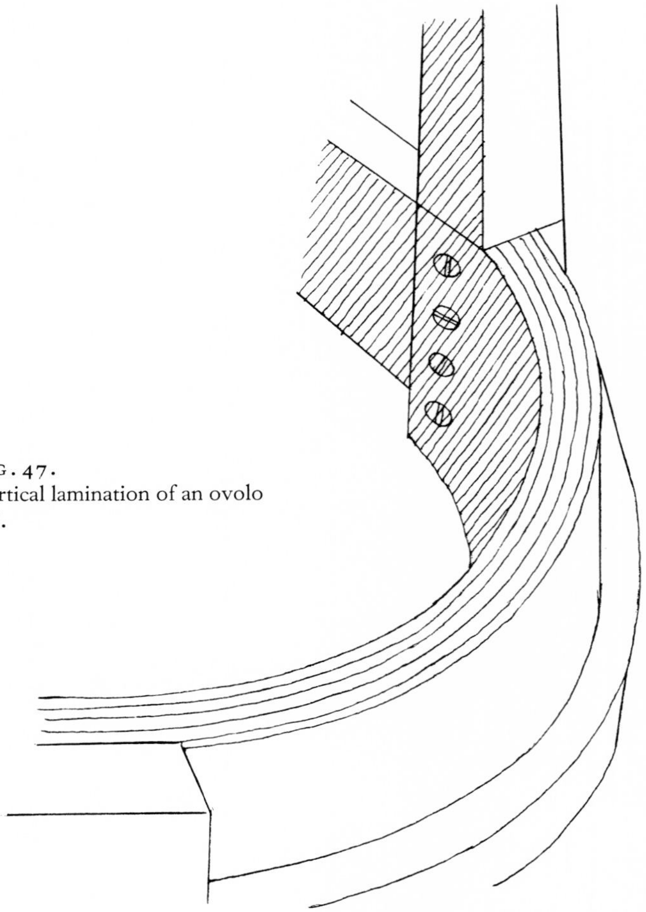

FIG. 47.
Vertical lamination of an ovolo
rail.

cators of regional origin, the other forms of rail construction draw only broad regional distinctions.

The data also reveal that within centers, given cabinetmakers used different forms of curved-rail construction and different numbers of horizontal laminations. For example, of the five square tables with ovolo corners (shape 2) by Joseph Short of Newburyport, the curved rails of three are of single-board construction, one has one horizontal lamination, and the other has two horizontal laminations.[43]

Hinged rails. A card table has a rear rail and a hinged rail; the latter is composed of one stationary rail and either one or two movable flying rails. The stationary rail is attached to the rear rail, and the flying rail or rails have a flyleg mortised to their outer end to support the top leaf in the open position. Three kinds of hinged rails were found on the tables in the study.

Hinged-rail design 1 has two parts, a stationary and a flying rail, and was used on tables with three fixed legs and one flyleg (fig. 48). Hinged-rail design 2 has three parts, a stationary and two flying rails, and was used on the tables with two flylegs and two fixed legs (fig. 49). Hinged-rail design 3 has two parts, a stationary and a flying rail, and was used on card tables with one fly and either four or five fixed legs. It is like hinge design 1 except that its flying rail is shorter so as to fit on the inside of the fixed right rear leg, and its boards are thinner to permit the hollow-square top of the flyleg to fit under and against the rear rail (fig. 50).

Hinged-rail design data show that, while no design was unique to a particular center, some regions used much more of some rail

FIG. 48.
Hinged-rail design 1.

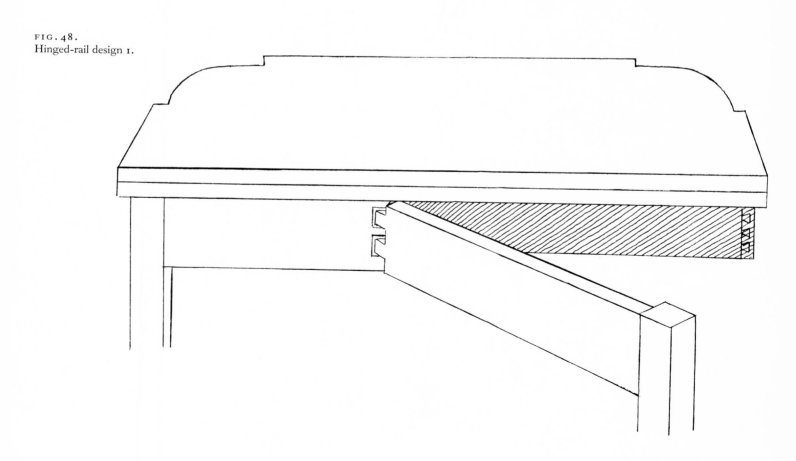

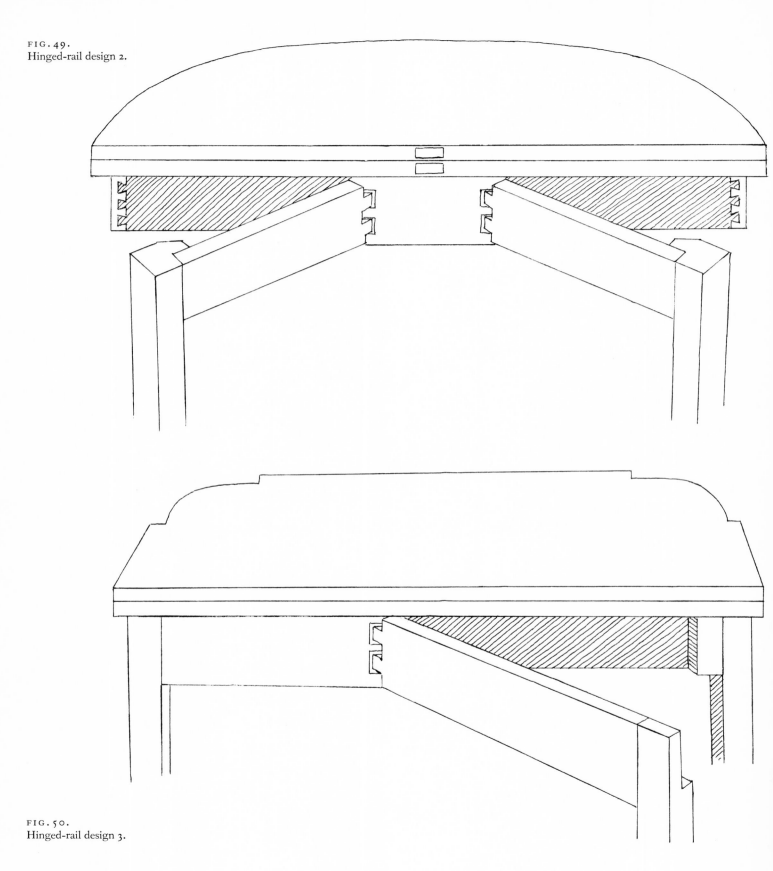

FIG. 49.
Hinged-rail design 2.

FIG. 50.
Hinged-rail design 3.

designs than others did (chart XII, 2). For example, design 1 was found almost invariably on tables that originated in urban New Hampshire, rural Massachusetts–New Hampshire, Newburyport, the Boston area, Providence, the Philadelphia area, and Annapolis. It was also found with high frequency on tables that originated in Salem and Baltimore. Design 2 is found on about half the card tables made in Newport and Baltimore and on more than a fifth of the tables made in Salem. Design 3 was found on all tables that originated in Connecticut, on 93 percent in New York, and almost half of those made in Newport.

Thus these data suggest, but do not define, the regions where tables might have originated. However, because of uniformity in the preferences of centers for hinge designs, they are useful in corroborating hypotheses based on other kinds of information about regional origins and about levels of specialization in the furniture industry.

To determine whether the regional uniformities were significant and, if they were, to speculate about the reason for their significance, the data on hinged rails were tested statistically. The first step was to hypothesize that within most regional centers, cabinetmakers had strong preferences, rather than random or chance preferences, for one particular hinged-rail design. This hypothesis was confirmed by statistical analysis.[44]

One can speculate that the consistent preferences of cabinetmakers within given regions for a particular hinged-rail design indicate that local specialists produced hinged rails and sold them to many shops. If a component was consistently produced in the same way within a region, it was reasoned, it probably was the output of a specialist. Conversely, if sizable numbers of a table component were produced in different ways within a region, they were probably made by craftsmen in the shops that used them. This interpretation is supported by findings that the construction of other parts of card tables from individual shops in the same region have a notable lack of consistency, as was demonstrated above for curved rails. Because the angles and shapes of dovetails and corner blocks vary significantly on different tables by the same maker, it is likely that different shop employees made them. Therefore, it is concluded that if cabinetmakers had also been producing the hinged rails for their tables, the types of hinged rails used within centers would have varied more than they do.

Back construction. An analysis of the hinged rail and the rear rail at the back of the table also reveals certain regional preferences (chart XII, 3). The rear rail, fastened to the two end rails, is the main supporting member of the frame at the back of the table and is the part to which the hinged rail is attached. The stationary part of the hinged rail had to be fastened to the rear rail in such a way that the teeth on the movable part of the hinged rail were free to turn inward as the flyleg was pulled backward. This fastening of the rear rail and the hinged rail was accomplished by two types of construction. The first is called filler construction because fillers, or narrow strips of wood (sometimes scrap), were inserted between the stationary part of the hinged rail and the rear rail to create a space for the teeth on the flying rail to move into (fig. 51). For the second, flush construction, the hinged rails were constructed of thick boards the width of the top of the flyleg, and its stationary part was fastened directly against the rear rail. Therefore, since there was no space between the rear rail and the hinged rail, it was necessary either to round the teeth or to cut a groove in the rear rail so that the flying rail could move (fig. 52).

Half or more of the tables produced in urban New Hampshire, rural Massachusetts–New Hampshire, Newburyport, Salem, the Boston area, and Annapolis have filler construction (chart XII, 3). On the other hand, all the tables that originated in Newport and Connecticut, the vast majority from Providence and New York, and two-thirds or

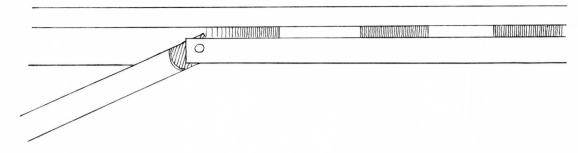

FIG. 51.
Filler back construction as seen from the underside of a table.

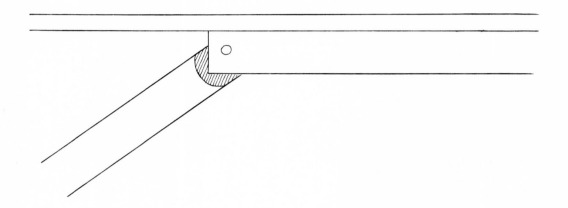

FIG. 52.
Flush back construction as seen from the underside of a table.

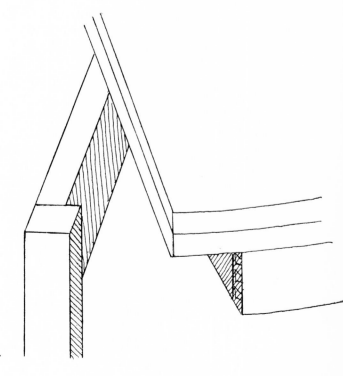

FIG. 53.
Plane flyleg construction.

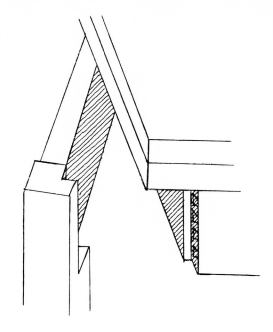

FIG. 54.
Overlapping flyleg construction.

more of the Philadelphia-area and Baltimore tables exhibit flush construction.

Flyleg. The top of the flyleg of Federal card tables was fashioned to allow it to fit neatly into the rear structure of the table. Ninety-eight percent of the tables in the study have flylegs that were constructed in one of three ways.[45] In plane flyleg construction, found only on tables with four legs, the top of the flyleg has a flat, or planar front surface which butts flat against the rear rail (fig. 53). In overlapping construction, also found only on four-leg tables, a rectangle about a half an inch deep was cut from the inside edge of the top of the flyleg. It provides a thin horizontal shelf that fits under the rear rail to support the weight of the table, and a vertical lip that fits snugly against the apron to hold the flyleg in place in the closed position (fig. 54). In additional flyleg construction, found only on tables with five or six legs, the flyleg has a hollow-square or rabbeted top, which permits the flyleg to fit under the rear rail (fig. 55).

Although no one flyleg construction is unique to a particular center, some constructions are found on 90 percent or more of the regional samples, as, for example, plane construction in all five of the Massachusetts and New Hampshire centers, overlapping construction in Providence, and additional flyleg construction in Connecticut and New York (chart XII, 4). Flyleg construction is thus useful in determining origin.

Because of the consistent regional preferences for flyleg construction as well as for shapes of straight legs, discussed above, regional data about flyleg construction and straight-leg shape were combined in order to test the hypothesis that this combination reflects consistent rather than random regional preferences (chart XIII). It was reasoned that since these two characteristics describe the construction of both the fixed and flylegs (or all of the legs of tables), consistency in their construction could suggest that regional specialists produced and sold

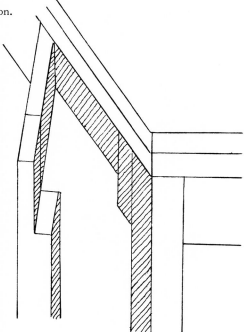

FIG. 55.
Additional flyleg construction.

sets of legs to cabinetmakers. Statistical tests of this hypothesis revealed that in eleven regions—all centers except Annapolis—cabinetmakers had consistent preferences for particular combinations of straight-leg shapes and flyleg construction.[46] It was therefore hypothesized that specialists produced sets. If this were not true, sets of legs would have had to be fashioned by cabinetmakers, who would have varied their combinations of construction and shape more randomly.

These findings are shown in chart XIII, where italic frequencies show the kinds of sets that specialists are believed to have made. It will be noted that Newburyport and Connecticut and nearly all New York and Providence tables had one kind of set; that two kinds were used in urban New Hampshire, rural Massachusetts–New Hampshire, Salem, and the Philadelphia area. Three types were used in the Boston area. In Baltimore one kind accommodated most of the tables.

Rear leaf-edge tenon. Cabinetmakers sometimes added tenons and mortises to the rears of leaf edges to keep the two leaves stable when the table was open (fig. 56).

Regional preferences ranged from no tenons to the invariable use of one or more. With the exception of urban New Hampshire, tenons were used much more sparingly in the Massachusetts and New Hampshire regions than in the other seven centers. In New York, for example, two and sometimes three tenons were used more frequently than one (chart XII, 5).

Medial brace. A brace was sometimes used between the front and rear rails to add rigidity to the table frame (fig. 57). It is found most frequently on tables with four legs of which two are flylegs, a characteristic of more than half the tables from Baltimore. It was also found on tables with one flyleg, including a few from Baltimore and other locales (chart XII, 6).

CONCLUSION. The details of the construction of the six parts of card tables that were analyzed in this study show that *only one* characteristic—vertically laminated rail construction found only on New York tables—is a completely reliable indicator of regional origin. Yet the ways in which cabinetmakers in various regions produced these details are suggestive of origin. New York makers al-

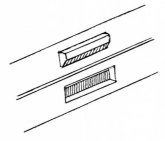

FIG. 56.
Rear leaf-edge tenon as seen from the back of a table.

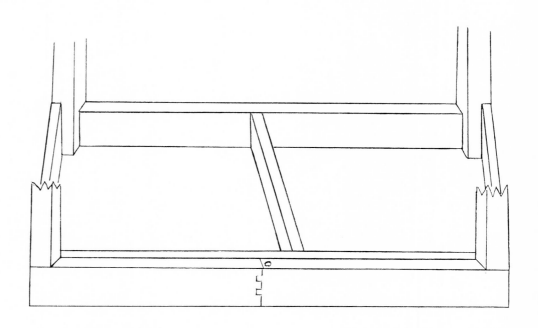

FIG. 57.
Medial brace as seen from the underside of a table.

ways used leaf-edge tenons, constructed curved rails with two or more horizontal laminations or with vertical laminations, and with rare exception used hinged-rail design 3, flush back construction, and the additional flyleg. If construction features do not often pinpoint origins, they nonetheless provide evidence that is helpful in arriving at accurate regional determinations.

Sturdiness

This study also analyzed the construction of curved rails, the back, flylegs, rear leaf-edge tenons, and medial braces to determine the degree of strength each contributed to the table. These five parts, it will be recalled from above, were constructed in different ways or used in different amounts in the various regions. Each of these different construction methods, and the number of times a feature was used, made a card table more or less sturdy. As the sturdiness of each construction increased, the cost of labor and materials increased also. Sturdiness was costly.

A comparison of the backs reveals that flush construction was stronger and required more materials and slightly more labor to fashion than filler construction. The latter used wood of thinner dimensions for the hinged rear rail and narrow strips of wood, sometimes scraps, to fill the space between the rear rail and the hinged rail. It was weaker than flush construction because any movement of the hinged rails was conducted to the frame of the table at only two points—where the fasteners went through the fillers to join the rear rail and hinged rail and at the left side of the rails where they joined the table's rail. The space which the filler created between the rear and the hinged rails enabled the teeth on the hinged rail to move inward without being rounded. Because the wood of the rail was thinner, it also took less time and effort to drive nails or screws through it. Flush construction

was stronger because the hinged rail was butted directly against the rear rail and any movement of the hinged rail was conducted uniformly to the frame of the table along the length of the rear rail from the center of the table to the left side. Flush construction required additional labor to round the teeth on the hinge or to make grooves in the back rail so that the flying rail could move. The thickness of the boards and their buttressed construction meant that they were less apt to warp or break and hence added sturdiness to the table.

Tenons on the rear leaf edge are a minor detail, but the shaping of each one and its corresponding mortise took additional time and materials. They provided a more even and sturdier playing surface when the table was open. Likewise, a medial brace took more time and material but added strength to the rail construction.

The three types of flyleg construction—plane, overlapping, and additional—also provided different degrees of sturdiness. The plane flyleg, on which the inner front surface of the top of the leg was flat, took less time to construct because a minimum of detailed work was required. The construction is weak because if the flyleg rail warps or the hinge wears with use, there is nothing to prevent the flat surface of the flyleg from wobbling or its top from pressing upward against the lower leaf and weakening its attachment to the rails. On the other hand, the rectangular sleeve on an overlapping flyleg provides a thin horizontal shelf that fits under the rear rail to support the weight of the table, and a vertical lip to hold the flyleg in place against the apron. Additional flyleg construction provided the most support, but it also cost the most because extra materials and labor were required to produce the other leg and to fashion a hollow-square or rabbeted top, which permitted the flyleg to fit under the rail.

The same criteria can be applied to the curved rails. Single-board construction resulted in an inherently weak rail because the short grain at the ends would be weak. The kerf rail is weak since the cuts in the wood to allow it to bend violate its structural strength. By applying muslin and glue to it, cabinetmakers compensated for this inherent weakness, but on several tables with kerf construction the rails had split, an indication that this form of construction is not necessarily strong. With horizontally laminated rails, as the number of laminations increased, the rails became stronger and the expense of making them increased, as data in the Philadelphia price book for 1795 indicate. For example, a 3-inch-high circular or serpentine rail between 2½ and 3½ feet long cost a total of 3 pence. But to produce a horizontally laminated rail of that width from two boards 1½ inches high, the costs were 2 pence for each board and 2 pence for gluing up the joint; thus, the total cost was 6 pence. To produce the horizontally laminated rail from three boards each of one-inch height, the costs were 1.5 pence for each board and 4 pence for gluing up the two joints; thus the total cost was 8.5 pence.[47] Therefore, as the number of horizontal laminations increased, the cost of labor and materials also increased. Horizontal lamination also increased shop overhead because clamps and cauls were costly, space had to be provided for gluing and clamping the rails and for spreading them out to dry, and fabricating skill was required.[48]

Vertically laminated rails are plywood-like and although they are thin, the direction of the grain of the wood in each layer is alternated for a balanced construction that has great strength.

The methods by which each of these five parts were constructed reveal the attitudes of cabinetmakers about constructing tables both sturdily and economically, but they do not indicate the extent to which sturdy methods were used in constructing all parts of the same table. To determine whether cabinetmakers in the same center had consistent attitudes about sturdy construction, a score based on a point system was computed to reveal the overall sturdiness of each table.[49] Mean sturdiness scores and the range of scores for tables of each origin are shown in chart XIV.

Tables produced in Newport, Providence, Connecticut, the Philadelphia area, and Baltimore are sturdier than those from Massachusetts and New Hampshire, but New York tables are the sturdiest of all. The mean for urban New Hampshire, rural Massachusetts-New Hampshire, Newburyport, Salem and the Boston area is lower than that of any of the other seven centers, and statistically each of their scores is significantly lower than the mean score of all tables in the study.

Turned-leg tables from rural Massachusetts-New Hampshire, Newburyport, Salem, and the Boston area were significantly less sturdy than those produced in either Philadelphia or New York. Because turned-leg tables, on the average, were manufactured later than straight-leg tables, comparison of their mean number of sturdiness points suggests that as the Federal period progressed, Massachusetts, New Hampshire, and New York cabinetmakers produced increasingly less sturdy tables, but Philadelphia craftsmen moved toward even stronger construction.

CONCLUSION. This analysis of five structural features shows that the sturdiness of card tables of the same origin was highly consistent but that sturdiness varied considerably from center to center. Thus cabinetmakers working in the same locality had similar attitudes about the economical use of labor and materials.

The use of less sturdy and hence less expensive construction methods reflects a need to cut costs to produce competitively priced furniture. The first to respond to these pressures were craftsmen in urban New Hampshire, rural Massachusetts–New Hampshire, Newburyport, Salem, and the Boston area. Cabinetmakers from these centers used more expeditious methods of construction, resulting in tables which were not so sturdy as those made elsewhere. Cabinetmakers everywhere must have felt the same need to safeguard their profit, and yet shops south of Massachusetts and New Hampshire were slower in developing methods by which to increase their productivity.

Customized and Custom-Made Tables

Statistics concerning straight-leg styles, fly-leg construction, hinged rails, and shapes of tables reveal that 80 to 85 percent of the card tables in the study follow standardized construction methods. These tables were ready-made, available from stock, or were basic models ordered with extra features, that is, customized. The remaining 15 to 20 percent of the tables might incorporate any of the customized extras, but they also included one or more features which are significantly different from the standard model. Because basic changes did not permit routine methods of production, tables with these features have been identified as custom-made.

CUSTOMIZED TABLES

A standard model could be "customized" in five ways by changing the amount or kind of ornamentation or by enhancing its suitability as a gaming table (chart IX): by adding baize to improve the playing surface; by shaping the top with pockets for counters and candles; by adding a drawer to the rear rail for storing cards and other card-playing accouterments; by changing the amount of relief, veneer, or inlay; or by chamfering or hollowing the lower leaf edge. Some of these features are noted in the price books as extras that could be added to the basic table for slightly more cost.

Baize was glued to the inner-leaf surfaces of some tables to facilitate the play. This entailed either sinking the surface of the table top (cat. 47) or lipping the perimeter with banding the thickness of the fabric

(cats. 17, 38). Baize was used on twenty-three tables in the study—one or more from each center except urban New Hampshire and rural Massachusetts–New Hampshire—but was found on all five tables from Annapolis (chart IX, 3B, i), where it may have been standard.

Carved pockets on the playing surface are found infrequently on Federal card tables. A unique example is a customized New York table (no. 279) by Charles Honoré Lannuier which has eight hollows, four for candlesticks and four for accouterments. Although this treatment was commonly found on Chippendale card tables, it may have been less popular in the Federal period because, as Ward reasons in his essay, Federal card tables were probably multipurpose and baize and pockets restricted their use to card playing.

A drawer inset in the rear rail was an added convenience. Its placement behind the flying rail entailed building a drawer, installing slides, and cutting an opening in the straight rear rail, which was otherwise a standard ready-made product. The addition of this feature therefore resulted in a customized rather than a custom-made table. It was found on a few tables made in Massachusetts–New Hampshire (cat. 15).

Customers who wanted more or different ornament, however, could and did order it. A table can be considered customized if it has ornament used in a way that was not the standard for a center. For example, string inlay appears on the perimeter of the top leaf of a table by Jacob Forster (cat. 24). By comparing that feature with statistics on chart IX, 1C, i, it can be seen that this practice was followed on only 4 percent of the Boston-area tables and hence it can be concluded that the Forster table was customized.

Cabinetmakers enhanced the overall lightness of their tables by reducing the thickness of the tops by chamfering or hollowing the lower leaf edge (cat. 8). Because this feature is found on small numbers of tables from eight regions, it was probably a customized extra wherever it was used (chart IX, 4A, i).

CUSTOM-MADE TABLES

Custom-made tables can be difficult to attribute to a particular region because they conform so irregularly to the standardized norms. Regional identification usually can be made only if the table is signed or documented, or if it has a feature which is known to be a highly significant indicator of regional origin, such as a unique turned capital or base.

It can be determined that a table of established origin was custom-made if it varies significantly from the established norms of the region where it was made in one of the following ways: if it is significantly smaller or larger than the standard 36-inch width (see Kane essay, above); is either a "rare" shape or a different shape from those popular in its region; has a shape of leg and flyleg construction atypical of its region; has an arrangement of legs atypical of its region; has a drawer in the front or side aprons. To produce any of these features the cabinetmaker had to deviate significantly from the production of a standard model. Tables of undersized or oversized width may have been ordered by customers who wanted to use them in narrow spaces or to accommodate a small or large number of players. Both variations from the norm of approximately 36-inch width required custom work because rails and tops had to be constructed to meet the customer's requirements. An oversize example is the 99-inch Salem or Boston table (cat. 17); an undersized one is the Baltimore table (cat. 54). Undersize tables were produced rarely, mostly in Baltimore, but small numbers of oversized tables were constructed in rural Massachusetts–New Hampshire, Salem, the Boston area, Providence, and Baltimore.

Rare-shaped tables are presumed to have been produced on special order because they do not conform to regional norms. The turned-leg table by Lannuier, with canted corners (shape 17, cat. 41), was unique to the study and was obviously custom-made. However, some tables of popular shape elsewhere could also be custom-made if they originated in a center where the form was unpopular. The Providence table (cat. 31) with elliptic front and serpentine ends (shape 6), by Joseph Rawson and Son, was of a shape popular in Boston and Salem but is unique among the Providence tables in the study. It can confidently be called a custom-made table because the Rawsons had to change their production methods to produce it.

It has been hypothesized that sets of legs of popular shapes and flyleg construction were manufactured by specialists and sold to local shops. Legs of different shape, or atypical legs, were produced for special customers by cabinetmakers in their own shops. For instance, a few customers in Salem, Providence, Baltimore, and Annapolis ordered a single-taper leg ending in a spade foot (chart XIII, 4A, B), which was atypical of regional norms. Examples are seen on the Salem or Boston table (cat. 17) and the Baltimore example (cat. 54). The single-taper leg with knopped foot (chart XIII, 6), was produced for a customer who wanted a table of distinctive appearance (fig. 30).

Some customers must have found the flyleg of ready-made tables not to their liking, because the leg arrangement of some tables does not conform to regional norms. For example, if one supposes that most tables were used by four people, two players at tables with three fixed legs and one flyleg had to straddle a leg. At tables with five and six legs and one flyleg, three people straddled a leg. However, four people could sit comfortably at tables with four legs and either no flyleg or two flylegs. Any deviation from local preferences in the number and arrangement of flylegs (chart XII, 2) required custom construction within the cabinet shop because the hinged rails and the set of legs available from the local specialists could not be used. Among such custom-made tables are the Newburyport example (cat. 11) with two fixed and two flylegs, and a New York example by an unknown maker with three fixed and one flyleg.[51]

A drawer in the front or end rail was not a standard feature of ready-made Federal-period tables. Although drawers inserted in the rear rails were customized features because they involved no major alterations of the standard model, drawers in the front and end rails were a different matter because a special rail to hold the drawer, and an opening into which it fit, had to be specially made. Additional work included constructing the drawer with a front shaped to the curve of the rail, ornamenting the front compatibly with the apron, and constructing the interior slides. Only eight tables with this feature were found in this study: one each from the Boston area, Newport, Connecticut, and Baltimore, and two each from Providence and the Philadelphia area.[52] The circular Philadelphia-area table without a folding top (cat. 50) has four drawers, and the Newport table by John Townsend (fig. 42) has a drawer in its right end.

Custom tables are likely to have more than one custom-made characteristic, because a table with one unusual feature sometimes required many specially made parts. A customer's specification for a table of regulation size that would comfortably seat eight people must have prompted Holmes Weaver of Newport to produce a unique six-legged card table which extends to become a perfect octagon.[53] To execute the order, Weaver used a standard hinged rail to hold the two flylegs, but he had to fashion five special rails for the apron and a uniquely shaped top. He also had to produce a set of six legs, four of which had to have five sides so that they fitted into the angle of the apron where they were fastened to the five adjoining rails. It is presumed that because he had to construct the legs anyway, he produced flylegs with a plane instead of the regionally popular overlapping top.

Custom-made tables reflect the preferences, needs, and priorities of customers that went beyond stock models: 15 to 20 percent of the tables in the study can be designated as custom-made. This figure indicates that although in large part the cabinetmaking business was geared for standardized production, the organization of the industry was still flexible enough for a patron and producer to carry on a dialogue. This was particularly true in rural areas where the size of the market was so small that cabinetmakers could not make a living by producing furniture in large quantities but tended to tailor their production to specific orders. In urban areas, however, cabinetmakers devoted most of their energy to ready-made furniture and derived only part of their income from custom work.

Conclusions

By systematically analyzing a large representative sample of Federal-period card tables, this study has generated verifiable data about the regional characteristics of this one form of furniture. Although the idea, or basic design for this kind of table, was adopted from England, cabinetmakers in twelve American regions either found similar or quite different solutions to the problems which the card table presented. Cabinetmakers in the same center usually were consistent in the solutions they found. This study has considered fifteen aspects, or solutions, for the basic design.

English design books and price books represented card tables with straight legs that could be tapered or tapered legs ending in spade feet. Practically everywhere in America in that period cabinetmakers exercised these two options, but in Massachusetts and New Hampshire they developed a distinctive variation of the tapered leg by making it a double taper, which in the Boston area was rendered in a singular way— the squat double taper. Such individual interpretations of basic ideas make these elements valuable indicators of regional origin.

Although in the fashioning of straight legs there was not a wide range of options from which to choose, turned legs offered innumerable possible combinations of shapes. From among these, eight popular capitals and nine popular bases were used most consistently in particular regions. This phenomenon is understandable since a few specialist turners apparently served many cabinetmakers in most regions.

Although many of the shapes of American Federal card tables were derived directly from England, by the early 19th century, New York and the Philadelphia area often favoured their own distinctive forms—double elliptic and treble elliptic in New York and kidney-end tables in Philadelphia.

During the Chippendale period, inlay as a form of ornament was eclipsed, but with the arrival of the neoclassical style it once more came into fashion. Faced with the problem of an adequate supply of ornamental inlay, American cabinetmakers had two possible solutions: they could manufacture it themselves or they could purchase it from domestic or foreign specialists.

Although some patterned inlay was probably made by cabinetmakers themselves, such large numbers of patterns were common to centers as to suggest that much of it was made by specialists who distributed it over wide areas. On the other hand, pictorial inlay can be more readily traced by analyzing its construction. The more simply made single-unit inlays were made for the most part by the shops that used them, and because they are idiosyncratic they are reliable indicators of regional origin. Many specialist-made integrated inlays are not closely bound to particular regions, but a systematic analysis of their occurrence defines the origin of many of them and separates them from others which very probably were imported from Europe.

Facade designs were closely linked to the shapes of tables and afforded American craftsmen much latitude in individual interpretations. The facades were of three basic types: one-unit, two-unit, and three-unit designs. The choice of type was dictated by the geometry of the tables. Plain one-unit designs suited the curved facades of circular tables, whereas the strong central axis of two- and three-unit designs suited the frontal orientation of rectangular tables. By repeating facade designs, individual cabinetmakers standardized their production, which leads to recognizable regional styles.

Most of the discussion of construction pertains to the functional problem of the design—constructing a movable leg to support one leaf of the table in the open position. Unlike the external aspects of the table, in which many options were exercised in the twelve regions, the solutions reached in construction were fewer. Curved rails were constructed in only four different ways, hinged rails in three, backs in two, and flylegs in three. Within regions, these choices were not random, however, because high degrees of consistency were found in the choices that were made. Cabinetmakers' decisions about how to build card tables were determined by their attitudes toward productivity, a factor that is evident in the sturdiness of their construction.

Identifying regional characteristics is a process of collecting and tabulating a large amount of detailed information on each example of the form, and organizing it to find the details that are shared. Some details, it was found, were shared by card tables from many regions and are therefore not useful in making regional attributions. The details that are peculiar to a number of tables help bring them together as a distinctive group and are profiles against which to compare tables of unknown origin. The profile is useful in answering the basic question of where a table was made, in judging whether it is an average or an exceptional example compared to its regional counterparts, and in facilitating comparisons of how cabinetmakers solved the same basic design problem in various regions.

1. For scholarship on Federal-period furniture and craftsmen, the most comprehensive bibliography was compiled by Charles F. Montgomery, *American Furniture: The Federal Period* (New York: Viking Press, 1966), pp. 484–89. More recently, Wendy A. Cooper, *In Praise of America* (New York: Alfred A. Knopf, 1980), pp. 267–73, lists many bibliographic references for research of the colonial and Federal periods. Many documentary studies conducted by students at the University of Delaware show 18th- and 19th-century cabinetmaking practices. By researching account books, William Michael Pillsbury described the operations of two family-run shops which produced turned components for large cabinetmaking shops ("The Providence Furniture-Making Trade, 1772–1834, as seen in the Account Books of Job Danforth and William, Samuel, and Daniel Proud" [unpublished Master's Thesis, University of Delaware, 1975]); and Morrison Heckscher's analysis of the business records of Samuel Ashton showed that he employed as many as eight journeymen at a time in his large Philadelphia shop ("The Organization and Practices of Philadelphia Cabinetmaking Establishments 1790 to 1820" [unpublished Master's Thesis, University of Delaware, 1964]). Marilynn A. Johnson's study of documents revealed that the New York cabinetmaker, John Hewitt, was a merchant-manager who produced little of the furniture and none of the varied commodities which he shipped to his Savannah warehouse and marketed in towns along the Hudson and Connecticut rivers ("John Hewitt," *Winterthur Portfolio 4* [Charlottesville: University Press of Virginia, 1971]). By researching the tools of a family of cabinetmakers Charles F. Hummel reconstructed the roles of rural craftsmen who produced many kinds of furniture in small units (*With Hammer in Hand: The Dominy Craftsmen of East Hampton, New York* [Charlottesville: The University Press of Virginia, 1968]). Wendell Garrett revealed the huge supplies of furniture which Providence cabinetmakers advertised for sale to the retail and wholesale markets ("Providence Cabinetmakers, Chairmakers, Upholsterers, and Allied Craftsmen, 1756–1838," *Antiques* 82, no. 4 [October 1966]: 514–19).

2. J.A. Hartigan, "Direct Clustering of a Data Matrix," *Journal of the American Statistical Association* 67 (1972): 123–29. The computer program for executing block clustering is described in W.J. Dixon, ed., *Biomedical Computer Programs* (Berkeley: University of California Press, 1975), pp. 339–56. This program brought together groups of tables sharing groups of statistically significant characteristics in a visual diagram which simultaneously identified tables with the same characteristics and revealed what those characteristics were.

3. Even though Henry J. Berkley, M.D., in "A Register of the Cabinet Makers and Allied Trades in Maryland, as Shown by the Newspapers and Directories, 1746–1820," *Maryland Historical Magazine* 25, no. 1 (March 1930): 1–27, listed a total of 316 cabinetmakers, chairmakers, carvers, and ebonists in Baltimore between 1796 and 1819, few appear to have labeled or branded their furniture. Berkley observed (p. 23) that John Simonson "was one of the few cabinetmakers whose label is still in existence." No piece of furniture by a documented Baltimore cabinetmaker, for example, is in Charles F. Montgomery's catalogue section (*American Furniture: The Federal Period*). The one fully documented Baltimore card table known to the writer is inscribed in chalk "John Needles" (see Montgomery, "John Needles, Baltimore Cabinetmaker," *Antiques* 65, no. 4 [April 1954]: 292–95). This is believed to have been custom-made because it did not cluster with other turned-leg tables and was consequently excluded from the study by the statistical procedure. It is believed that turned-leg tables meeting the criteria of this study were not ready-made in Baltimore but that painted tables with turned legs may have been. The data suggest that wherever they worked, cabinetmakers specialized in straight- or turned-leg tables. Perhaps in Baltimore they gave customers a choice of straight-leg tables which were heavily inlaid or turned-leg tables that were copiously painted.

While the penciled inscription on one straight-leg table (no. 367) may be that of a known Baltimore cabinetmaker, no other tables in the Baltimore sample are documented. Because the characteristics of the tables in the Baltimore sample are closely related, their common origin is established; this origin is assumed to be Baltimore because of information concerning their provenance, which is noted and described in the list of Baltimore tables.

4. While the 108 variables which had already been used in block clustering were believed by statisticians at that time to be the greatest number attempted in any known research, it was nevertheless possible that the addition of more variables might reveal the origin of some unidentified tables. Therefore the 108 characteristics were randomly broken into three subsamples, each with 36 characteristics, by means of which block clustering consistently brought together the same groups of tables. These results indicate that the 12 regional groups identified by the 108-characteristic analysis were reasonably well established and that the further addition of variables would probably not identify the origin of clusters with no documented example or of tables that fell into no cluster. Probably among these tables of unidentified origin are some produced

south of Maryland, of which none of documented origin was found. These analyses also resulted in the exclusion of tables with characteristics which were unlike those of the Federal period. Among these were one table by William King of Salem and the other by Amzi Chapin owned by the Loomis family of Bloomfield, Connecticut (see Dean A. Fales, *The Furniture of Historic Deerfield* [New York: E.P. Dutton, 1976], p. 134, fig. 277).

5. R.I. Jennrich, "Stepwise Discriminant Analysis," in K. Enslein, A. Ralston, and H.S. Wilf, eds., *Statistical Methods for Digital Computers* (New York: Wiley, 1977), Vol. III, pp. 76–95. The computer program for executing stepwise discriminant analysis is described in Dixon, *Biomedical Computer Programs*, pp. 411–52; 31 characteristics were required to identify the origin of straight-leg tables and 28 to identify the origin of turned-leg tables.

6. Three exceptions, each with a fixed leg at the four corners, provide for the extension of the leaves by a pivot permitting the top to swivel (see cat. 41), by a slide leg in the center of the rear, and by framed back legs which are pulled back. For examples of the latter two see Montgomery, *American Furniture: The Federal Period*, p. 331, fig. 303, and p. 332, fig. 305.

7. Patricia E. Kane, *Furniture of the New Haven Colony, The Seventeenth-Century Style* (New Haven: New Haven Colony Historical Society, 1973), p. 6, notes that turners were sometimes referred to as "dish turners." Cooper, *In Praise of America*, p. 124, states that between 1630 and 1730 there were 21 turners and blockmakers in Charlestown and 16 turners and 9 chairmakers in Boston and notes that the inventory of Edward Browne, the Ipswich turner, included trays, dishes, trenchers, and pails. Pillsbury, "The Providence Furniture-Making Trades," pp. 61–63, notes that Samuel and Daniel Proud, turners and chairmakers of Providence, supplied chairmakers, chaisemakers, clockmakers, pewterers, printers, and cabinetmakers with components and that Job Danforth, cabinetmaker, supplied cabinetmakers with turned components.

8. Margaret Burke Clunie, "Joseph True and the Piecework System in Salem," *Antiques* 111, no. 5 (May 1977): 1006–13.

9. *Plain and Elegant, Rich and Common: Documented New Hampshire Furniture, 1750–1850* (Concord, New Hampshire: New Hampshire Historical Society, 1979), p. 131, no. 55.

10. No. 36. See Dean A. Fales, *The Furniture of Historic Deerfield*, p. 139, figs. 288, 288a.

11. The writer is indebted to Patricia E. Kane for tracing the origin of regional preferences for table shapes to information in the following price books. *The Cabinet-Makers' London Book of Prices and Designs of Cabinet Work* (also called *The London Cabinet Book of Prices*), 1788; rev. eds. 1793, 1803. *The Prices of Cabinet Work with Tables and Designs*, London, 1797. *Supplement to the Cabinet-Makers' London Book of Prices and Designs of Cabinet-work*, 1805. *The London Cabinet-Makers' Union Book of Prices*, London, 1811. *The Journeymen Cabinet and Chair Makers' New-York Book of Prices*, printed by T. and J. Swords, 1796. *The New-York Book of Prices for Cabinet and Chair Work Agreed Upon by the Employers*, printed by Southwick and Crooker, 1802. *The New-York Revised Prices for Manufacturing Cabinet and Chair Work*, printed by Southwick and Pelsue, 1810. *Additional Prices Agreed Upon by the New-York Society of Journeymen Cabinet Makers*, 1815. *The New-York Book of Prices for Manufacturing Cabinet and Chair Work*, printed by J. Seymour, 1817. *New-York Revised Prices for Manufacturing Cabinet and Chair Work*, printed by Daniel D. Smith, 1817. *The Philadelphia Cabinet and Chair-Makers' Book of Prices*, copyrighted John Lindsay, 1794. *The Journeymen Cabinet and Chair-Makers' Philadelphia Book of Prices*, 2nd ed. 1795. *The Philadelphia Cabinet and Chair-Makers' Book of Prices*, printed by Richard Folwell, 1796. *The Cabinet-Makers Philadelphia and London Book of Prices*, Snowden and McCorkle Press, 1796. *The Journeymen Cabinet and Chair Makers' Pennsylvania Book of Prices*, printed for the Society, 1811.

12. Square tables included in the study have some high-style ornament such as veneer, inlay, beading, or carving and should not be confused with the plain square card tables of local wood which rural cabinetmakers produced and customarily painted.

13. *The New-York Book of Prices for Cabinet and Chair Work Agreed Upon by the Employers*, 1802, p. 21; *The New York Book of Prices for Manufacturing Cabinet and Chair Work*, 1817, p. 34; *The Journeymen Cabinet and Chair Makers' Pennsylvania Book of Prices*, 1811, p. 33.

14. *The Journeymen Cabinet and Chair Makers' Pennsylvania Book of Prices*, 1811, p. 36.

15. *The Cabinet-Makers' London Book of Prices* . . . 1788, pp. 56–57; rev. ed., 1793, pp. 96–97. *The Prices of Cabinet Work with Tables and Designs*, London, 1797, pp. 91–92.

16. *The New-York Revised Prices for Manufacturing Cabinet and Chair Work*, 1810, p. 25. *The New-York Book of Prices for Manufacturing Cabinet and Chair Work*, 1817, p. 35.

17. *The Journeymen Cabinet and Chair Makers' Pennsylvania Book of Prices*, 1811, p. 35.

18. *The Cabinet Makers' London Book of Prices* . . . 1788, pp. 56–59; rev. ed. 1793, pp. 96–102. *The Prices of Cabinet Work with Tables and Designs*, London, 1797, pp. 91–97. *The London Cabinet-Makers' Union Book of Prices*, 1811, pp. 139–50.

19. *The Journeymen Cabinet-Makers' New-York*

Book of Prices, 1796, pp. 35–37. *The New-York Book of Prices for Cabinet and Chair Work*, 1802, pp. 20–23. *New-York Revised Prices for Manufacturing Cabinet and Chair Work*, 1810, pp. 24–25. *The New-York Book of Prices for Manufacturing Cabinet and Chair Work*, 1817, pp. 34–36.

20. *The Journeymen Cabinet and Chair Makers' Pennsylvania Book of Prices*, 1811, pp. 33–36.

21. Nos. 66, 206, 371, 374.

22. No. 229.

23. No. 262.

24. *The Cabinet-Makers' London Book of Prices . . .*, rev. ed., 1793, pp. 99–100. *The Price of Cabinet Work with Tables and Designs*, London, 1797, pp. 94–95. *The London Cabinet-Makers' Union Book of Prices*, 1811, p. 144.

25. Nos. 228, 280.

26. *New-York Book of Prices for Cabinet and Chair Work*, 1802, p. 22.

27. Nos. 50, 51, 308, 349.

28. *The Journeymen Cabinet and Chair Makers' Pennsylvania Book of Prices*, 1811, pp. 36–37.

29. To determine the regional popularity of relief ornament, "one" was counted each time it occurred as a vertical divider on the front apron and as a frame around the perimeter of the pilasters. A "one" was also counted each time it was used on the leaf edge, at the skirt, at the center of the front apron, at the center of the front pilaster, on the shaft, and at the cuff.

30. The degree to which veneer was utilized was determined by counting the number of individual pieces of veneer starting from "o" for a solid wood apron to "6" for an apron with three units, each with two veneers.

31. In *American Furniture: The Federal Period*, Montgomery notes (p. 13) that Thomas Barrett's inventory of 1800 shows that he had supplied at least 15 Baltimore cabinet shops with inlay and (p. 40) that John Dewhurst was listed as a banding and stringing maker in the 1809 Boston directory. In the Concord, New Hampshire, *Gazette*, Porter Blanchard, the Concord cabinetmaker, advertised on May 11, 1811, for cabinetmakers to learn the art of making banding and stringing.

32. To determine the extent to which plain inlay was used on the average table from each center, "one" was counted for its occurrence on each of the following nine places on straight-leg tables: upper-leaf edge, perimeter of the top, perimeter of the inner leaves, skirt, each front apron panel, vertical divider of the front apron, front pilaster frame, shaft, and cuff. For turned-leg tables, five places were counted: upper-leaf edge, skirt, front-apron panel, vertical divider of the front apron, and front pilaster frame. No turned-leg table was found with string inlay on the perimeter of the top or inner leaves, on the shafts, or at a place comparable to the cuff of straight-leg tables.

33. These flute inlays are associated with Newport, Providence, and Connecticut, possibly the work of a specialist who dispensed them in the three regions. Flute (inlay 110) is found on one Providence table (cat. 32) and one Newport table (no. 231). A second very similar flute is found on two Newport tables (fig. 42 and no. 235). Two other flutes are found on two Newport tables (nos. 227, 233) and one Connecticut table (no. 254). However, another flute inlay is found on a Boston-area table by Jacob Forster (no. 142).

34. Each time pictorial inlay was found at one of the following ten places on straight-leg tables, "one" was tallied for its occurrence: center of top, perimeter of the top, interior leaves, front apron center, front apron corners, and any other places on the apron, front of pilasters, side of front pilasters, shaft, and cuff. Because pictorial inlay was found on only two turned-leg tables in the study, the frequency of its use on this form was disregarded.

35. Nos. 46, 57, 90.

36. No. 292.

37. Other inlays are a flower on a stem and an intersecting husk, each unique to one Newburyport table (nos. 49, 51); a quarter-round patera on one Salem table (no. 105); an eagle on an Annapolis table (no. 370); and a patera shared by one Newburyport (no. 60) and one Philadelphia-area table (no. 309).

38. Charles F. Montgomery, *American Furniture: The Federal Period*, p. 36.

39. Nos. 1,6.

40. Robert Courtenay advertised imported shells for inlaying in mahogany furniture. *Baltimore Daily Repository*, October 19, 1793, quoted in Alfred Coxe Prime, comp., *The Arts and Crafts in Philadelphia, Maryland and South Carolina, Part II, 1786–1800* (1932; reprint, New York: Da Capo Press, 1969), p. 209.

41. The six documented tables by Joseph Short of Newburyport (cat. 9); two by John Dolan of New York (cat. 43); two by John Shaw of Annapolis that are plain (cat. 55, no. 372) and three others by Shaw (cat. 56, nos. 371, 374) that are facade 2; three by Jacob Forster of Charlestown (cat. 24); two by Rogers and Atwood (cat. 10); and two by Elisha Tucker of Boston (nos. 136, 165).

42. In the few instances of tables with two or more curved rails of different construction, only the strongest was tabulated.

43. Nos. 45, 47, 53, 55, 56.

44. The probabilities are greater than 99 out of 100 that hinged-rail designs were consistent in all areas except Newport, where the probability is insignificant (90 out of 100). This statistical test, chi square, is described in Henry E. Garrett, *Statistics in Psy-*

chology and Education, 3rd ed. (New York: Longmans, Green, 1951), pp. 241–46.

45. The exceptions are tables with no flyleg. These are described in note 6 above.

46. The probabilities are highly significant (99 out of 100) in ten centers, significant (95 out of 100) in urban New Hampshire, but insignificant (80 out of 100) in Annapolis: chi-square tests, according to Garrett, *Statistics in Psychology and Education*, pp. 241–46.

47. *The Journeymen Cabinet and Chair-Makers' Philadelphia Book of Prices*, 2nd ed., 1795; Table No. XX (n.p.). The writer is indebted to Patricia Kane for bringing this reference to his attention.

48. Forest Products Laboratory, Forest Service, U.S. Dept. of Agriculture, *Wood Handbook* (Agriculture Handbook no. 72) [Washington D.C.: U.S. Government Printing Office, 1955], pp. 247–49.

49. Points were assigned for each element that exceeded the minimal requirements of card table construction. Zero points were assigned for filler construction of the hinged rail, plane flyleg, no tenon, no medial brace, kerf and single-board construction of the curved rails; one point for flush construction of the hinged rail, for the overlapping flyleg, for each tenon, for the medial brace, and for each horizontal lamination of the table's strongest curved rail (one to six); two points for additional flyleg construction; and seven points for vertical lamination of the curved rail. Each table's sturdiness score was the total number of points awarded. Total number of sturdiness points per straight-leg table range from zero to thirteen with the mean at 3.22. Total number of sturdiness points per turned-leg tables range from zero to ten with the mean at 2.45.

50. No. 279.

51. No. 278.

52. Nos. 183, 229, 251, 252, 255, 295, 309, 362.

53. No. 228.

A Regional Survey
of American Federal-Period Card Tables: Selections from the Study

Benjamin A. Hewitt with the assistance of Barbara McLean Ward

Card table by John Dunlap II,
Antrim, New Hampshire (cat. 4).

Card table by Samuel Barnard,
Salem, Massachusetts (cat. 19).

Card table, unknown maker, Boston area (cat. 26).

Card table attributed to Holmes Weaver, Newport, Rhode Island (cat. 29).

Notes to the catalogue

Tables marked with a dagger (†) have labels in such poor condition that they were not reproduced.

All measurements are given in centimeters rounded to the nearest whole number.

Pictorial inlays not reproduced on pp. 76-80 are described in the catalogue entries.

Some patterned inlays are not readily visible in the catalogue illustrations and their locations have therefore been designated within brackets [ ]. All patterned inlays are reproduced in color on pp. 74-75.

The "no . . ." refers to the list of tables at the end of the catalogue.

Card table attributed to Thomas Howard, Pawtuxet and Providence, Rhode Island (cat. 33).

Card table, unknown maker, New York (cat. 40).

Card table, unknown maker,
Philadelphia area (cat. 45).

Card table, unknown maker,
Baltimore (cat. 52).

Urban New Hampshire

Similarities were found in the form, ornament, and construction of this small but distinctive sample which includes documented card tables made in two New Hampshire towns many miles apart. They are tables from Keene by Eliphalet Briggs (cat. 1), and from Concord by Robert Choate and George Whitefield Martin (cat. 3), and by Levi Bartlett.[1] The sample is wholly comprised of straight-leg tables.

Urban New Hampshire cabinetmakers were especially fond of square tables with elliptic front (shape 4), and showed a strong preference for integrated, patterned, and plain inlays which a Concord inlay maker, Porter Blanchard, may have supplied. They generally used one-unit facades with imaginatively arranged contrasting veneers (cats. 1, 2) framed by patterned inlay on the leaf edge and skirt and by bold pictorial inlay on the pilasters. Although they inlaid plain stringing on one or two sides of each shaft, they usually left the rear pilasters and end aprons plain.

Mean number of construction points ranging from one to three, three fixed and one flyleg, single-taper or pointed double-taper legs, and white pine and cherry as secondary woods are helpful clues in attributing the origin of tables to urban New Hampshire. These features include either filler or flush back construction, design 1 hinged-rail construction, and plane flyleg construction. A medial brace was found on one table and leaf-edge tenons were found on most tables in this sample.

1. *Plain and Elegant, Rich and Common, Documented New Hampshire Furniture, 1750–1850* (Concord, New Hampshire: New Hampshire Historical Society, 1979), p. 140.

Cat. 1

1

CARD TABLE (*no. 3*)
Eliphalet Briggs (1788–1853)
Keene, New Hampshire
Yale University Art Gallery,
Mabel Brady Garvan Collection

Primary woods: mahogany, rosewood.
Secondary wood: white pine.
Dimensions: H. 75 cm; W. 86 cm; D. 42 cm.
Form and Ornament: Shape 2, single-taper
legs; patterned inlay 56, pictorial inlay of
inset-integrated urn (similar to 134) on
pilasters; facade 4.
Construction: Flush back and plane flyleg
construction, hinged-rail design 1, one leaf-
edge tenon, no medial brace, one horizontal lamination in the curved rails,
three points.
Notes: Eliphalet Briggs was a partner in the
firm of Smith and Briggs, owners of a
cabinet shop and turning mill in Keene, in
1812. After Smith's death, Briggs advertised independently in the chair- and
cabinetmaking business several times during 1815–16. In 1819 he entered another
partnership, this time with Joseph Brown,
to produce gravestones; in 1824 he and his
brother John advertised, "the manufacture"
of numerous forms of furniture at their
"warehouse," where they did "all kinds
of job work at short notice."[1] The contrasting veneer and the use of inset-
integrated inlay on the pilasters are characteristic of urban New Hampshire.

1. *New Hampshire Sentinel* (Keene), November 11,
1819; February 12, 1824.

The author is indebted to Charles S. Parsons for
providing this information on Eliphalet Briggs.

2

CARD TABLE (*no. 4*)
Unknown maker
Urban New Hampshire
The Currier Gallery of Art

Primary woods: cherry, birch. *Secondary
woods:* white pine, cherry.
Dimensions: H. 70 cm; W. 90 cm; D. 43 cm.
Form and Ornament: Shape 4, single-taper
legs; no patterned inlay, pictorial inlay of
simple-integrated column (much like 133)
on pilasters; miscellaneous facade.
Construction: Flush back and plane flyleg
construction, hinged-rail design 1, no leaf-
edge tenons, no medial brace, one horizontal lamination in the curved rails,
one point.
Notes: To create the facade of this table
the cabinetmaker carefully selected and
skillfully mitered ten pieces of veneer
around three richly figured ovals to create
subtle distinctions in texture and explicit
contrasts in color. He also put an oval
within a mitered rectangle on the end aprons
and inset the front pilasters with simple-
integrated column inlays, a popular motif
probably produced by a specialist inlay
maker in Concord. The square shape with
elliptic front, the use of contrasting veneer,
and pictorial inlay on the pilasters suggest
that the table originated in urban New
Hampshire.

3

CARD TABLE (*no. 5*)
Robert Choate (1770–?) and George
Whitefield Martin (1771–1810)
Concord, New Hampshire
New Hampshire Historical Society

Primary wood: mahogany. *Secondary woods:*
cherry, white pine.
Dimensions: H. 73 cm; W. 91 cm; D. 45 cm.
Form and Ornament: Shape 1, single-taper
legs; no patterned inlay, pictorial inlays of
single-unit bellflower (similar to 118) on
front legs, and 12-part inset-integrated

Cat. 2

Cat. 3

patera (like 122) at center of front and side aprons; facade 5C.

Construction: Filler back and plane flyleg construction, hinged-rail design 1, two leaf-edge tenons, no medial brace, one horizontal lamination in the curved rails, three points.

Notes: The partnership of Choate and Martin in Concord lasted from 1794 to 1796, when Choate continued alone as a cabinet- and chairmaker,[1] and Martin may have moved to Salem. He was in partnership there in 1802 with Edmund Johnson, Samuel Barnard (see cat. 19) and Jonathan Marston, cabinetmakers, in the purchase of the schooner *Friendship*[2] and land in the northfield of Salem.[3] On this table the ornamental preferences of northeastern Massachusetts, where Choate and Martin had lived before their partnership, are seen in the facade design, the plain string inlay outlining the legs, and the absence of cuffs on the legs—all ornamental features of the table by Samuel and William Fiske of Salem, Massachusetts (cat. 15).

1. *Plain and Elegant . . . New Hampshire Furniture,* p. 143.
2. Registered March 27, 1802, *Essex Institute Historical Collections* 40 (1904): 195.
3. Deed of William Dennis to Edmund Johnson et al., October 18, 1802, Essex County Registry of Deeds, vol. 171, p. 81.

Rural Massachusetts–New Hampshire

Documented card tables from this region originated in Massachusetts from Hingham in the east, Greenfield in the west, and Springfield in the south; and from Bedford, New Hampshire, in the north. Most cabinetmakers in these small towns probably operated modest shops in which they performed most of the craft functions themselves and produced furniture to the specifications of individual customers. Nevertheless, their tables have many similarities in form, ornament, and construction. Both straight- and turned-leg tables comprise the sample.

STRAIGHT-LEG TABLES

Most tables from this region are square with ovolo corners (shape 2) and square with elliptic front (shape 4). Cabinetmakers most frequently used simple one-unit facade designs in which the color of one wood predominated and some miscellaneous designs were also used (cat. 4). While the makers inlaid most leaf edges and skirts and ornamented most front pilasters with contrasting veneer or pictorial inlay, they rarely ornamented the rear pilasters or inset single-unit or plain inlay into more than one side of the front legs, regardless of whether they were single taper or pointed double taper in form.

Most important in attributing straight-leg tables to this region is the use of cherry, birch, or maple as primary wood, a characteristic of nearly the entire rural Massachusetts–New Hampshire sample, and evidence of the non-urban use of locally available woods rather than imported mahogany. White pine and cherry, followed by maple and birch, were the secondary woods. Construction was economical, with filler back construction, plane flyleg construction, and hinged-rail design 1 most frequently used. Curved rails were produced with single-board and the rare kerf construction and with varied numbers of horizontal lamination.

TURNED-LEG TABLES

Capital 7, shaft 4, and base 7, turnings unique to the region, identify the origin of more than half the turned-leg tables from rural Massachusetts–New Hampshire. Because many miscellaneous turnings (capital 8, base 9) were also found there, turnings are not always useful for identifying tables from this area. However, local preferences for square tables with serpentine front, serpentine ends and ovolo corners over colonettes (shape 7), a small number of construction points ranging from zero to two, and the use of cherry as a secondary wood, are helpful indicators in establishing that rural Massachusetts–New Hampshire was the region of origin. Preferences for three-unit facades liberally inset with patterned inlays and veneered with woods of contrasting color and texture (cat. 8) and for mahogany as a primary wood are to be expected on many turned-leg tables from this area.

4
CARD TABLE (*no. 13*)†
John Dunlap II (1784–1869)
Antrim, New Hampshire
Yale University Art Gallery, gift of
Benjamin A. Hewitt, B.A. 1943
Reproduced in color on p. 108

Primary wood: cherry. *Secondary woods:* maple, white pine.
Dimensions: H. 74 cm; W. 91 cm; D. 45 cm.
Form and Ornament: Shape 4, pointed double-taper legs; patterned inlays 10 [leaf edge, skirt, center of top], 17 [perimeter of top], pictorial inlays 122, 128, and inset-integrated round 12-point patera on top, 3-point quarter patera at each

Cat. 4

corner of top, oval 12-point patera at apron center, and single-unit buds-on-vine on front legs; miscellaneous facade design.
Construction: Filler back and plane flyleg construction, hinged-rail design 1, no leaf-edge tenons, no medial brace, one horizontal lamination in the curved rails, one point.
Notes: Dunlap's unusual rear rail construction provides almost unmistakable evidence of his workmanship. Dovetailed to the right end rail, the rear rail runs to about an inch from the left end rail and provides little strength for the rear of the table. By nailing the rear rail to the stationary part of the hinge and screwing the hinge to the top, Dunlap made the top an integral part of the rear structure. The one table in the study with this construction which originated outside of New Hampshire is labeled by John Shaw of Annapolis.[1]

1. See no. 371.

Cat. 4. Detail of top.

5
CARD TABLE (*no. 22*)
Pelatiah Bliss (1770–1826)[1]
Springfield, Massachusetts
Connecticut Valley Historical Museum, Springfield, Massachusetts

Primary wood: cherry. *Secondary woods:* white pine, cherry.
Dimensions: H. 73 cm; W. 91 cm; D. 45 cm.
Form and Ornament: Shape 2, single-taper legs; no patterned inlay, pictorial inlays 144 and a simple-integrated 20-point patera (much like 135) at center of apron; facade 6A.

Construction: Flush back and plane flyleg construction, hinged-rail design 1, no leaf-edge tenons, no medial brace, three horizontal laminations in the curved rails, four points.
Notes: All four-leg cherry tables in the study originated in Massachusetts or New Hampshire, where they were especially popular in rural areas. Their construction and ornament usually reflect makers' individual preferences rather than regional styles, as in this table where Bliss constructed his curved rails with multilaminations and made the apron unusually deep. Leaving the leaf edges and pilasters plain and beading the skirt, he emphasized wood color. He relieved the heaviness of the apron with a bold central patera.

1. *Springfield Republican*, August 9, 1826; John Homer Bliss, *Genealogy of the Bliss Family in America* (Boston: Printed by the author, 1881), p. 135.

6
CARD TABLE (*no. 31*)
Unknown maker
Rural Massachusetts–New Hampshire
John Whitmore

Primary woods: cherry, mahogany, light wood inlay. *Secondary woods:* maple, white pine.
Dimensions: H. 72 cm; W. 90 cm; D. 44 cm.
Form and Ornament: Shape 24, pointed

Cat. 5

Cat. 6

double-taper legs; patterned inlays 51, 52, 99 [upper leaf edge], 100, no pictorial inlay; facade 5B.

Construction: Filler back and plane flyleg construction, hinged-rail design 1, no leaf-edge tenons, no medial brace, one horizontal lamination in the curved rails, one point.

Notes: Cherry as the primary wood and a simple one-unit facade—a central oval panel contrasting in color and texture to the veneer—are common characteristics of tables from this area. Patterned inlay was often inset on the leaf edges and skirts and sometimes around the panels on the pilasters. The inlaid panels on the rear and side pilasters and on two sides of the front and rear legs, however, show an atypical extravagance in the use of ornament.

7

CARD TABLE (*no. 33*)
Isaiah Wilder (1782–1867)
Hingham, Massachusetts; Surrey and Keene, New Hampshire
New Hampshire Historical Society, gift of William L. Warren

Primary wood: mahogany. *Secondary wood:* white pine.
Dimensions: H. 73 cm; W. 89 cm; D. 45 cm.
Form and Ornament: Shape 7, turned legs with capital 7 and base 7; patterned inlay 30 [at apron center], no pictorial inlay; miscellaneous facade design.
Construction: Filler back and plane flyleg construction, hinged-rail design 1, no leaf-edge tenons, no medial brace, single-board construction of the curved rails, no points.

Notes: These turned legs with shallow ogee capital, curving ringed shaft, and squat taper under quarter-circle round at the base were probably produced by a local specialist. Identical legs appear on a table branded T. Green[1] and identical turnings appear on thinner legs for a painted table also by Wilder. Since this table bears the stamp "I. Wilder, j," and Wilder dropped the designation "Jr." after his move to New Hampshire, this table was probably made prior to 1821, when Wilder was active in Hingham, Massachusetts.[2]

1. Dean A. Fales Jr., *The Furniture of Historic Deerfield* (New York: E. P. Dutton, 1976), p. 139, figs. 288, 288a.
2. *Plain and Elegant . . . New Hampshire Furniture*, p. 131, no. 55.

8

CARD TABLE (*no. 39*)
Alden Spooner (1784–1877)[1]
Athol, Massachusetts
Yale University Art Gallery, gift of Benjamin A. Hewitt, B.A. 1943, in memory of Charles F. Montgomery for inspiring *The Work of Many Hands*

Primary woods: maple, cherry. *Secondary wood:* white pine.
Dimensions: H. 73 cm; W. 95 cm; D. 46 cm.
Form and Ornament: Shape 8, turned legs with capital 8 and base 9; patterned inlays 3, 5, 31, no pictorial inlay; facade 12E.

Cat. 7

Cat. 8

Construction: Flush back and plane flyleg construction, hinged-rail design 1, no leaf-edge tenons, no medial brace, single-board construction of the curved rails, one point. *Notes:* Successfully imitating urban Massachusetts styles, Spooner composed a complex three-unit facade with varied shapes, colors, and textures of veneer which he bordered with patterned inlays. The shallowly ringed colonettes and ball feet are similar to other turnings from rural Massachusetts–New Hampshire. The legs may have been made to resemble the ring-over-hollow turning (capital 3) preferred by Boston–Salem area specialists, although the hollow turning is very narrow.

1. Born in Petersham, Massachusetts, to Clapp and Mary Spooner. *Vital Records of Petersham* (Worcester, 1904), p. 47. Died in Athol. William G. Lord, *History of Athol, Massachusetts* (Athol: published by the author, 1953), p. 282.

Newburyport

The considerable number of card tables from Newburyport in the study in proportion to its small population during the Federal period, suggests that Newburyport shops produced tables for export. One table with regional characteristics indicating Newburyport origin bears the chalk inscription of New York cabinetmaker Joel Ketchum (no. 69). Although the consistent construction of the straight legs and hinged rails on Newburyport tables suggests that specialists produced components for some shops, the rare shapes of both straight- and turned-leg tables indicate that many makers were producing custom-made tables for local residents.

STRAIGHT-LEG TABLES

Newburyport tables are most commonly square with ovolo corners (shape 2) but many of intricate rare shapes also survive. Legs are always single taper, frequently inlaid with plain string on one side. The makers characteristically chose restrained ornament by using simple one-unit facade designs comprised of one or two veneers (cats. 9, 10). To lightly accent the shapes they customarily used inlay on the leaf edges and skirt, and they preferred panels of contrasting veneer on the pilasters. All pictorial inlays used in Newburyport were of the integrated type and were probably imported.

Tables from Newburyport can be recognized by the use of white pine, birch, and maple for secondary woods, and by the economy of their construction (construction points range from zero to four). Back construction is either flush or filler and flylegs are of plane construction. Hinged-rail design 1 is invariably found on ready-made tables and the curved rails are most often single-board construction.

Singular turnings (capital 8, base 9) and shape 9, square with elliptic and hollow front, half elliptic and hollow ends, ovolo corners (cat. 12), suggest a Newburyport origin. This hypothesis is strengthened by the use of white pine, birch, and maple as secondary woods, one-unit facade designs of dark overall appearance, rare use of inlay, and much molded relief ornament. The last includes rounded leaf edges, beaded skirts, and sometimes raised molding applied to the apron to create simple three-unit facades. While most tables have colonettes, the pilasters of other tables are usually plain or reeded, and the rear pilasters of most are plain. Major construction features are the same as for straight-leg tables.

9
CARD TABLE (*no. 54*)
Joseph Short (1771–1819)
Newburyport, Massachusetts
Yale University Art Gallery, gift of
Benjamin A. Hewitt, B.A. 1943, in honor
of Patricia E. Kane for making *The
Work of Many Hands* a reality

Primary wood: mahogany. *Secondary woods:*
white pine, cherry.
Dimensions: H. 73 cm; W. 90 cm; D. 44 cm.
Form and Ornament: Shape 6, single-taper
legs; patterned inlay 70, no pictorial inlay;
facade 1.
Construction: Filler back and plane flyleg
construction, hinged-rail design 1, no leaf-
edge tenons, no medial brace, single-board
construction of the curved rails, no points.
Notes: The six labeled tables by Joseph
Short in the study reveal his highly stand-

Cat. 9

ardized production.[1] Except for this example, they are square with ovolo corners (shape 2); they have plain aprons (facade 1) with darker mahogany pilaster panels which are of three shapes, plain stringing inlaid at the leaf edges and bordering the edges of the legs, and patterned inlay around the skirt. The rear legs of all are inlaid on one side, the front legs of five are inlaid on one side, and the front legs of one are inlaid on two sides. Cuffs are inset on only two tables.

1. See nos. 45, 47, 53–56.

by specializing in this rare shape, which corresponds to that of their only other known documented example.[2] On both they bordered the birdseye maple panels with mahogany crossbanding, inset identical shells in the pilasters, inlaid the skirt and cuffs with patterned inlay, inlaid the leaf edges with plain stringing, and inlaid the borders of one side of both front and rear legs with plain stringing. They customized the playing surface of this table by adding baize but left the other plain.

1. Susan Makiewicz, "A Focus on the Decorative Arts of Newburyport," *Custom House Maritime Museum Antiques Show* (1979): 23–24.
2. See no. 46.

10

CARD TABLE (*no. 57*)
Ebenezer Rogers (1783–1866) and
Thomas Atwood (1782–1818)[1]
Newburyport, Massachusetts
Timothy Fuller Marquand

Primary woods: mahogany, maple. *Secondary wood:* white pine.
Dimensions: H. 74 cm; W. 90 cm; D. 44 cm.
Form and Ornament: Shape 23, single-taper legs; patterned inlay 2, pictorial inlay 142; facade 3.
Construction: Flush back and plane flyleg construction, hinged-rail design 1, no leaf-edge tenons, no medial brace, single-board construction of the curved rails, one point.
Notes: Rogers and Atwood may have standardized their production of card tables

11

CARD TABLE (*no. 62*)
Unknown maker
Newburyport, Massachusetts
Yale University Art Gallery,
Mabel Brady Garvan Collection

Primary wood: mahogany. *Secondary woods:* chestnut, maple.
Dimensions: H. 73 cm; W. 93 cm; D. 46 cm.
Form and Ornament: Shape 1, single-taper legs; no patterned inlay, pictorial inlay 146, and an inset-integrated inlay of a thistle on stem on pilasters; facade 2.
Construction: Filler back and plane flyleg construction, hinged-rail design 2, one leaf-edge tenon, no medial brace, single-board construction of the curved rail, one point.

Cat. 10

Cat. 11

Notes: Single-taper legs, a simple facade design, and imported inset-integrated inlay on the pilasters suggest that this table originated in Newburyport. Because Newburyport ready-made tables usually have only one flyleg, this example, with two, must have been made on special order for a customer who wanted a table at which four people could sit without having to straddle the legs. The inset-integrated shell on the top also cost extra; it was made by a specialist in another center or abroad because local demand for pictorial inlay was too small to support the services of an expert capable of making such intricate patterns.

12
CARD TABLE (*no. 68*)
Charles Short (1792–1872+)
Newburyport, Haverhill, Andover, and Salem, Massachusetts
Mr. and Mrs. John M. Keese IV

Primary woods: mahogany, birch. *Secondary woods:* white pine, maple.
Dimensions: H. 75 cm; W. 93 cm; D. 43 cm.
Form and Ornament: Shape 9, turned legs with capital 8 and base 9; no patterned inlay, no pictorial inlay; facade 1.
Construction: Filler back and plane flyleg construction, hinged-rail design 1, no leaf-edge tenons, no medial brace, single-board construction of the curved rails, no points.

Notes: Charles Short was one of a large family of Newburyport woodworkers, some of whom were piecework turners.[1] In producing this table he conformed to local preferences for this curvate shape with plainly veneered aprons and cockbeading on the skirt. Because the capital and base turnings of all but two of the Newburyport tables in this study are unique, it suggests that most makers, like Short, probably turned the legs themselves.

1. Martha G. Fales, "The Shorts, Cabinetmakers of Newburyport," *Essex Institute Historical Collections* 102 (June 1966): 229-30.

13
CARD TABLE (*no. 74*)
Unknown maker
Newburyport, Massachusetts
Patrick M. Spadaccino Jr.

Primary woods: mahogany, maple. *Secondary woods:* white pine, maple.
Dimensions: H. 75 cm; W. 92 cm; D. 41 cm.
Form and Ornament: Shape 6, turned legs with capital 8 and base 9; patterned inlays 30 [adjacent central facade rectangle], 51 [around facade oval], 72 [leaf edge and skirt], pictorial inlay similar to 123; facade 12C.
Construction: Flush back and plane flyleg construction, hinged-rail design 1, no leaf-edge tenons, no medial brace, one horizontal lamination in the curved rails, three points.
Notes: The color-contrastive veneers of the facade and the inset-integrated shells on the pilasters may be likened to those of the Rogers and Atwood table (cat. 10). In form, elliptic front and serpentine ends, it corresponds to the table by Joseph Short (cat. 9). The atypical but delicate turnings were found on one other table of corresponding shape and construction, suggesting origin in the same unknown shop.[1]

1. See no. 70.

Cat. 12

Cat. 13

Salem

During the Revolution, when Boston Harbor was effectively closed by the British blockade, Salem and other ports along the North Shore enjoyed an era of prosperity which lasted through the Federal period. Neoclassical Salem furniture was undoubtedly strongly influenced by cabinetmakers who moved there to take advantage of Salem's growth. These newcomers probably came from Boston, Charlestown, Ipswich, and towns in southern and eastern New Hampshire. All of the documented card tables, except one which was produced in nearby Lynn, can be ascribed to Salem. Both straight- and turned-leg tables were manufactured there.

STRAIGHT-LEG TABLES

Tables with elliptic front and serpentine ends (shape 6), with an oval within a mitered rectangle on the facade (facade 12), with patterned inlay used at many places, and with veneers of different colors, shapes, and dimensions are likely to have originated in Salem. Many cabinetmakers enhanced their tables by paneling pilasters with contrasting veneer and by insetting patterned inlay on leaf edges and skirts. They used little ornament on the end aprons and on the legs, which regardless of their single or double taper were often plain except for inlaid cuffs. Pictorial inlays, rarely used, were generally of the specialist-made inset-integrated type.

Secondary woods of Salem straight-leg tables are usually white pine and either birch or maple; the number of construction points ranges from zero to three; some tables have a specialist-made, three-part hinged rail (design 2) for two flylegs. Filler back construction, plane flyleg construction, and curved rails of either a single board or with one horizontal lamination are generally characteristic of Salem tables.

Medial braces were not found on any of the tables in this sample.

TURNED-LEG TABLES

Tables with turned legs having base 2a and the combination of capital 2 and base 2b are reliably attributed to Salem. Shape 7 serpentine front, serpentine ends, ovolo corners over colonettes, was the most popular. The facades of many tables look like those of straight-leg tables because they are ornamented with many veneers of contrasting color and shape, and are likely to be conspicuously inlaid with patterned string. However, an important group of Salem tables was produced with restrained ornament, usually the plainly veneered facades 1 or 11.[1]

1. One such table is seen in Charles F. Montgomery, *American Furniture: The Federal Period* (New York: Viking Press, 1966), p. 334, pl. 309.

14
CARD TABLE (*no. 81*)
Mark Pitman (1779–1829)
Salem, Massachusetts
Yale University Art Gallery, gift of
Mr. and Mrs. Charles F. Montgomery

Primary woods: mahogany, birch, rosewood
Secondary woods: white pine, birch.
Dimensions: H. 74 cm; W. 92 cm; D. 44 cm.
Form and Ornament: Shape 4, single-taper

legs; patterned inlays 1 [around facade oval], 2 [leaf edge, skirt], 66 [cuffs], 81 [adjacent facade rectangle], no pictorial inlay; facade 12C.

Construction: Filler back and plane flyleg construction, hinged-rail design 1, no leaf-edge tenons, no medial brace, one horizontal lamination in the curved rails, one point.

Notes: Even though square tables with elliptic fronts (shape 4) were not especially popular in Salem, Pitman's choice and placement of ornament epitomize Salem preferences. At the center of the facade he placed an oval within a mitered rectangle, highlighted the front pilasters with contrasting veneer, used patterned inlays at five places, plainly veneered the end aprons, and inset patterned inlay on the cuffs of otherwise plain legs.

15
CARD TABLE (*no. 89*)
Samuel Fiske (1769–1797) and
William Fiske (1770–1844)
Salem, Massachusetts
Robert and Barbara Sallick

Primary wood: mahogany. *Secondary woods:* white pine, birch.
Dimensions: H. 72 cm; W. 91 cm; D. 45 cm.
Form and Ornament: Shape 1, single-taper legs; no patterned inlay, pictorial inlay simple-integrated 16-part patera at center of front and side aprons; facade 5C.
Construction: Filler back and plane flyleg construction, hinged-rail design 2, one leaf-edge tenon, no medial brace, one horizontal lamination in the curved rails, two points.
Notes: Ready-made tables with two flylegs were produced in Salem, where three-part hinged-rails were manufactured. The

Cat. 14

Fiskes customized this table with a drawer in the rear (now missing), a rare characteristic found principally on Massachusetts and New Hampshire tables produced in the early Federal period. After his father's death in 1797, William Fiske worked briefly for the Sandersons in Salem and then moved to Roxbury, a thriving center for craftsmen clustered around the Willard clockworks.[1]

1. Ethel Hall Bjerkoe, *The Cabinetmakers of America* (Garden City, New York: Doubleday & Co., 1957), p. 93.

16
CARD TABLE (*no. 100*)
Thomas Needham III (1780–1858)
Salem, Massachusetts
Yale University Art Gallery, gift of
Benjamin A. Hewitt, B.A. 1943

Primary woods: mahogany, maple. *Secondary woods:* white pine, birch.
Dimensions: H. 74 cm; W. 91 cm; D. 46 cm.
Form and Ornament: Shape 2, single-taper legs; no patterned inlay, no pictorial inlay; facade 1.

Construction: Flush back and plane flyleg construction, hinged-rail design 1, no leaf-edge tenons, no medial brace, one horizontal lamination in the curved rails, two points.
Notes: Unlike most Salem tables with complex facades highlighted by patterned inlays and contrasting veneers, this table may represent Thomas Needham's attempt to appeal to customers who wanted a useful and inexpensive table. With its simple square shape, ovolo corners, plainly veneered facade, a panel of contrasting veneer on the pilasters, and cockbeading on the skirt, it is representative of a ready-made form, as is also seen on a published example of his work.[1]

1. This table, not located for inclusion in the study, is pictured in Ruth Bradbury Davidson, "American Gaming Tables," *Antiques* 64, no. 4 (October 1953): 294–96.

17
CARD TABLE (*no. 101*)
Unknown maker
Salem or Boston, Massachusetts
Museum of Fine Arts, Boston,
M. and M. Karolik Collection

Primary woods: mahogany, boxwood, ebony. *Secondary woods:* white pine, maple.
Dimensions: H. 75 cm; W. 124 cm; D. 61 cm.
Form and Ornament: Shape 1, single-taper legs with spade feet; patterned inlay 57 [perimeter of top], pictorial inlay of an inset-integrated shell on top; miscellaneous facade design.
Construction: Filler back and plane flyleg construction, hinged-rail design 1, two leaf-edge tenons, medial brace, two horizontal laminations in the curved rails, five points.
Notes: This table, with elaborate carving of the type usually associated with Samuel McIntire (1757–1811) of Salem, is one of a pair probably made in Boston or Salem to the specifications of Elizabeth Derby

Cat. 15

Cat. 16

West.[1] An example of outstanding crafts-manship and exquisite design, it has two unusual construction features which indi-cate that it was custom made: its large size requiring specially made hinged rails, and its carved (rather than standard produc-tion) legs.[2] The carved decoration was probably executed to be compatible with the large rooms of Mrs. West's home, Oak Hill, a mansion which demanded fur-niture of ample proportions.

1. Wendy A. Cooper, *In Praise of America: American Decorative Arts, 1650–1830* (New York: Alfred A. Knopf, 1980), pp. 132, 136.
2. Because of doubt about the exact origin of this table, it was arbitrarily included in the Salem data in the charts.

18
CARD TABLE (*no. 104*)
William Hook (1777–1867)
Salem, Massachusetts
Museum of Fine Arts, Boston, gift of
Mrs. John B. M. Mactaggart

Primary wood: mahogany. *Secondary woods:* white pine, maple.
Dimensions: H. 74 cm; W. 93 cm; D. 46 cm.
Form and Ornament: Shape 7, turned legs with capital 2 and base 2a; patterned inlay 30 [skirt, around facade oval, and adjacent to facade rectangle], no pictorial inlay; facade 12C.
Construction: Filler back and plane flyleg construction, hinged-rail design 1, one leaf-edge tenon, no medial brace, single-board construction of the curved rails, one point.
Notes: According to family tradition William Hook was the maker of this table.[1]

Cat. 17

Cat. 18

Cat. 19

Hook was a member of the network of Salem cabinetmakers who produced components for and purchased furniture from one another and often exported their products on jointly owned ships. The legs of this table were probably bought from Joseph True, who supplied Hook and eleven other cabinetmakers with components between 1810 and 1820.[2] The turnings of the ringed-drum capital and the attenuated bulbous foot are found on much Salem furniture and afford reliable evidence on which to base a regional attribution.

1. Richard H. Randall Jr., *American Furniture in the Museum of Fine Arts, Boston* (Boston: Museum of Fine Arts, 1965), p. 132.
2. Margaret Burke Clunie, "Joseph True and the Piecework System in Salem," *Antiques* 111, no. 5 (May 1977): 1006–13.

19
CARD TABLE (*no. 121*)
Samuel Barnard (1776–1858)[1]
Salem, Massachusetts
Patrick M. Spadaccino Jr.
Reproduced in color on p. 108

Primary wood: mahogany. *Secondary woods:* white pine, birch.
Dimensions: H. 73 cm; W. 90 cm; D. 43 cm.
Form and Ornament: Shape 24, turned legs with capital 3 and base 3; patterned inlays 1 [around facade oval], 30 [pilasters], 42, 91, no pictorial inlay; facade 12C.

Construction: Flush back and plane flyleg construction, hinged-rail design 1, no leaf-edge tenons, no medial brace, one horizontal lamination in the curved rails, three points.
Notes: Barnard is called "cabinetmaker of Salem" in six deeds in the Essex County Registry of Deeds, Salem, Massachusetts.[2] Along with Josiah Austin and Elijah Sanderson, other Salem cabinetmakers, he consigned furniture to Joseph Henderson, master of the schooner *Good Intent* bound for the West Indies, in August 1805.[3] On his invoice Barnard drew "SB" which was to be marked on each case.[4] The same mark is on the flying rail of this table. The legs of the table were supplied by a turner who may have moved from Boston to Salem, because the capital and base turnings are common to both origins.

1. Samuel Barnard "of Salem" was born in Watertown, July 22, 1776, son of Major Samuel Barnard and Elizabeth Bond: Henry Bond, M.D., *Genealogies of the Families and Descendants of the Early Settlers of Watertown, Massachusetts*, 2nd ed. (Boston: N. E. Historic-Genealogical Society, 1860), p. 16. Barnard died June 14, 1858, in Watertown, Massachusetts, at the home of D. A. Tainter, his brother-in-law, at the age of 82: The Commonwealth of Massachusetts, State Department of Public Health, Registry of Vital Records and Statistics, Vol. 121, p. 167, no. 14 and *New England Historical and Genealogical Register* 12 (October 1858): 363.
2. Vol. 169, p. 214, January 29, 1802; Vol. 171, p. 81, October 18, 1802; Vol. 174, p. 7, January 5, 1804; Vol. 176, p. 216, August 9, 1805; Vol. 179, p. 209, December 8, 1806; Vol. 183, p. 147, February 11, 1808.
3. Henry W. Belknap, "Furniture Exported by Cabinet Makers of Salem," *Essex Institute Historical Collections* 85 (October 1949): 351.
4. Barnard to Henderson, Elijah Sanderson Manuscripts: Commercial Papers, 1785–1822, p. 13, Essex Institute, Salem, Massachusetts.

Boston Area

Boston was New England's largest Federal-period city and the hub from which its styles emanated. Because of numerous similarities in card tables from all of the Massachusetts and New Hampshire centers it seems likely that many more Boston cabinetmakers and their apprentices moved to urban New Hampshire, rural Massachusetts-New Hampshire, Newburyport, and Salem than documentary research has revealed. Some Boston influence is evident in the Providence sample but little in Newport or Connecticut. The Boston area, including the towns of Charlestown, East Sudbury, Quincy, and Dorchester, produced both straight- and turned-leg tables.

STRAIGHT-LEG TABLES

Three table shapes—circular (1), square with ovolo corners (2) and square with elliptic front and serpentine ends (6)—comprise nearly the entire output of Boston straight-leg tables. The rare squat double-taper leg (cat. 24) is reliable evidence of Boston origin, but pointed double-taper and single-taper styles were also produced in large numbers. Little relief ornament is found on Boston straight-leg tables. However, plain and patterned inlays were more popular in the Boston area than in any of the other centers, and about equal amounts of single-unit and integrated pictorial inlays were used. Both inlay types were generally placed on the pilasters and many of the integrated inlays were probably produced locally. Legs were customarily inlaid with plain stringing—on one or two sides of the front and on one side of the rear shaft.

Equal numbers of Boston tables have one- and three-unit facades. On those with one unit, the predominating color of ma-

Cat. 20

hogany veneer is most frequently relieved by a panel of stringing (facade 2, see cat. 24) but is rarely plain. Those with three units are almost invariably facade 12, which creates colorful or textural contrasts of oval, triangular, and rectangular shapes. Regardless of facade design, pilaster ornament is most often of contrasting veneer. Boston straight-leg tables invariably have three fixed and one flyleg of plane construction and hinged-rail design 1; most of their curved rails are horizontally laminated. While no Boston table with a medial brace was found, about half have a leaf-edge tenon. Construction points range between zero and four. Birch and maple were popular secondary woods.

TURNED-LEG TABLES

Most Boston turned-leg tables are square with serpentine front, serpentine ends, ovolo corners over colonettes (shape 7). Three-fourths of the turned-leg tables are readily identified by one of two turnings (base 6 or base 8). Each of four other turnings popular in Boston—capitals 2, 3, 6, and base 3—was used by one other center, but the Boston preference for curving shafts (shaft 2) suggests a distinction. Patterned inlay was most popular and much plain stringing was also used.

Three-unit facades were especially popular. These are usually very colorful because they frequently employ four or more pieces of veneer which are set off by patterned or plain inlay. The latter inlays were usually inset on leaf edges and skirts. Either of two facade designs (11 or 12) was found on a third of the tables. Facade 11, of three rectangles divided by banding or patterned inlay (cat. 25), is not as lively as facade 12, on which oval, triangular, and rectangular pieces of veneer are combined to form pleasing contrasts of shapes, colors, and textures (cat. 27). The construction of Boston turned-leg tables is much like that of straight-leg tables. Two

characteristics, filler construction of the back and maple or birch as the secondary wood, are particularly suggestive of Boston origin.

20
CARD TABLE (*no. 133*)
Unknown maker
Boston area
Yale University Art Gallery,
Mabel Brady Garvan Collection

Primary woods: mahogany, maple. *Secondary woods:* white pine, cherry.
Dimensions: H. 75 cm; W. 92 cm; D. 45 cm.
Form and Ornament: Shape 6, pointed double-taper legs; patterned inlay 81, no pictorial inlay; facade 3.
Construction: Filler back and plane flyleg construction, hinged-rail design 1, one leaf-edge tenon, no medial brace, two horizontal laminations in the curved rails, three points.
Notes: The shape of this table, its pointed double-taper legs, the contrasting veneer on its pilasters, and the panels on the end aprons, all point to its manufacture in the Boston area. Veneered legs, a rare embellishment of American card tables, reflect the personal preference of patrons who were willing to pay extra for additional ornament. For this Boston example the buyer must have specified that three sides of the front and two sides of the rear legs be veneered with birdseye maple and inlaid with light and dark stringing to match the facade and end aprons and pilasters.

21
CARD TABLE (*no. 180*)
Unknown maker
Boston area
Yale University Art Gallery,
Mabel Brady Garvan Collection

Primary woods: mahogany, maple, rosewood. *Secondary woods:* white pine, maple.

Dimensions: H. 75 cm; W. 91 cm; D. 45 cm.
Form and Ornament: Shape 6, pointed double-taper legs; patterned inlays 3 [leg], 79 [around rectangular apron panels], pictorial inlays 129, 134; facade 12B.
Construction: Filler back and plane flyleg construction, hinged-rail design 1, one leaf-edge tenon, no medial brace, one and two horizontal laminations in the front and end curved rails respectively, three points.
Notes: This cabinetmaker heightened the contrasts inherent in this popular three-unit facade with a colorful eagle inlaid in a mitered rosewood rectangle flanked by striped maple panels with dark patterned inlay. Classical urns ornament the pilasters, patterned inlay borders the tapering shafts—a rare feature—and inlaid cuffs mark the second taper. By repeating his panels on the end aprons, the maker underscored the table's serpentine lines.

22
CARD TABLE (*no. 178*)
Unknown maker
Boston area
Yale University Art Gallery,
Mabel Brady Garvan Collection

Primary wood: mahogany. *Secondary woods:* birch, white pine.
Dimensions: H. 75 cm; W. 87 cm; D. 45 cm.
Form and Ornament: Shape 2, pointed double-taper legs; patterned inlays 23 [leaf edge], 56 [skirt and cuffs], pictorial inlays 129, 134; facade 5C.
Construction: Filler back and plane flyleg construction, hinged-rail design 1, no leaf-edge tenons, no medial brace, kerf construction of the curved rails, three points.
Notes: By inlaying an eagle surrounded by a hollow-corner rectangle in a bifurcated veneer, this maker tried to produce a fa-

Cat. 21

cade of one unit that looked like and cost less than a three unit facade (see cat. 21, with identical inlays). Composed of few elements and unified by a single veneer, one-unit facades were produced more economically because they required less painstaking labor.

examples which are usually abundantly inlaid (cat. 38).

1. Smith and Hitchings are first mentioned in the Boston directories in 1803, *The Boston Directory* (Boston: John West, 1803). By 1805 they are listed separately, *The Boston Directory* (Boston: Edward Cotton, 1805).

23
CARD TABLE (*no. 137*)
John Smith and Samuel Hitchings (in partnership ca. 1803–1804)[1]
Boston, Massachusetts
Yale University Art Gallery, gift of
Mr. and Mrs. Charles F. Montgomery

Primary wood: mahogany. *Secondary wood:* white pine.
Dimensions: H. 74 cm; W. 88 cm; D. 43 cm.
Form and Ornament: Shape 2, single-taper legs; no patterned inlay, no pictorial inlay; facade 4.
Construction: Flush back and plane flyleg construction, hinged-rail design 1, one leaf-edge tenon, no medial brace, one horizontal lamination in the curved rails, three points.
Notes: This type of facade, a wide-oval panel of veneer bordered by inlay and enclosed by mitered veneer, was found most frequently in conjunction with this shape. The Boston group presents a restrained appearance with side and end aprons plainly veneered in comparison with New York

24
CARD TABLE (*no. 138*)
Jacob Forster (1764–1838)
Charlestown, Massachusetts
Yale University Art Gallery, gift of
Benjamin A. Hewitt, B.A. 1943

Primary wood: mahogany. *Secondary woods:* white pine, cherry.
Dimensions: H. 74 cm; W. 88 cm; D. 44 cm.
Form and Ornament: Shape 1, squat double-taper legs; patterned inlay 52 [perimeter of top], pictorial inlay of simple-integrated patera on front pilasters; facade 2.
Construction: Flush back and plane flyleg construction, hinged-rail design 1, no leaf-edge tenons, no medial brace, one horizontal lamination in the curved rails, two points.
Notes: The study shows that all circular card tables with squat double-taper legs, pilasters with pictorial inlay, and simply veneered facades with rectangular panels of plain stringing, can be attributed to

Cat. 22

Cat. 23

Jacob Forster.[1] Forster probably manufactured and supplied other makers with legs of this rare shape because they are found on a few Boston-area tables, one of which is branded "I BROOKS," perhaps an unknown cabinetmaker.[2]

1. Forster's other documented examples are nos. 135, 142, of which the former has single-taper legs and a facade with plain inlay only at the horizontal perimeters. Attributions are nos. 144, 152, 158, 160.
2. No. 161.

25
CARD TABLE (no. 204)[†]
Samuel Adams and William Todd
(in partnership 1798–1800)
Boston, Massachusetts
Historic Deerfield, Inc., Deerfield,
Massachusetts

Primary woods: mahogany, birch. *Secondary woods:* white pine, birch.

Dimensions: H. 73 cm; W. 96 cm; D. 46 cm.
Form and Ornament: Shape 7, turned legs with capital 8 and base 8; patterned inlay 96, no pictorial inlay; facade 11.
Construction: Filler back and plane flyleg construction, hinged-rail design 1, no leaf-edge tenons, no medial brace, single-board construction of the curved rails, no points.
Notes: The three-unit facade of matched veneer rectangles outlined by crossbanding (and here with lunette inlay) was popular in Boston. The reel-over-taper base turning is found on the legs of several Boston tables believed to have been supplied to a number of shops by one turner; however, the capital turning on this table is unique in this study. The two-year partnership of Adams and Todd establishes a narrow date range for the table's manufacture, which makes it the earliest documented turned-leg table in the study.

Cat. 24

Cat. 25

Cat. 26

26

CARD TABLE (*no. 198*)
Unknown maker
Boston area
Yale University Art Gallery,
Mabel Brady Garvan Collection
Reproduced in color on p. 109

Primary woods: mahogany, birch. *Secondary woods:* white pine, maple.
Dimensions: H. 75 cm; W. 93 cm; D. 47 cm.
Form and Ornament: Shape 7, turned legs with capital 6 and base 6; patterned inlays 95, 97, no pictorial inlay; facade 11.
Construction: Filler back and plane flyleg construction, hinged-rail design 1, no leaf-edge tenons, no medial brace, single-board construction of the curved rails, no points.
Notes: The unknown maker of this table used the same shape and facade design as on the preceding Adams and Todd table (both popular in the Boston area), and

probably purchased lunette inlay from the same specialist (cat. 25) but bought legs from a different turner. The base turning (ring over hollow over ring over taper) was found only on Boston-area tables, and the capital, an ogee with deep curves, was used frequently in Boston but rarely in rural Massachusetts or New Hampshire.

27

CARD TABLE (*no. 207*)
Unknown maker
Boston area
Yale University Art Gallery, gift of Mrs. Clark R. McIlwaine in memory of her mother, Margaret Tyler Clark

Primary woods: mahogany, maple.
Secondary wood: white pine.
Dimensions: H. 76 cm; W. 93 cm; D. 45 cm.

Cat. 27

Form and Ornament: Shape 7, turned legs with capital 3 and base 3; no patterned inlay, no pictorial inlay; facade 12c.

Construction: Filler back and plane flyleg construction, hinged-rail design 1, one leaf-edge tenon, no medial brace, single-board construction of the curved rails, one point.

Notes: Boston preferences in turned-leg tables are epitomized in the shape, facade, and turnings of this table. Close relationships between Boston and Salem craftsmen are suggested by the Barnard example (cat. 19), but distinctions are evident in its use of patterned inlays on the facade and in its turnings—the Barnard table having a straight taper and a less graceful base.

Newport

The population of Newport declined after the Revolution, when the town lost its commercial preeminence to Providence. Cabinetmakers such as John Townsend (1732–1809) and Stephen (1764–1804) and Thomas Goddard (1765–1858) who had attained distinction for their custom work in the Chippendale style, interpreted the neoclassical style conservatively. For the most part they and other Newport cabinetmakers produced circular card tables ornamented with simple one-unit facades and single-unit inlays produced in their own shops. Only straight-leg tables are known to have been made there.

Most Newport tables have an elegant and austere appearance created by richly figured bifurcated mahogany veneer and by inlays on pilasters and legs. Lightwood profiles of urns, flutes, tassels, and icicles project starkly on the plain surfaces. Usually two sides of the front legs and two sides of the rear legs were inlaid with stringing. The ornament on front and rear pilasters is generally matched.

Newport card tables are readily distinguished from the output of the eleven other centers by the use of white pine, birch, maple, cherry, chestnut, and tulip poplar, and by two kinds of legs and hinged rails—five fixed and one flyleg of additional construction or two fixed and two flylegs of overlapping construction. Flush back construction and horizontally laminated curved rails are characteristic. The range of construction points is from six to seven.

28

CARD TABLE (*no. 232*)
Stephen Goddard (1764–1804) and
Thomas Goddard (1765–1858)
Newport, Rhode Island
The Metropolitan Museum of Art,
Rogers Fund, 1929

Primary wood: mahogany. *Secondary woods:* white pine, chestnut.
Dimensions: H. 71 cm; W. 91 cm; D. 45 cm.
Form and Ornament: Shape 1, single-taper legs; no patterned inlay, pictorial inlays 125, and single-unit urn on pilasters; facade 2.
Construction: Flush back and additional flyleg construction, hinged-rail design 3, no leaf-edge tenons, no medial brace, three horizontal laminations in the curved rails, six points.
Notes: Equal numbers of Newport tables in the study have two fixed–and two flylegs and five fixed–and one flyleg. In the interest of symmetry, Newport cabinetmakers added this sixth stationary leg at the left rear. Perhaps because it served no useful purpose and increased the cost of ready-made tables, this form achieved limited popularity in Newport and was produced only on special order in other regions. This is the only known documented example of a six-leg Newport table, but it is believed that the form was produced ready-made by other Newport cabinetmakers.

29

CARD TABLE (*no. 236*)
Attributed to Holmes Weaver (1769–1848)
Newport, Rhode Island
Benjamin A. Hewitt
Reproduced in color on p. 109

Primary wood: mahogany. *Secondary woods:* white pine, cherry.
Dimensions: H. 72 cm; W. 87 cm; D. 43 cm.
Form and Ornament: Shape 1, single-taper legs; no patterned inlay, pictorial inlays 101, 124; facade 2.
Construction: Flush back and overlapping flyleg construction, hinged-rail design 2, one leaf-edge tenon, no medial brace, four horizontal laminations in the curved rails, seven points.
Notes: This table was probably part of a set with a matching table[1] and a pembroke table,[2] inlaid with engraved single-unit urns on the pilasters, tassels on the shafts, and flowers on a lightwood prism inlay extending from the cuff line to the floor. These inlays are believed to have been produced in Weaver's own shop. Another circular card table has corresponding inlays on the pilasters and shafts but raised banding at the cuff.[3] The inlays are like those on a pembroke table labeled by Weaver to which he added drapery inlay at the top of the shafts.[4]

1. Illustrated in *Fine Americana, American Paintings and Chinese Export Porcelain* (New York: Christie, Manson & Woods International, Inc., June 24-25, 1980), pp. 183-84, lot 691.
2. Illustrated in Stanley Stone, "Rhode Island Furniture at Chipstone: Part I," *Antiques* 91, no. 2 (February 1967): 210.
3. No. 237.
4. Edwin J. Hipkiss, *Eighteenth-Century American Arts: The M. and M. Karolik Collection* (Boston: Museum of Fine Arts, 1941), pp. 126-27, cat. 67.

Cat. 28

Cat. 29. Detail of leg.

Cat. 29

Providence

After the Revolution many Massachusetts and Newport cabinetmakers settled in Providence, a growing and prospering center of commerce.[1] Either eastern Massachusetts or Newport influences are evident in the shape and ornament of card tables, and their construction blends the practices of the two regions. All tables in the sample have straight legs.

Most Providence tables are either circular (shape 1) with restrained one-unit facades of the type associated with Newport, or square with ovolo corners (shape 2) with complex and lively three-unit facades similar to those on Salem and Boston tables (cats. 19, 27). As in Newport, plain stringing was preferred to patterned inlay. It is often found on leaf edges and skirts and was used to liberally ornament two or three sides of the front shafts and one or two sides of the rear. For pilasters, legs, and facades, some cabinetmakers produced their own single-unit inlays but others used imported integrated inlays. Like some Newport makers, Providence cabinetmakers sometimes created a cuff with raised crossbanding, a characteristic rarely found in other centers.

Hinged rail design 1 (for tables with three fixed and one movable leg) and overlapping flyleg construction readily distinguish Providence tables from the entire output of all other New England centers and New York. White pine, birch, maple, cherry, and chestnut as secondary woods further differentiate Providence tables from

Cat. 30

those made in the Philadelphia area, Baltimore, and Annapolis. Back construction is usually flush, and the curved rails are usually horizontally laminated. While few tables have a medial brace, most have tenons.

1. Wendell D. Garrett, "Providence Cabinetmakers, Chairmakers, Upholsterers, and Allied Craftsmen, 1756–1838," *Antiques* 90, no. 4 (October 1966): 514-19.

30
CARD TABLE (*no. 240*)
Joseph Rawson Sr. (w. ca. 1790; d. 1835)
Providence, Rhode Island
The Henry Francis du Pont Winterthur Museum

Primary wood: mahogany. *Secondary woods:* white pine, maple.
Dimensions: H. 72 cm; W. 91 cm; D. 45 cm.
Form and Ornament: Shape 2, single-taper legs; patterned inlay 81, no pictorial inlay; facade 12C.
Construction: Flush back and overlapping flyleg construction, hinged-rail design 1, no tenons, no medial brace, four horizontal laminations in the curved rails, six points.
Notes: This table, with three fixed legs and one flyleg of overlapping construction, typifies Providence workmanship. Three generations of the Rawson family produced furniture in Providence from 1741 until 1894. The earliest member of the family to

do so, Grindall Rawson, was succeeded by his son Joseph about 1800. In 1808 when Joseph's son Samuel joined him as his partner, the firm became known as Joseph Rawson and Son. From 1815, when they were joined by Joseph's sons William and Edward, until 1828 they operated as "Joseph Rawson and Son's" (sic). The Rawsons' huge shop employed 25 apprentices in 1800, and in 1818 William and Edward advertised furniture from their "manufactory in the North" in a Charleston, South Carolina, newspaper.[1]

1. Eleanore Bradford Monahon, "The Rawson Family of Cabinetmakers in Providence, Rhode Island," *Antiques* 118, no. 1 (July 1980): 134-47.

31
CARD TABLE (*no. 253*)
Joseph Rawson and Son (w. ca. 1808–1815)
Providence, Rhode Island
Yale University Art Gallery, gift of Benjamin A. Hewitt, B.A. 1943

Primary wood: mahogany. *Secondary woods:* white pine, maple.
Dimensions: H. 73 cm; W. 94 cm; D. 45 cm.
Form and Ornament: Shape 6, single-taper legs; patterned inlays 1 [around facade oval], 64 [adjacent to facade rectangle], 72 [skirt], 93 [leaf edge], no pictorial inlay; facade 12C.
Construction: Filler back and plane flyleg construction, hinged-rail design 1, no leaf-edge tenons, no medial brace, single-board construction of the curved rails, no points.
Notes: The craftsmen who cut the patterns from which the facade of this and the earlier Rawson table (cat. 30) were ornamented must have worked at some time in Salem or Boston where this type of central oval within mitered rectangle was so popular. The Rawsons continued to use this design for at least 25 years.[1] This table's flyleg construction indicates that it was produced on special order for a customer requesting a table with elliptic front and

serpentine ends, a shape otherwise found only in Salem, Boston, and Newburyport.

1. A turned-leg table with this facade and the Rawson label used between 1815 and 1828 appeared in Eleanore Bradford Monahon, "Providence Cabinetmakers of the Eighteenth and Early Nineteenth Centuries," *Antiques* 87, no. 5 (May 1965): 576. This table was excluded from the study because its median date of production is after 1820.

salers from that city exported many tables to New York,[1] and the label is probably that of the retailer, rather than of the maker. Between 1791 and 1795 George Shipley's manufactory and wholesale mahogany business was located at 161 Water Street, the address on this label.[2] An expansive wholesaler and retailer, Shipley supplied cabinetmakers with precut lumber, imported woods, and hardware, upholsterers with cloth, and masons and plasterers with implements and supplies. For retail customers he advertised furniture, china, pewter, and landscape paintings.[3]

1. Joseph K. Ott, "Rhode Island Furniture Exports 1783–1800 Including Information on Chaises, Buildings, Other Woodenware and Trade Practices," *Rhode Island History* 36, no. 1 (February 1977): 3–13.
2. Martha Gandy Fales, "George Shipley: His Furniture and His Label," *Antiques* 79, no. 4 (April 1961): 376.
3. Rita Susswein Gottesman, comp., *The Arts and Crafts in New York 1800–1804* (New York: The New-York Historical Society, 1965), pp. 152–53.

32
CARD TABLE (*no. 243*)
Unknown maker
Providence, Rhode Island
Labeled by George Shipley (d. 1801)
New York, New York
Benjamin A. Hewitt

Primary woods: mahogany, cherry. *Secondary woods:* white pine, cherry.
Dimensions: H. 72 cm; W. 92 cm; D. 45 cm.
Form and Ornament: Shape 1, single-taper legs; no patterned inlay, pictorial inlays 110 and icicles on the front legs; facade 1.
Construction: Flush back and overlapping flyleg construction, hinged-rail design 1, one leaf-edge tenon, no medial brace, two horizontal laminations in the curved rails, five points.
Notes: Despite its New York label, the construction with four legs and overlapping flyleg, plain facade, and flute and icicle inlay define its Providence origin. Whole-

Cat. 31

Cat. 32

33
CARD TABLE (*no. 241*)
Attributed to Thomas Howard (1774–1833)
Pawtuxet and Providence, Rhode Island
Private collection
Reproduced in color on p. 112

Primary wood: mahogany. *Secondary woods:* maple, white pine.
Dimensions: H. 75 cm; W. 91 cm; D. 46 cm.
Form and Ornament: Shape 2, single-taper legs; patterned inlays 3 [leaf edge], 81 [around facade rectangle], 93 [skirt], pictorial inlays 132, 140; facade 10E.
Construction: Flush back and overlapping flyleg construction, hinged-rail design 1, one leaf-edge tenon, no medial brace, two horizontal laminations in the curved rails, five points.

Notes: One of a pair, this table and its mate, inset with single-unit inlays produced by shop employees, are among the few documented examples of Thomas Howard's furniture. The tables descended through the Carrington family to the present owners along with a bill of sale indicating that the tables were made for General Edward Carrington in 1817.[1] Howard grew wealthy by selling his own as well as imported furniture to both retail and wholesale customers. He also dealt in ivory, lumber, and other materials required by varied craftsmen, and was involved in the export business and real estate speculation.[2]

1. The bill of sale is among the Carrington Papers, Rhode Island Historical Society, Providence, Rhode Island.
2. Eleanore Bradford Monahon, "Providence Cabinetmakers," *Rhode Island History* 23, no. 1 (January 1964): 1-22.

Cat. 33

Connecticut

After the Revolution, the once flourishing coastal and riverside towns of Connecticut were quickly eclipsed by the burgeoning metropolis of New York. The two documented tables in the study from this region originated in Hartford (cat. 36) and New London (cat. 35), two towns which had populations of the size of Salem, Massachusetts, during the prewar years. Because of the distance between Hartford and New London, and the large number of undocumented tables in the sample, the region encompassing these two towns has been given the broad designation of Connecticut. Construction characteristics in this sample are highly consistent. It is not understood how manufacturing developed in these two distant towns, but specialist-made components very similar to those used in New York are evident in tables from the

region. All the Connecticut tables in the study have straight legs.

Connecticut cabinetmakers preferred square (shape 3) and circular (shape 1) tables with single-taper legs, and simple one-unit and miscellaneous facade designs with a wide variety of ornament. Both integrated inlays produced by specialists and single-unit inlays made within cabinet shops are found. Relief ornament, such as scratchbeaded or rounded leaf edges and beaded skirts was favored and pilasters were ornamented with simple string panels, contrasting veneer, or pictorial inlay. Shafts were invariably ornamented, usually on two sides of the front and one side of the rear legs with veneer, pictorial inlay, or plain stringing and sometimes the legs were molded from the leaf edge to the floor.

Their four fixed- and one flyleg (hinged-rail design 3) distinguish Connecticut

Cat. 34

tables from those of every other center except New York, from which they are differentiated by fewer construction points (four to seven). Connecticut tables have flush back construction, additional flyleg construction, and horizontal laminations in the curved rails. Medial braces are found on few tables from this region but most have rear leaf-edge tenons.

34
CARD TABLE (*no. 257*)
Unknown maker
Connecticut
Litchfield Historical Society

Primary wood: cherry. *Secondary woods:* white pine, cherry.
Dimensions: H. 76 cm; W. 90 cm; D. 44 cm.
Form and Ornament: Shape 3, single-taper legs; no patterned inlay, pictorial inlays, four designs of inset-integrated paterae, one with 12 points at apron center, one with 12 points on pilasters, four quarter patera with 6 points at corners of the top, and one with 28 points at center of the top, icicle inlay on legs; miscellaneous facade.
Construction: Flush back and additional flyleg construction, hinged-rail design 3, one leaf-edge tenon, no medial brace, no curved rails, four points.
Notes: Although simply constructed square tables with relief ornament were popular in Connecticut, the unusual perforated apron and gadrooned skirt reflect the work of a skillful craftsman accustomed to producing expensive special-order furniture in the pre-Revolutionary craft tradition. His extravagant use of paterae on the top, the pilasters, and apron center suggest that an affluent customer ordered a unique table with fashionable ornament. Icicle inlay, a popular motif in Connecticut, Providence, Newport, and Springfield, Massachusetts, may have been produced by a specialist who supplied many shops in southern New England. Cherry as a primary wood is in-

dicative of Connecticut origin on five-leg tables and of rural Massachusetts–New Hampshire origin on four-leg tables.

35
CARD TABLE (*no. 258*)
Attributed to Richard Fosdick
(w. 1790–1815)
New London, Connecticut
New London County Historical Society

Primary wood: mahogany. *Secondary woods:* white pine, chestnut.
Dimensions: H. 75 cm; W. 89 cm; D. 44 cm.
Form and Ornament: Shape 3, single-taper legs; no patterned inlay, no pictorial inlay; facade 2.
Construction: Flush back and additional flyleg construction, hinged-rail construction 3, one leaf-edge tenon, no medial brace, no curved rails, four points.
Notes: This table is believed to be one of the pair Richard Fosdick delivered to Thomas Shaw of New London shortly before the latter's death in 1795,[1] and it suggests an early date for the production of Connecticut ready-made tables.[1] Square tables were the least expensive to construct and a popular form. While some were customized with inlays and carving for which customers paid extra, this example with simple ornament was probably a stock item.

1. Minor Myers Jr. and Edgar de N. Mayhew, *New London County Furniture 1640–1840* (New London, Connecticut: The Lyman Allyn Museum, 1974), p. 82.

36
CARD TABLE (*no. 263*)
B. C. Gillett (w. ca. 1812)
Hartford, Connecticut
Wadsworth Atheneum, Hartford,
The Henry and Walter Keney Fund

Primary wood: mahogany. *Secondary woods:* white pine, cherry.
Dimensions: H. 73 cm; W. 92 cm; D. 45 cm.

Cat. 35

Cat. 36

Form and Ornament: Shape 1, single-taper legs; no patterned inlay, pictorial inlay of single-unit bellflower on legs; facade 2.
Construction: Flush back and additional flyleg construction, hinged-rail design 3, no leaf-edge tenons, no medial brace, three horizontal laminations in the curved rails, six points.
Notes: Gillett must have been familiar with New York styles. Unlike most Connecticut makers who preferred solid wood tops and rounded leaf edges, Gillett veneered the white pine leaves of this table with mahogany, applied crossbanding to the square edges, and inlaid the perimeter of the top with plain stringing. An inlaid oval on the apron, replicates the central apron panel which New York makers often surrounded with a mitered rectangle (facade 4).

New York

New York made a speedy postwar recovery from British occupation to become a fashionable cosmopolitan city. For a short time the nation's capital, by 1797 it achieved great commercial importance and by 1820 its population numbered more than 120,000 people. New York straight-leg card tables are elegant interpretations of neoclassical designs, and the grace, delicacy, and restrained ornament of New York turned–leg tables show French taste skillfully interpreted by immigrant cabinetmakers.

STRAIGHT-LEG TABLES

Straight–leg tables are likely to have an elegant appearance due to the use of fine quality woods and the careful workmanship of specialist inlay makers. Usually mahogany veneers are richly figured, bellflowers precisely cut, and paterae deftly shaded. Legs bear panels of fanciful shape, corners of the leaf edges have plain stringing, and the tops are bordered by treble or quadruple stringing. Most popular in New York were one–unit facades, such as facade 4, with an oval surrounded by treble stringing and mitered veneer which created a subtle play of textures and shapes. It was also common practice in New York to panel all aprons. The single-taper legs are ornamented on two sides of the rear and two or three sides of the front. Shape 2, square with ovolo corners, was the most popular for New York straight-leg tables.

Five-leg construction readily distinguishes all New York straight-leg tables from those produced everywhere but in Connecticut, from which most are reliably distinguished by their greater number of construction points and the unique construction of curved rails with vertical laminations. New York cabinetmakers invariably used rear leaf-edge tenons to compensate for warpage of the secondary woods under the veneer on the leaves, flush back construction, and curved rails with multiple laminations.

TURNED-LEG TABLES

New York turned-leg tables are reliably distinguished by either a capital 1 or base 1. Because these tables are higher than those from other regions and their aprons are a little shorter, they are likely to appear lighter, or less bulky. Their delicacy is further enhanced by thin, finely reeded legs and by double and treble elliptic forms (shapes 10, 11). These sophisticated shapes are more evident than the subtle distinctions in the dark mahogany veneer on the facades and pilasters. The crossbanding and raised banding which sometimes frame the facades and pilasters and the carving applied to the center of the facades may blend with the mahogany veneer to make

aprons appear plain (cats. 41, 42). With few exceptions, leaf edges are unobtrusively veneered and skirts are crossbanded or beaded. Invariably the curved rails have many horizontal laminations, the rear edges of the veneered leaves have tenons, the frames are supported by five legs, and the back construction is flush.

37
CARD TABLE (*no. 267*)
Unknown maker
New York, New York
Yale University Art Gallery,
Mabel Brady Garvan Collection

Primary wood: mahogany. *Secondary woods:* white pine, tulip, maple.
Dimensions: H. 75 cm; W. 91 cm; D. 45 cm.
Form and Ornament: Shape 2, single-taper

Cat. 37

legs; patterned inlays 2, 5 [combined on skirt], 68 [cuffs], pictorial inlays 107, 116, inset-integrated flowers in urn at center of facade, and flutes adjacent to ovolo corners; facade 13.

Construction: Flush back and additional flyleg construction, hinged-rail design 3, one leaf-edge tenon, no medial brace, vertically laminated curved rails, eleven points.

Notes: While this table's three-unit facade with pictorial inlay at the center and veneered panels of boldly contrasting colors and shapes is atypical, its construction with five legs and vertically laminated rails defines its New York origin. Also representative of New York preferences are the flute inlays adjoining the ovolo corners, inlays on the pilasters, single-unit bellflowers on the shafts, patterned inlay on the skirt, and treble–string inlay bordering the veneered top.

38
CARD TABLE *(no. 269)*
Attributed to William Whitehead
(w. 1792–1800)[1]
New York, New York
Benjamin A. Hewitt

Primary wood: mahogany. *Secondary woods:* white pine, maple.
Dimensions: H. 73 cm; W. 91 cm; D. 45 cm.
Form and Ornament: Shape 2, single-taper legs; no patterned inlay, pictorial inlays 116, 119, 120, 148; facade 4.
Construction: Flush back and additional flyleg construction, hinged-rail design 3, two leaf-edge tenons, medial brace, four horizontal laminations in the curved rails, ten points.
Notes: The maker of this table selected from the inlay maker's stock treble-string inlay to border the ovals on the apron, 12-point paterae for the pilasters, flutes for the rails adjacent to the ovolo corners, and three bellflowers for the front legs. The composition of the inlays on this table, particu-

larly the V-shape and looped stringing used in conjunction with the bellflowers, resembles that on a labeled sideboard by William Whitehead, to whom this table is attributed.[2] The label reveals that Whitehead's address was 75 Pearl Street, New York City, where he was located between 1794 and 1800, and it seems probable that he manufactured this table at that time.

1. Whitehead's name appears in the New York directories from 1792 to 1800.
2. Illustrated in *American Antiques From Israel Sack Collection*, Vol. III (Washington, D.C.: Highland House Publishers, Inc., 1972), p. 650, no. 1449.

39
CARD TABLE *(no. 273)*
Label of Charles Courtright[1]
New York, New York
Gracie Mansion

Primary wood: mahogany. *Secondary woods:* white pine, cherry.
Dimensions: H. 76 cm; W. 92 cm; D. 45 cm.
Form and Ornament: Shape 1, single-taper legs; no patterned inlay, no pictorial inlay; facade 4.
Construction: Flush back and additional flyleg construction, hinged-rail design 3, two leaf-edge tenons, no medial brace, two horizontal laminations in the curved rails, seven points.
Notes: Conforming to New York preferences, this table has facade 4 with an oval panel bordered by treble stringing and enclosed by mitered veneer. The softwood top is veneered with mahogany and bordered with treble stringing, the edges are crossbanded, the corners are inlaid with plain stringing, and the feet are finished off with cuffs of plain inlay and banding. With its plain pilasters and simple string inlay on the shaft, this table is unusually spare for New York.

1. No information about Charles Courtright has been discovered in a search of New York City

Cat. 38

Cat. 39

records, and the typography of his label calls its date into question. The words "Made and Sold By" and "New York" in the label are printed in a sans serif typeface, and it is generally accepted that sans serif type was not made prior to 1816, and was not in common use until the 1830s (see Nicolete Gray, *Nineteenth Century Ornamented Typefaces* [Berkeley, California: University of California Press, 1976], p. 194, and Stanley Morison, *On Type Designs: Past and Present* [London: Ernest Benn, 1962], pp. 62-3). The writers would like to thank Howard I. Gralla for bringing this information to their attention.

40
CARD TABLE (*no. 274*)
Unknown maker
New York, New York
Benjamin A. Hewitt
Reproduced in color on p. 112

Primary wood: mahogany. *Secondary woods:* white pine, cherry.
Dimensions: H. 74 cm; W. 94 cm; D. 48 cm.
Form and Ornament: Shape 20, single-taper legs; no patterned inlay, pictorial inlays of a simple-integrated Prince of Wales feather on the pilasters and flutes on the apron adjacent to the ovolo corners (similar to 119); facade 4.
Construction: Flush back and additional flyleg construction, hinged-rail design 3, two leaf-edge tenons, no medial brace, two, three, and four horizontal laminations respectively in the curved rails at the ends, front, and corners, nine points.
Notes: This table's successful combination of serpentine and ovolo shapes required

meticulous design and painstaking craftsmanship. This form is described in the *New-York Book of Prices for Cabinet & Chair Work* (1802), but this is the only example of the handsome design found in the study, suggesting that the table was custom-made for a fastidious patron. Its construction is entirely in keeping with New York practice. Furniture ornamented with Prince of Wales feather inlay, found here on the pilasters, is often attributed to Michael Allison, who used it on a pembroke table bearing his label.[1] Probably made by a specialist inlay maker, it was available to many cabinetmakers, and consequently provides only the basis for a New York attribution.

1. Advertisement, Ginsburg and Levy, Inc., *Antiques* 52, no. 2 (August 1947): 85.

41
CARD TABLE (*no. 280*)
Charles Honoré Lannuier (1779–1819)
New York, New York
The Henry Francis du Pont Winterthur Museum

Primary wood: mahogany. *Secondary woods:* white pine, tulip, cherry.
Dimensions: H. 76 cm; W. 91 cm; D. 45 cm.
Form and Ornament: Shape 17, turned legs with capital 1 and base 1; no patterned inlay, no pictorial inlay; facade 10A.
Construction: No flylegs, no hinged rail, three leaf-edge tenons, no medial brace, no curved rails.[1]
Notes: The shape and swivel top of this table are unique to the study, but the uniform color and subtle three-unit facade design and capital and base turnings 1 are representative of New York styles. Lannuier reduced construction costs by introducing a pivot, thus eliminating a flyleg and hinged rails. This is the earliest known documented example of this simple construction, which became widely used in the latter part of the Federal period.

Cat. 40

Cat. 41

1. Computing sturdiness points for this table is inappropriate because Lannuier's custom construction did not involve the use of hinged rails and flylegs.

42
CARD TABLE (*no. 282*)
Unknown maker
New York, New York
The Brooklyn Museum, gift of
Mrs. J. Amory Haskell

Primary wood: mahogany. *Secondary wood:* white pine.
Dimensions: H. 75 cm; W. 91 cm; D. 45 cm.
Form and Ornament: Shape 10, turned legs with capital 1 and base 1; no patterned inlay, no pictorial inlay; facade 10B.
Construction: Flush back and additional flyleg construction, hinged-rail design 3, two leaf-edge tenons, medial brace, three horizontal laminations in the curved rails, nine points.

Notes: Carving, such as the central drapery plaque, was produced by a carver, a specialist who served the cabinetmaking industry. This table, in the style of Duncan Phyfe, may in fact have originated in his large shop where he sometimes employed as many as a hundred craftsmen. Nevertheless, the legs are similar to those on two tables by John T. Dolan (cat. 43, no. 287) and one by Charles Honoré Lannuier (cat. 41), although the brass paw feet are an unusual, refined touch.

43
CARD TABLE (*no. 285*)
John T. Dolan (w. 1805–1813)
New York, New York
Museum of the City of New York, gift of Doctors C. Ray and Winifred Hope Franklin

Primary woods: mahogany, satinwood.
Secondary woods: white pine, cherry.
Dimensions: H. 79 cm; W. 92 cm; D. 45 cm.
Form and Ornament: Shape 11, turned legs with capital 1 and base 1; no patterned inlay, no pictorial inlay; facade 1.
Construction: Flush back and additional flyleg construction, hinged-rail design 3, three leaf-edge tenons, no medial brace, three horizontal laminations in the curved rails, nine points.
Notes: By bifurcating a piece of mahogany into two slices and veneering them so that their figures meet at the center and run

Cat. 42

Cat. 43

symmetrically across the front apron, Dolan produced a richly textured but plain facade. He customized the playing surface with ovals of satinwood to simulate pockets for chips. His only other documented card table (no. 287) is identical in form, construction, facade design, turnings, and brass casters, but its playing surface is plain and its pilasters bear rectangular panels of mahogany veneer.

Philadelphia Area

Philadelphia, the largest urban center in America before the Revolution, boasted a population of 92,000 by 1800 but was soon surpassed by New York. Most of the craftsmen who produced its Chippendale-style furniture, often regarded as the golden age of Philadelphia furniture, had died or retired by the time the neoclassical style came into fashion. Their successors, a new generation of craftsmen, produced card tables of curvate forms. Because the tables in the study from as far away as West Chester and Trenton were found to have the characteristics of those produced in Philadelphia, this region is referred to as the Philadelphia area.

Cat. 44

Shape 5, kidney-end with serpentine middle, nearly exclusive to this region, was by far the most popular shape for Philadelphia-area straight-leg card tables. Legs are always single taper, with two sides of the front and one side of the rear legs usually inset with plain stringing. Most tables are uniformly dark in color except for light lines of plain string inlay on their one-unit facades and on their leaf edges and skirts to faintly define the shapes. Pilasters and shafts, either plain or paneled with stringing, usually distinguish Philadelphia from Baltimore tables, with which they are sometimes confused.

Useful in distinguishing Philadelphia-area straight-leg tables from almost all of the output of other regions is their invariable construction with three fixed and one movable leg, the unique use of walnut as primary wood on a small number of tables, and oak or taeda pine as secondary wood. Philadelphia-area cabinetmakers preferred sturdy tables with multilaminated curved rails, rear leaf-edge tenons, and flush back construction.

TURNED-LEG TABLES

Almost all Philadelphia-area turned-leg tables are reliably distinguished by one of four characteristics: capital 4a and 4b or 5 or base 4 or 5. Makers of turned-leg tables also preferred curvate shapes like the highly popular shape 12, square with elliptic front and serpentine corners, uniformly dark-color plainly veneered aprons, and subtle ornament such as reeding, beading, and crossbanding to define the shapes of the leaf edges and skirt and to ornament pilasters. They too used very sturdy construction—almost invariably one or more leaf-edge tenons, flush back construction, and curved rails with three or more horizontal laminations.

44
CARD TABLE (*no. 299*)
Unknown maker
Philadelphia area
Gift of Mr. and Mrs. Samuel Schwartz
to the Diplomatic Reception Rooms,
Department of State

Primary wood: walnut. *Secondary woods:* white pine, oak.
Dimensions: H. 78 cm; W. 91 cm; D. 46 cm.
Form and Ornament: Shape 5, single-taper legs; patterned inlay 57 [pilasters], pictorial inlay inset-integrated shell at apron center; facade 12B.
Construction: Flush back and overlapping flyleg construction, hinged-rail design 1, two leaf-edge tenons, no medial brace, three horizontal laminations in the curved rails, seven points.
Notes: The shape and the use of walnut as the primary wood define this as a ready-made Philadelphia table. Its three-unit facade with shell and its lozenge-shaped inlays indicate that it was customized. The cabinetmaker embellished the aprons with unusual geometric panels of stringing. Because no specialist is believed to have produced patterned and pictorial inlays in Philadelphia, the shell on the apron and the rope-twist inlay on the pilasters must have been imported.

45
CARD TABLE (*no. 302*)
Unknown maker
Philadelphia area
Yale University Art Gallery,
Mabel Brady Garvan Collection
Reproduced in color on p. 113

Primary wood: walnut. *Secondary woods:* tulip, white pine.
Dimensions: H. 73 cm; W. 93 cm; D. 45 cm.
Form and Ornament: Shape 5, single-taper legs; no patterned inlay, no pictorial inlay; facade 1.

Construction: Flush back and overlapping flyleg construction, hinged-rail design 1, no leaf-edge tenons, no medial brace, one horizontal lamination in the curved rails, three points.

Notes: Usually emphasizing form rather than ornament, Philadelphia-area cabinet-makers produced many curvate card tables with plain facades. To subtly accent the curving shapes of straight-leg tables they inset the leaf edges and skirts with plain inlay, and to relieve the monotony of their plain facades they often used stringing on the pilasters. Most bordered the shafts with plain inlay down to the banded or inlaid cuffs.

46

CARD TABLE (*no. 323*)
Unknown maker
Philadelphia area
Yale University Art Gallery, gift of
Benjamin A. Hewitt, B.A. 1943

Primary wood: mahogany. *Secondary woods:* oak, white pine.
Dimensions: H. 74 cm; W. 93 cm; D. 43 cm.
Form and Ornament: Shape 10, turned legs with capital 4a and base 4; no patterned inlay, no pictorial inlay; facade 1.
Construction: Flush back and overlapping flyleg construction, hinged-rail design 1, two leaf-edge tenons, no medial brace, three horizontal laminations in the curved rails, seven points.
Notes: At first glance Philadelphia and New York double-elliptic tables (shape 10) look much alike. Their color, unobtrusive relief ornament, and plainly veneered facades are similar. Philadelphia examples are distinguished by four legs whereas New

Cat. 45

Cat. 46

Cat. 47

York examples have five. Specialists in each area also produced capitals and bases for legs of distinctive configuration.

47
CARD TABLE (*no. 312*)
Unknown maker
Philadelphia area
Benjamin A. Hewitt

Primary wood: mahogany. *Secondary woods:* white pine, maple.
Dimensions: H. 74 cm; W. 91 cm; D. 46 cm.
Form and Ornament: Shape 12, turned legs with capital 4a and base 4; no patterned inlay, no pictorial inlay; facade 1.
Construction: Flush back and overlapping flyleg construction, hinged-rail design 1, one leaf-edge tenon, no medial brace, three horizontal laminations in the curved rails, six points.
Notes: Reeding on the leaf edges and crossbanding on the skirt accentuate the curvate shapes of Philadelphia tables without detracting from their uniform color. Many legs like these were produced by specialists who varied the number of rings on the capital, sometimes added a groove or ring on or below the bulb at the base, ended the foot with a taper or round spade rather than a ball, and occasionally reeded only the front and sides of the shafts.

48
CARD TABLE (*no. 313*)
Alexander Shaw (w. 1801–1807)
Philadelphia, Pennsylvania
Private collection

Primary wood: mahogany. *Secondary woods:* oak, white pine.
Dimensions: H. 74 cm; W. 91 cm; D. 44 cm.
Form and Ornament: Shape 5, turned legs with capital 5 and base 5; no patterned inlay, no pictorial inlay; facade 1.
Construction: Flush back and overlapping flyleg construction, hinged-rail design 1,

no leaf-edge tenon, no medial brace, three horizontal laminations in the curved rails, six points.
Notes: Ornament on this plainly veneered table with kidney ends and serpentine middle is confined to its rounded leaf edges and beaded skirt. The shape is found on a small number of turned and many straight-leg Philadelphia tables (cats. 44, 45). Plain tapering shafts, a unique regional characteristic, are found in combination with either this capital or this base.

49
CARD TABLE (*no. 324*)
Unknown maker
Philadelphia area
Benjamin A. Hewitt

Primary wood: mahogany. *Secondary woods:* oak, white pine.
Dimensions: H. 73 cm; W. 92 cm; D. 45 cm.
Form and Ornament: Shape 12, turned legs with capital 8 and base 5; no patterned inlay, no pictorial inlay; facade 1.
Construction: Flush back and additional flyleg construction, hinged-rail design 3, one leaf-edge tenon, no medial brace, three horizontal laminations in the curved rails, seven points.
Notes: The shape, the reeded leaf edges, the plain facade, and the use of oak and white pine as secondary woods reveal that this table was produced in the Philadelphia area, where five-leg tables like this were made on special order. Here the turner produced legs with atypical capitals (8), but the same base (5) is found on four-leg tables by other makers (cat. 48).

Cat. 48

Cat. 49

50

CARD TABLE (no. 326)
Unknown maker
Philadelphia area
Benjamin A. Hewitt

Primary wood: mahogany. *Secondary woods:* tulip, white pine.
Dimensions: H. 77 cm; W. 81 cm; D. 81 cm.
Form and Ornament: Shape 1, turned legs with capital 4a and base 4; no patterned inlay, no pictorial inlay.
Construction: The construction of this table is so atypical that only one of the normal categories apply: four horizontal laminations in the curved rails.[1]

Notes: The overall dark color and plain ornament of this table suggest it was made in the Philadelphia area, a hypothesis confirmed by the capital and base turnings typical of those produced by Philadelphia turners. The special features of this custom-made table suggest that the customer who ordered it was an avid card player. With a nonfolding top it stood ready for immediate use. Its baize-covered surface restricted it to games, and the four locked drawers provided private repositories for each player's money and counters. The brass casters ensured easy movability.

1. Computing points for this table is inappropriate because of its atypical construction.

Cat. 50

Baltimore

After 1780, when Baltimore was made an official port of entry, many Irish, Scottish, and English cabinetmakers settled there. A flourishing commercial center, Baltimore's population rose dramatically from only 6,000 before the Revolution to 63,000 by 1820. Its prosperity, coupled with the arrival of talented immigrant craftsmen, is seen in the great popularity of circular card tables and the abundant use of ornament, in imitation of the most fashionable English card tables of the period. The sample is comprised wholly of straight-leg tables.

Baltimore tables are usually circular (shape 1) and have single-taper legs inlaid on two sides; they are likely to be ornamented with demilune inlays such as shells and 12-point paterae on the top, simple one-unit facades lightly paneled with string inlay, inlays of open blossoms on pilasters, and bellflowers with long central petals on shafts. Patterned inlay was often used on skirts and sometimes on leaf edges. Exquisite pictorial inlays were readily available from such local specialists as Thomas Barrett, and contrasting veneer was unpopular in Baltimore.

The invariable use of oak or taeda pine distinguishes Baltimore tables from the entire production of the eight New England regions and New York. Four-leg tables with two flylegs (hinged-rail design 2) or a medial brace are far more likely to have originated in Baltimore than in the Philadelphia area. Their square or hollow upper-leaf edge differentiates them from Annapolis work. Back construction is usually of flush type and flyleg construction of overlapping type. Most tables have leaf-edge tenons and horizontally laminated curved rails. The construction points of Baltimore tables range from zero to ten.

51
CARD TABLE (*no. 366*)
Unknown maker
Baltimore, Maryland
Thomas and Rebecca Colville

Primary wood: mahogany. *Secondary woods:* white pine, oak.
Dimensions: H. 74 cm; W. 90 cm; D. 45 cm.
Form and Ornament: Shape 1, single-taper legs; patterned inlays 5 [skirt and cuffs], 57 [top and facade], pictorial inlays 111, 115; facade 2.
Construction: Filler back and overlapping flyleg construction, hinged-rail design 2, one leaf-edge tenon, one medial brace, three horizontal laminations in the curved rails, six points.
Notes: Baltimore manufacturing preferences are epitomized by the choice of secondary woods, two flylegs with overlapping construction, multilaminated rails, and a medial brace. The work of a local inlay maker is evident in the 12-point patera on the top and the bellflowers with long center petals on the shafts. The circular shape and simply paneled facade with bold oval inlays on the pilasters further exemplify local stylistic preferences.

52
CARD TABLE (*no. 365*)
Unknown maker
Baltimore, Maryland
The Brooklyn Museum, H. Randolph Lever Fund
Reproduced in color on p. 113

Primary wood: mahogany. *Secondary woods:* white pine, cherry.
Dimensions: H. 73 cm; W. 91 cm; D. 45 cm.
Form and Ornament: Shape 1, single-taper legs; patterned inlays 2 [top swags and facade panel], 46 [perimeter of top], pictorial inlays 117, 143, and inset-integrated lily-of-the-valley on pilasters; facade 4.
Construction: Flush back and overlapping flyleg construction, hinged-rail design 1,

Cat. 51

Cat. 52

Cat. 52. Detail of top.

bellflower (cats. 37, 38). The swags on the top and the patterned inlay around the apron ovals reflect the expertise of a inlayer.

one leaf-edge tenon, no medial brace, five horizontal laminations in the curved rails, eight points.
Notes: The colorful acorns, oak leaves, and pods on the top of this table and the carefully executed lily-of-the-valley on the pilasters are foremost examples of the Baltimore inlay maker's ample stock, which may have also included the single-unit bellflowers on the shafts. Their shape can be compared to the popular New York

53
CARD TABLE (*no. 345*)
Unknown maker
Baltimore, Maryland
The Metropolitan Museum of Art,
gift of George Coe Graves, 1932

Primary woods: mahogany, satinwood.
Secondary woods: white pine, poplar, oak.
Dimensions: H. 75 cm; W. 91 cm; D. 44 cm.
Form and Ornament: Shape 2, single-taper legs; patterned inlays 51 [rope twist of tassel on leg], 68 [skirt and cuffs], pictorial inlays of inset-integrated acorns and oak leaves on pilasters, and single-unit bellflowers and tassels on shafts; facade 3.
Construction: Flush back and plane flyleg construction, hinged-rail design 2, one leaf-

Cat. 53

edge tenon, one medial brace, one horizontal lamination in the curved rails, four points.

Notes: The motifs of oak leaves and acorns, bellflowers, and tassels have been found on other Baltimore pieces and their placement emphasizes the vertical lines of the design. By bordering a rectangle of mahogany veneer with satinwood crossbanding, the cabinetmaker produced a simple facade which echoed the contrasting colors of the woods in the shafts. Like many Baltimore makers, he bordered the top and interior with plain inlay and used patterned inlay to outline the skirt.

54
CARD TABLE (*no. 347*)
Unknown maker
Baltimore, Maryland
The Baltimore Museum of Art, gift of
Mrs. Harry B. Dillehunt Jr. in memory
of her husband

Primary wood: mahogany. *Secondary wood:* oak.

Dimensions: H. 74 cm; W. 78 cm; D. 38 cm.

Form and Ornament: Shape 2, single-taper legs with spade feet; patterned inlays 51 [leaf edge], 58 [top], 69 [skirt], 94 [facade panel], no pictorial inlay; facade 2.

Construction: Filler back and overlapping flyleg construction, hinged-rail design 2, one leaf-edge tenon, medial brace, three horizontal laminations in the curved rails, six points.

Notes: Card tables of unusually narrow width were custom made because special patterns were required to construct the tops and rails. The client who commissioned this table may have wanted it for two-handed games or to fit a narrow space. The spade feet, two flylegs, and carved bellflowers and open blossoms, which are translations in carved form of Baltimore inlays, must have increased the cost of the table.

Cat. 54

Annapolis

Annapolis was never as large a city as many of the other centers discussed here. However, the existence of a small but distinctive number of labeled card tables from Annapolis makes it significant to this study. Because all five of the tables analyzed have either the label of John Shaw or a strong attribution to him, it has been possible to determine Shaw's (but not the region's) characteristic methods of production. Documentary evidence that Shaw was a large-scale manufacturer of furniture is lacking, but between 1786 and 1793 Archibald Chisholm and William Waters advertised for journeymen cabinet- and chairmakers to work at their "manufactory" indicating that Annapolis could support the cabinetmaking business, at least on a modest scale.[1] Two of the five Shaw tables appear to represent his ready-made tables dating from about 1790, and three are believed to represent custom-made tables produced after 1795. All five have straight legs.

The two ready-made tables are square (shape 3) and retain elements of the Chippendale style—such as the legs which are barely tapered and are chamfered on the inside corners. The two are identically constructed and ornamented (cat. 55), and the date 1790 is penciled on the label of one (no. 372). Characteristic of these ready-made tables are plainly veneered aprons (facade 1), cockbeaded skirts, plain legs, and one flyleg of plane construction.[2]

Of the other three tables in the study, two have characteristics which definitely place them in the category of custom-made furniture. One, a circular table (no. 370) with the date 1796 penciled on the label, has spade feet, frequently found on custom-made tables from other regions. The second, square with serpentine front, serpentine ends, and canted corners (shape 13), is dated 1801 (no. 371), and has an unusually short rear rail (cat. 4). Since this construction was not found on Shaw's other four tables, it was concluded that it was not his usual method of production and that therefore the table was custom-made. The third table (cat. 56) is also shape 13 and has the same facade design as the second table, but its rear-rail construction spans the distance between the end rails. That this table was ready-made cannot be proved unless others like it can be found and their construction studied.

Ornamental details on these three tables show that by the mid-1790s Shaw was working in the neoclassical style. This is evident in the inlaid panels on the labeled circular card table Shaw made in 1796, by the curvate serpentine tables he made about 1801 (cat. 56), and by other labeled and dated Shaw pieces.[3] His three neoclassical card tables are constructed with one overlapping flyleg.

Some characteristics of Shaw's card tables do, however, remain constant throughout the entire decade. All five have rounded leaf edges, and in every case the secondary woods include oak and taeda pine. They also have baize-covered interiors which, although such covering has been found to be peculiar to customized work in other regions, may have been Shaw's standard practice.

1. Alfred Coxe Prime, comp., *The Arts and Crafts in Philadelphia, Maryland, and South Carolina: Part II, 1776–1800* (1932; reprint, New York: Da Capo Press, 1969), p. 172.
2. Six other square tables with Shaw's label have been mentioned to the writer by another researcher but they were unavailable for this study.
3. Lu Bartlett, "John Shaw, Cabinetmaker of Annapolis," *Antiques* 111, no. 2 (February 1977): 362–77.

55
CARD TABLE (*no. 373*)
John Shaw (1745–1829)
Annapolis, Maryland
Hammond-Harwood House, Annapolis

Primary wood: mahogany. *Secondary woods:* oak, taeda pine, walnut.
Dimensions: H. 76 cm; W. 91 cm; D. 46 cm.
Form and Ornament: Shape 3, single-taper legs; no patterned inlay, no pictorial inlay, facade 1.
Construction: Filler back and plane flyleg construction, hinged-rail design 1, one leaf-edge tenon, no medial brace, no curved rails, one point.
Notes: Shaw produced plain square tables in this simple style during the early Federal period. One table, of slightly smaller proportions and molded Marlborough legs but otherwise similar to this example, has the label of Shaw and Chisholm, a partnership which existed in 1783–84.[1] Another table, nearly identical, bears a label with the penciled date 1790 (no. 372).

1. Bartlett, "John Shaw, Cabinetmaker," p. 367, fig. 5.

Cat. 55. Label of John Shaw.

56
CARD TABLE (*no. 374*)
Attributed to John Shaw (1745–1829)
Annapolis, Maryland
The Baltimore Museum of Art, gift of Mr. and Mrs. Francis C. Taliaferro

Primary wood: mahogany. *Secondary woods:* oak, taeda pine.
Dimensions: H. 73 cm; W. 88 cm; D. 44 cm.
Form and Ornament: Shape 13, single-taper legs; patterned inlay 39, pictorial inlay of inset-integrated vase with flowers on pilasters; facade 2.
Construction: Filler back and overlapping flyleg construction, hinged-rail design 1, one leaf-edge tenon, no medial brace, one horizontal lamination in the curved rails, three points.
Notes: A mate to this table bears the label of John Shaw.[1] They are believed to have been made about 1801, the penciled date on the label of another Shaw table of identical form which also has the same facade design, plain inlay bordering the legs, rounded leaf edges, and a baize-lined interior (no. 371). Comparison with the previous table made a decade earlier (cat. 55) reveals Shaw's later turn to more neoclassical forms and ornament.

1. See *Baltimore Furniture* (Baltimore: Baltimore Museum of Art, 1947), no. 11.

Cat. 55

Cat. 56

List of Tables Included in the Study

Table number	Table shape	Maker	Owner

*Label or inscription of the cabinetmaker who is believed to have been the retailer rather than the manufacturer of the table.

Urban New Hampshire (Tables with straight legs)

1	4	Levi Bartlett, Concord	Private collection
2	2	Unknown	Essex Institute
3	2	Eliphalet Briggs, Keene	Yale University Art Gallery
4	4	Unknown	The Currier Gallery of Art
5	1	Robert Choate and George Whitefield Martin, Concord	New Hampshire Historical Society
6	4	Unknown	Private collection
7	26	Unknown	Private collection
8	3	Unknown	Private collection

Rural Massachusetts–New Hampshire (Tables with straight legs)

9	4	Unknown	Private collection
10	4	John Dunlap II, Antrim, NH	Private collection
11	2	John Dunlap II, Antrim, NH	Private collection
12	2	Unknown	Private collection
13	4	John Dunlap II, Antrim, NH	Yale University Art Gallery
14	4	Attributed to John Dunlap II, Antrim, NH	Yale University Art Gallery
15	4	Unknown	The Society for the Preservation of New England Antiquities
16	4	Unknown	Historic Deerfield, Inc.
17	2	Unknown	Private collection
18	2	Unknown	Smithsonian Institution
19	2	Label of Archelaus Flint, Charlestown, MA[1]	Private collection
20	1	Unknown	The Society for the Preservation of New England Antiquities
21	2	Unknown	Private collection
22	2	Pelatiah Bliss, Springfield, MA	Connecticut Valley Historical Museum
23	1	Unknown	Private collection
24	2	Attributed to Samuel Dunlap, Bedford, NH	Private collection
25	2	Unknown	The Society for the Preservation of New England Antiquities
26	3	Daniel Clay, Greenfield, MA	Historic Deerfield, Inc.
27	3	Unknown	Historic Deerfield, Inc.
28	4	John Dunlap II, Antrim, NH	Private collection
29	4	Attributed to Dan Dunlap, Antrim, NH, area	Private collection
30	4	Unknown	The Society for the Preservation of New England Antiquities
31	24	Unknown	John Whitmore

Rural Massachusetts–New Hampshire (Tables with turned legs)

32	7	Oliver Batchelor, New Ipswich, NH	Private collection
33	7	Isaiah Wilder, Hingham, MA, Surrey and Keene, NH	New Hampshire Historical Society
34	7	Unknown	Private collection
35	7	Unknown	The Currier Gallery of Art
36	7	Unknown	Historic Deerfield, Inc.
37	8	Unknown	The White House
38	7	Unknown	Yale University Art Gallery
39	8	Alden Spooner, Athol, MA	Yale University Art Gallery
40	8	Unknown	Historic Deerfield, Inc.
41	7	Unknown	Woodlawn Plantation
42	7	Unknown	Woodlawn Plantation
43	7	Unknown	Private collection
44	9	J. Fairbanks, Harvard, MA	Old Sturbridge Village

Newburyport (Tables with straight legs)

45	2	Joseph Short	The Henry Francis du Pont Winterthur Museum
46	23	Ebenezer Rogers and Thomas Atwood	Private collection
47	2	Joseph Short	Private collection
48	6	Unknown	Mount Vernon Ladies' Association of the Union
49	1	Unknown	The Brooklyn Museum
50	19	Unknown	The Society for the Preservation of New England Antiquities
51	19	Unknown	The Society for the Preservation of New England Antiquities
52	15	Unknown	Rhode Island Historical Society
53	2	Joseph Short	Western Reserve Historical Society
54	6	Joseph Short	Yale University Art Gallery
55	2	Joseph Short	Private collection
56	2	Joseph Short	Private collection
57	23	Ebenezer Rogers and Thomas Atwood	Timothy Fuller Marquand
58	1	Unknown	Worcester Art Museum
59	2	Unknown	Museum of the City of New York
60	1	Unknown	Private collection
61	2	Unknown	The Society for the Preservation of New England Antiquities
62	1	Unknown	Yale University Art Gallery
63	6	Label of Archelaus Flint, Charlestown, MA	Private collection
64	1	Unknown	Essex Institute
65	23	Unknown	The Society for the Preservation of New England Antiquities
66	13	Unknown	Essex Institute

List of Tables Included in the Study

Table number	Table shape	Maker	Owner
Newburyport (Tables with turned legs)			
67	8	Unknown	Private collection
68	9	Charles Short, Newburyport, Haverhill, Andover, and Salem, MA	Mr. and Mrs. John M. Keese IV
69	9	Signed in chalk, "Joel Ketchum, New York City"*	Private collection
70	6	Unknown	Yale University Art Gallery
71	7	Unknown	Private collection
72	4	Unknown	Wadsworth Atheneum
73	9	Unknown	Yale University Art Gallery
74	6	Unknown	Patrick M. Spadaccino Jr.
75	9	Unknown	Jumel Mansion
76	9	Unknown	Private collection
77	7	Unknown	Private collection
Salem (Tables with straight legs)			
78	1	Unknown	The Society for the Preservation of New England Antiquities
79	4	Attributed to Mark Pitman	The Henry Francis du Pont Winterthur Museum
80	6	Unknown	The Henry Francis du Pont Winterthur Museum
81	4	Mark Pitman	Yale University Art Gallery
82	6	Emery Moulton, Lynn, MA	Private collection
83	6	Unknown	Worcester Art Museum
84	6	Unknown	The Brooklyn Museum
85	2	Unknown	Essex Institute
86	6	Unknown	The Newark Museum
87	4	Unknown	Historic Deerfield, Inc.
88	2	Samuel Fiske	Private collection
89	1	Samuel and William Fiske	Robert and Barbara Sallick
90	6	Unknown	Connecticut Valley Historical Museum
91	15	Unknown	Smithsonian Institution
92	6	Unknown	The Henry Francis du Pont Winterthur Museum
93	6	Unknown	Connecticut Valley Historical Museum
94	6	Unknown	Museum of Fine Arts, Springfield
95	15	Unknown	Private collection
96	24	Unknown	Private collection
97	1	Unknown	Essex Institute
98	1	Unknown	Private collection
99	1	Unknown	Private collection
100	2	Thomas Needham III	Yale University Art Gallery
101	1	Unknown	Museum of Fine Arts, Boston
Salem (Tables with turned legs)			
102	7	Unknown	Private collection
103	7	Unknown	Old Sturbridge Village
104	7	William Hook	Museum of Fine Arts, Boston
105	7	Unknown	The Metropolitan Museum of Art
106	7	Unknown	The Society for the Preservation of New England Antiquities
107	2	Unknown	The Society for the Preservation of New England Antiquities
108	7	Unknown	The White House
109	7	Unknown	The Henry Francis du Pont Winterthur Museum
110	7	Unknown	Private collection
111	7	Unknown	Private collection
112	7	Unknown	The Baltimore Museum of Art
113	7	Unknown	The Society for the Preservation of New England Antiquities
114	7	Unknown	The Society for the Preservation of New England Antiquities
115	7	Unknown	The Henry Francis du Pont Winterthur Museum
116	6	Unknown	The Henry Francis du Pont Winterthur Museum
117	6	Unknown[2]	Essex Institute
118	6	Unknown	Diplomatic Reception Rooms, Dept. of State
119	6	Unknown	Decatur House
120	7	Unknown	Patrick M. Spadaccino Jr.
121	24	Samuel Barnard	Private collection
122	6	Unknown	Private collection
123	8	Unknown	Private collection
124	8	Nehemiah Adams	Private collection
125	7	Unknown	Private collection
Boston Area (Tables with straight legs)			
126	2	Unknown	Private collection
127	6	Unknown	Museum of Fine Arts, Boston
128	6	Unknown	The Metropolitan Museum of Art
129	23	Unknown	Museum of the City of New York
130	2	Unknown	The Society for the Preservation of New England Antiquities
131	6	Unknown	The Society for the Preservation of New England Antiquities

List of Tables Included in the Study

Table number	Table shape	Maker	Owner
132	2	Unknown	Diplomatic Reception Rooms, Dept. of State
133	6	Unknown	Yale University Art Gallery
134	1	Unknown	Yale University Art Gallery
135	1	Jacob Forster, Charlestown, MA	The Henry Francis du Pont Winterthur Museum
136	6	Elisha Tucker	The Henry Francis du Pont Winterthur Museum
137	2	John Smith and Samuel Hitchings	Yale University Art Gallery
138	1	Jacob Forster, Charlestown, MA	Yale University Art Gallery
139	2	Label of Boston Cabinet Manufactory, signed by Thomas Seymour	Private collection
140	1	Stephen Badlam	Private collection
141	1	Thomas Foster	Private collection
142	1	Jacob Forster, Charlestown, MA	Private collection
143	2	Samuel Davis	Private collection
144	1	Attributed to Jacob Forster, Charlestown, MA	Private collection
145	1	Unknown	Worcester Art Museum
146	2	Unknown	Wadsworth Atheneum
147	2	John Smith and Samuel Hitchings	Museum of Fine Arts, Boston
148	2	Unknown	The Society for the Preservation of New England Antiquities
149	6	Unknown	The Society for the Preservation of New England Antiquities
150	2	Unknown	Diplomatic Reception Rooms, Dept. of State
151	2	Unknown	Historic Deerfield, Inc.
152	1	Attributed to Jacob Forster, Charlestown, MA	Historic Deerfield, Inc.
153	1	Unknown	Historic Deerfield, Inc.
154	6	Unknown	The Henry Francis du Pont Winterthur Museum
155	6	William Leverett	Private collection
156	2	William Leverett	Private collection
157	1	Unknown	The Society for the Preservation of New England Antiquities
158	1	Attributed to Jacob Forster, Charlestown, MA	Private collection
159	2	Unknown	Private collection
160	1	Attributed to Jacob Forster, Charlestown, MA	Private collection
161	2	Branded, I Brooks	Private collection
162	2	Unknown	Private collection
163	1	Unknown	The Newark Museum
164	2	Unknown	Private collection
165	6	Elisha Tucker	Honolulu Academy of Arts
166	6	Unknown	Diplomatic Reception Rooms, Dept. of State
167	5	Unknown	Private collection
168	1	Unknown	Private collection
169	1	Unknown	Private collection
170	1	Unknown	Private collection
171	2	Unknown	The Brooklyn Museum
172	2	Unknown	The Society for the Preservation of New England Antiquities
173	6	Unknown	Private collection
174	23	Unknown	Museum of Fine Arts, Boston
175	6	Unknown	Museum of Fine Arts, Boston
176	6	Unknown	The Society for the Preservation of New England Antiquities
177	2	Unknown	Historic Deerfield, Inc.
178	2	Unknown	Yale University Art Gallery
179	6	Unknown	Yale University Art Gallery
180	6	Unknown	Yale University Art Gallery
181	2	Unknown	Private collection
182	2	Unknown	Essex Institute
183	6	Unknown	Essex Institute
184	6	Unknown	The Society for the Preservation of New England Antiquities
185	6	Unknown	The Henry Francis du Pont Winterthur Museum
186	6	Label of Archelaus Flint, Charlestown, MA	Private collection
187	6	Unknown	Woodlawn Plantation
188	2	Unknown	Museum of the City of New York
189	2	Unknown	Yale University Art Gallery
190	2	Unknown	Private collection
191	2	Unknown	The Society for the Preservation of New England Antiquities
192	2	Unknown	Museum of Fine Arts, Boston
193	1	John Seymour & Son	Private collection
194	23	Unknown	Museum of Fine Arts, Boston

Boston Area (Tables with turned legs)

195	7	Unknown	The Society for the Preservation of New England Antiquities
196	7	Unknown	The Henry Francis du Pont Winterthur Museum
197	7	Unknown	Yale University Art Gallery
198	7	Unknown	Yale University Art Gallery
199	25	Unknown	The Henry Francis du Pont Winterthur Museum
200	8	Unknown	Private collection
201	7	Unknown	The Society for the Preservation of New England Antiquities

List of Tables Included in the Study

Table number	Table shape	Maker	Owner
202	7	Unknown	The White House
203	7	Unknown	The White House
204	7	Samuel Adams and William Todd	Historic Deerfield, Inc.
205	7	Unknown	Historic Deerfield, Inc.
206	13	Unknown	The Society for the Preservation of New England Antiquities
207	7	Unknown	Yale University Art Gallery
208	7	Unknown	The Henry Francis du Pont Winterthur Museum
209	7	Unknown	Museum of Fine Arts, Springfield
210	7	Unknown	Hammond-Harwood House
211	7	Unknown	Museum of Fine Arts, Boston
212	7	Unknown	The Society for the Preservation of New England Antiquities
213	7	Unknown	The White House
214	7	Unknown	The White House
215	7	Unknown	Historic Deerfield, Inc.
216	4	Unknown	Yale University Art Gallery
217	8	Unknown	Yale University Art Gallery
218	8	Samuel S. Noyes, East Sudbury, MA	The Henry Francis du Pont Winterthur Museum
219	8	Unknown	Private collection
220	6	Unknown	The White House
221	6	Unknown	The White House
222	4	Unknown	Private collection
223	6	Unknown	Private collection
224	16	Unknown	Private collection
225	7	Unknown	Private collection
226	7	Unknown	Private collection

Newport (Tables with straight legs)

227	1	John Townsend	The Henry Francis du Pont Winterthur Museum
228	18	Holmes Weaver	Private collection
229	14	John Townsend	Mr. and Mrs. Stanley Stone
230	2	Holmes Weaver	Private collection
231	1	Unknown	Private collection
232	1	Stephen and Thomas Goddard	The Metropolitan Museum of Art
233	1	Unknown	Historic Deerfield, Inc.
234	1	Attributed to Stephen and Thomas Goddard	Rhode Island Historical Society
235	1	Attributed to John Townsend	Private collection
236	1	Attributed to Holmes Weaver	Benjamin A. Hewitt
237	1	Attributed to Holmes Weaver	Private collection

Providence (Tables with straight legs)

238	1	Unknown	Worcester Art Museum
239	1	Unknown	Worcester Art Museum
240	2	Joseph Rawson Sr.	The Henry Francis du Pont Winterthur Museum
241	2	Attributed to Thomas Howard	Private collection
242	1	Unknown	Private collection
243	1	Label of George Shipley, NY*	Benjamin A. Hewitt
244	1	Unknown	The Brooklyn Museum
245	15	Unknown	Diplomatic Reception Rooms, Dept. of State
246	15	Unknown	Diplomatic Reception Rooms, Dept. of State
247	1	Unknown	Historic Deerfield, Inc.
248	1	Unknown	Historic Deerfield, Inc.
249	2	Unknown	Rhode Island Historical Society
250	1	Unknown	Private collection
251	2	Unknown	Private collection
252	2	Unknown	Private collection
253	6	Joseph Rawson & Son	Yale University Art Gallery

Connecticut (Tables with straight legs)

254	3	Unknown	Yale University Art Gallery
255	2	Unknown	The Henry Francis du Pont Winterthur Museum
256	3	Unknown	Private collection
257	3	Unknown	Litchfield Historical Society
258	3	Attributed to Richard Fosdick, New London	New London County Historical Society
259	2	Unknown	The Newark Museum
260	1	Unknown	The Henry Francis du Pont Winterthur Museum
261	1	Unknown	The Brooklyn Museum
262	14	Unknown	Private collection
263	1	B. C. Gillett, Hartford	Wadsworth Atheneum

New York (Tables with straight legs)

264	2	Unknown	The Henry Francis du Pont Winterthur Museum
265	4	Unknown	Private collection
266	2	Unknown	Museum of the City of New York

List of Tables Included in the Study

Table number	Table shape	Maker	Owner
267	2	Unknown	Yale University Art Gallery
268	1	Unknown	The Henry Francis du Pont Winterthur Museum
269	2	Attributed to William Whitehead	Benjamin A. Hewitt
270	2	Unknown	Mount Vernon Ladies' Association of the Union
271	2	Unknown	The Metropolitan Museum of Art
272	1	Unknown	The Newark Museum
273	1	Label of Charles Courtright	Gracie Mansion
274	20	Unknown	Benjamin A. Hewitt
275	2	Unknown	Private collection
276	4	Unknown	Private collection
277	2	Unknown	Private collection
278	1	Unknown	Private collection

New York (Tables with turned legs)

279	3	Charles Honoré Lannuier	The Henry Francis du Pont Winterthur Museum
280	17	Charles Honoré Lannuier	The Henry Francis du Pont Winterthur Museum
281	11	Unknown	Private collection
282	10	Unknown	The Brooklyn Museum
283	11	Unknown	Museum of the City of New York
284	10	Unknown	Museum of the City of New York
285	11	John T. Dolan	Museum of the City of New York
286	11	Unknown	Museum of the City of New York
287	11	John T. Dolan	Gracie Mansion
288	11	Unknown	Gracie Mansion
289	10	Unknown	The Henry Francis du Pont Winterthur Museum
290	10	Unknown	Kaufman Americana Foundation

Philadelphia Area (Tables with straight legs)

291	1	Unknown	The Society for the Preservation of New England Antiquities
292	1	Unknown	The Henry Francis du Pont Winterthur Museum
293	5	S.T. Bellejeau, West Chester, PA	The Henry Francis du Pont Winterthur Museum
294	5	Unknown	Private collection
295	3	Henry Rigby	Private collection
296	21	Unknown	The Newark Museum
297	1	Unknown	The Newark Museum
298	1	Unknown	The White House
299	5	Unknown	Diplomatic Reception Rooms, Dept. of State
300	1	S. Brock	Gracie Mansion
301	1	Unknown	Maryland Historical Society
302	5	Unknown	Yale University Art Gallery
303	2	Unknown	Private collection
304	5	Unknown	Private collection
305	5	Unknown	Private collection
306	5	Unknown	Private collection
307	5	Unknown	Private collection
308	19	Unknown	Private collection
309	1	Unknown	Private collection

Philadelphia Area (Tables with turned legs)

310	22	Unknown	Yale University Art Gallery
311	10	Unknown	Private collection
312	12	Unknown	Benjamin A. Hewitt
313	5	Alexander Shaw	Private collection
314	12	Unknown	Private collection
315	23	William Kerwood, Trenton, NJ	Private collection
316	12	Unknown	Private collection
317	12	Unknown	Museum of Fine Arts, Boston
318	12	Unknown	The Society for the Preservation of New England Antiquities
319	12	Unknown	The White House
320	12	Unknown	Gracie Mansion
321	4	Unknown	The Metropolitan Museum of Art
322	5	Unknown	Woodlawn Plantation
323	10	Unknown	Yale University Art Gallery
324	12	Unknown	Benjamin A. Hewitt
325	12	Unknown	Benjamin A. Hewitt
326	1	Unknown	Benjamin A. Hewitt

Baltimore (Tables with straight legs)

327	2	Unknown	Yale University Art Gallery
328	1	Unknown	The Henry Francis du Pont Winterthur Museum
329	5	Unknown	Private collection
330	21	Unknown	Private collection
331	5	Unknown	Hammond-Harwood House

List of Tables Included in the Study

Table number	Table shape	Maker	Owner
332	1	Unknown	Rhode Island Historical Society
333	1	Unknown	The Henry Francis du Pont Winterthur Museum
334	1	Unknown	The Henry Francis du Pont Winterthur Museum
335	21	Unknown	The Henry Francis du Pont Winterthur Museum
336	2	Unknown	The Henry Francis du Pont Winterthur Museum
337	4	Unknown	Private collection
338	1	Unknown	Private collection
339	1	Unknown	Maryland Historical Society
340	1	Unknown	Maryland Historical Society
341	1	Unknown	Hammond-Harwood House
342	1	Unknown	The Brooklyn Museum
343	1	Unknown	Museum of Fine Arts, Boston
344	2	Unknown	Museum of Fine Arts, Boston
345	2	Unknown	The Metropolitan Museum of Art
346	1	Unknown	The Metropolitan Museum of Art
347	2	Unknown	The Baltimore Museum of Art
348	2	Unknown[3]	The Baltimore Museum of Art
349	19	Unknown[1]	The Baltimore Museum of Art
350	1	Unknown	The Baltimore Museum of Art
351	1	Unknown	The Baltimore Museum of Art
352	1	Unknown	The Baltimore Museum of Art
353	1	Unknown	The White House
354	1	Unknown	The White House
355	1	Unknown	The White House
356	1	Unknown	The White House
357	1	Unknown	Diplomatic Reception Rooms, Dept. of State
358	1	Unknown	Diplomatic Reception Rooms, Dept. of State
359	1	Unknown[5]	Diplomatic Reception Rooms, Dept. of State
360	1	Unknown	Diplomatic Reception Rooms, Dept. of State
361	1	Unknown	Private collection
362	2	Unknown	Yale University Art Gallery
363	1	Unknown	The Henry Francis du Pont Winterthur Museum
364	1	Unknown	Private collection
365	1	Unknown	The Brooklyn Museum
366	1	Unknown	Thomas and Rebecca Colville
367	2	Inscribed L. Thomas, possibly Lambert Thomas	Private collection
368	1	Unknown	The Newark Museum
369	19	Unknown	Private collection

Annapolis (Tables with straight legs)

370	1	John Shaw	Diplomatic Reception Rooms, Dept. of State
371	13	John Shaw	Private collection
372	3	John Shaw	Private collection
373	3	John Shaw	Hammond-Harwood House
374	13	Attributed to John Shaw	The Baltimore Museum of Art

Notes

1. Of the three tables in the study with the label of Archelaus Flint (see also nos. 63 and 186), the Charlestown, Massachusetts, cabinetmaker, one has the characteristics of the Boston area, one of rural Massachusetts–New Hampshire, and one of Newburyport. The label on each indicates that Flint was a retailer as well as a manufacturer: "House Furniture of the most approved fashion and best kind, made, sold, and exchanged by Archelaus Flint, Cabinet Maker, at his shop in Main Street, near the square, Charlestown."
2. While this table was attributed by Charles F. Montgomery (see *American Furniture: The Federal Period, 1788-1825* [New York: Viking Press, 1966], p. 334, no. 309) to Nehemiah Adams, the writer believes it was made by another Salem cabinetmaker because it has a plainly veneered facade and is shape 6, whereas the one known documented table by Nehemiah Adams (illustrated in Margaret Burke Clunie, "Joseph True and the Piece Work Sys-

tem in Salem," *Antiques* 111, no. 5 [May 1977]: 1010, fig. 5) has an oval within a rectangle at the center of the apron and is shape 8.
3. Originally owned by William E. Hooper, Baltimore, a contemporary of Charles Carroll of Carrollton. Illustrated in Baltimore Museum of Art, *Baltimore Furniture* (Baltimore: Baltimore Museum of Art, 1947), p. 33, no. 7.
4. Attributed to an unknown Baltimore cabinetmaker because the ornament on the top leaf edges, pilaster, legs, and cuffs and the shapes of the panels on the pilasters and legs match those of a pembroke table in the writer's collection inscribed in chalk "Baltimore March 29 1800."
5. A wedding present to George Coulson and his wife in 1796 when they moved into the house at the corner of Pratt and Albemarle Streets, Old Town, Baltimore. Illustrated in Baltimore Museum of Art, *Baltimore Furniture*, p. 26, no. 2.

List of Patterned Inlays and the Tables on Which They Appear (For illustrations of the patterned inlays, see pp. 74-75.)

Inlay nos.	Tables
1	Nos. 43, 71, 77, 81 (cat. 14), 82, 105, 110, 115, 121 (cat. 19), 184, 186, 189, 192, 253 (cat. 31), 304, 340, 368
2	Nos. 1, 40, 57 (cat. 10), 79, 81 (cat. 14), 93, 114, 173, 183, 186, 187, 192, 200, 215, 267 (cat. 37), 346, 361, 365 (cat. 52)
3	Nos. 12, 19, 25, 39 (cat. 8), 180 (cat. 21), 187, 241 (cat. 33), 255
4	No. 336
5	Nos. 39 (cat. 8), 46, 267 (cat. 37), 366 (cat. 51)
6	No. 19
7	Nos. 11, 14, 105, 166
8	Nos. 82, 340, 349, 353, 356
9	No. 135
10	Nos. 13 (cat. 4), 128
11	No. 371
12	No. 356
13	Nos. 115, 190
14	No. 106
15	No. 364
16	Nos. 29, 190
17	No. 13 (cat. 4)
18	No. 218
19	Nos. 336, 359
20	No. 333
21	No. 186
22	Nos. 70, 71, 82, 105, 127, 149, 155, 174, 182, 220, 221, 238, 327
23	Nos. 37, 43, 77, 118, 159, 165, 173, 178 (cat. 22), 186, 215
24	Nos. 8, 10, 14, 83, 86, 93, 94, 135, 186, 222
25	Nos. 136, 165, 218
26	No. 364
27	No. 98
28	No. 360
29	No. 30
30	Nos. 33 (cat. 7), 38, 41, 52, 74 (cat. 13), 104 (cat. 18), 110, 114, 121 (cat. 19), 131, 149, 166, 173, 175, 187, 201, 203, 205, 212, 223
31	Nos. 1, 6, 28, 39 (cat. 8), 94, 103, 173, 248, 255
32	No. 343
33	Nos. 90, 174, 367
34	No. 52
35	No. 195
36	No. 105
37	No. 139
38	Nos. 9, 85, 90, 91, 95, 154, 181
39	No. 374 (cat. 56)
40	No. 248
41	Nos. 90, 230
42	No. 121 (cat. 19)
43	Nos. 48, 63, 216
44	No. 194
45	No. 328
46	No. 365 (cat. 52)
47	No. 359
48	No. 14
49	No. 29
50	Nos. 43, 145, 224
51	Nos. 7, 8, 19, 31 (cat. 6), 35, 48, 74 (cat. 13), 108, 127, 139, 217, 220, 221, 311, 345 (cat. 53), 347 (cat. 54), 358
52	Nos. 21, 31 (cat. 6), 115, 138 (cat. 24), 142, 153, 171, 173, 176, 194, 202
53	No. 305
54	Nos. 2, 181
55	No. 271
56	Nos. 1, 3 (cat. 1), 8, 41, 178 (cat. 22), 222, 225, 245
57	Nos. 101 (cat. 17), 244, 299 (cat. 44), 334, 340, 366 (cat. 51), 367
58	Nos. 347 (cat. 54), 348, 361
59	Nos. 21, 171
60	No. 308
61	Nos. 16, 149, 190, 271
62	No. 85
63	No. 106
64	Nos. 12, 253 (cat. 31), 264
65	Nos. 70, 82, 129, 189, 225, 349
66	Nos. 81 (cat. 14), 96, 154, 190, 246, 330
67	Nos. 15, 212
68	Nos. 267 (cat. 37), 330, 345 (cat. 53), 357, 367, 370
69	No. 347 (cat. 54)
70	Nos. 54 (cat. 9), 339
71	Nos. 45, 53, 55, 56, 83, 107, 127, 211

Inlay nos.	Tables
72	Nos. 46, 74 (cat. 13), 176, 177, 187, 230, 253 (cat. 31)
73	Nos. 40, 87
74	No. 334
75	Nos. 41, 189
76	Nos. 339, 353
77	No. 190
78	Nos. 189, 275
79	Nos. 85, 150, 180 (cat. 21), 191, 218, 341, 368
80	No. 106
81	Nos. 48, 79, 81 (cat. 14), 96, 133 (cat. 20), 136, 154, 173, 177, 182, 240 (cat. 30), 241 (cat. 33), 255, 262
82	Nos. 77, 276
83	Nos. 19, 25, 43
84	No. 128
85	Nos. 174, 194
86	No. 52
87	No. 249
88	No. 262
89	No. 304
90	Nos. 52, 189, 222
91	Nos. 6, 37, 121 (cat. 19), 129, 136, 165
92	Nos. 141, 193, 242
93	Nos. 41, 241 (cat. 33), 253 (cat. 31)
94	No. 347 (cat. 54)
95	Nos. 108, 110, 198 (cat. 26), 199, 202
96	Nos. 40, 139, 204 (cat. 25)
97	Nos. 198 (cat. 26), 205
98	No. 214
99	No. 31 (cat. 6)
100	No. 31 (cat. 6)

List of Pictorial Inlays and the Tables on Which They Appear (For illustrations of the pictorial inlays, see pp. 76-80.)

Inlay nos.	Tables
101	Nos. 236 (cat. 29), 237
102	No. 341
103	No. 11
104	No. 246
105	No. 292
106	No. 360
107	Nos. 246, 267 (cat. 37), 270, 271, 275, 335
108	No. 354
109	No. 154
110	Nos. 231, 243 (cat. 32)
111	Nos. 346, 361, 366 (cat. 51)
112	No. 362
113	No. 335
114	Nos. 338, 341, 350, 357, 359, 360
115	Nos. 336, 346, 361, 366 (cat. 51)
116	Nos. 267 (cat. 37), 268, 269 (cat. 38) 270, 277, 278
117	No. 365 (cat. 52)
118	No. 134
119	Nos. 269 (cat. 38), 270, 277
120	Nos. 269 (cat. 38), 277, 278
121	No. 328
122	Nos. 11, 12, 13 (cat. 4), 99, 158, 163, 238
123	Nos. 74, 156, 189
124	Nos. 236 (cat. 29), 237
125	Nos. 232 (cat. 28), 234
126	No. 352
127	Nos. 146, 193 (fig. 27)
128	Nos. 10, 11, 13 (cat. 4), 14, 28, 29
129	Nos. 150, 156, 178 (cat. 22), 180 (cat. 21)
130	No. 270
131	No. 359
132	No. 241 (cat. 33)
133	No. 1
134	Nos. 150, 178 (cat. 22), 180 (cat. 21), 245
135	No. 227
136	Nos. 2, 51, 182, 262
137	No. 342
138	No. 356
139	Nos. 335, 343
140	No. 241 (cat. 33)
141	Nos. 338, 350, 357
142	Nos. 46, 57 (cat. 10), 90
143	Nos. 355, 365 (cat. 52)
144	No. 22 (cat. 5)
145	No. 235
146	No. 62 (cat. 11)
147	Nos. 338, 341, 350
148	Nos. 269 (cat. 38), 277, 278
149	Nos. 333, 357
150	No. 245
151	No. 242

Chart I
Regional Frequencies of Straight-Leg Shapes
(Expressed as percentages of each region's output)

	UNH	RMNH	Nbry	Sal	BoAr	Nwpt	Prov	Conn	NY	PhAr	Balt	Ann
Number of tables	8	23	22	24	69	11	16	10	15	19	43	5
1. Single taper	63	61	100	64	40	91	87	100	100	100	81	80
2. Pointed double taper	37	39		31	48							
3. Squat double taper					11							
4. Single taper, five-sided				5			13				19	20
5. Single taper with spade foot						9						
6. Single taper with knopped foot				1								

Chart II
Regional Frequencies of Capitals, Bases, and Shafts of Turned-Leg Card Tables and Mean Numbers of Reeds on Reeded Shafts
(Expressed as percentages of each region's output)

		RMNH	Nbry	Sal	BoAr	NY	PhAr
Number of tables		13	11	24	32	12	17
Percentage frequencies of each region's total production							
	Capitals						
1.	Hollow over ring over hollow					92	
2.	Ringed drum			67	22		
3.	Rings over hollow			29	44		
4a, b.	Shallow rings over hollow						81
5.	Hollow over taper						13
6.	Ogee, deep curves	15			28		
7.	Ogee, shallow curves	46					
8.	Miscellaneous, or significant variation from one of above	39	100	4	6	8	6
	Bases						
1.	Flat ogee					92	
2a.	Attenuated bulbous foot			22			
2b.	Short bulbous foot			28	6		
3.	Slender ogee under ring, plain turning, ring			50	19		
4.	Hollow, bulb, and taper						81
5.	Slender hollow, bulb, and taper						13
6.	Ring over hollow over ring over taper				56		
7.	Squat taper, under quarter-circle round	23					
8.	Taper under reel				16		
9.	Miscellaneous, or significant variation from one of above	77	100		3	8	6
	Shafts						
1.	Reeded, straight taper	54	64	67	41	92	38
2.	Reeded, curving taper	23	36	33	59		31
3.	Plain, curving taper						19
4.	Ringed, curving taper	23					
5.	Fluted, straight taper					8	12
Mean number of reeds, reeded shaft		11.3	11.5	12.2	11.3	14.9	12.3

Chart III
Regional Frequencies of Popular and Rare Shapes of Straight-leg Card Tables
(Expressed as percentages of each region's output)

	UNH	RMNH	Nbry	Sal	BoAr	Nwpt	Prov	Conn	NY	PhAr	Balt	Ann	All Tables
Number of tables	8	23	22	24	69	11	16	10	15	19	43	5	265
Popular shapes													
1. Circular (shape 1)	12.5	8.7	22.7	25.0	26.1	72.7	50.0	30.0	26.7	36.7	65.1	20.0	34.1
2. Square, ovolo corners (shape 2)	25.0	39.1	31.8	12.5	39.1	9.1	31.3	20.0	53.3	5.3	16.2		27.2
3. Square (shape 3)	12.5	8.7						40.0		5.3	2.3	40.0	4.2
4. Square, elliptic front (shape 4)	37.5	39.1		12.5					13.3		2.3		6.8
5. Kidney end, serpentine middle (shape 5)					1.4					42.1	4.7		4.2
6. Square, elliptic front, serpentine ends (shape 6)			13.6	37.5	29.0		6.2						12.5
Percent, popular shapes	87.5	95.6	68.1	87.5	95.6	81.8	87.5	90.0	93.3	89.4	90.6	60.0	89.0
Rare shapes													
7. Square, serpentine front, serpentine ends, canted corners (shape 13)			4.6									40.0	1.1
8. Square, serpentine front, serpentine ends (shape 14)						9.1		10.0					0.8
9. Square, round corners (shape 15)			4.6	8.3			12.5						1.9
10. Square, canted corners, eight equal sides (shape 18)						9.1							0.7
11. Square, serpentine front, ovolo corners (shape 19)			9.1							5.3	4.7		1.9
12. Square, serpentine front, serpentine ends, ovolo corners (shape 20)									6.7				0.4
13. Kidney end, round middle (shape 21)										5.3	4.7		1.1
14. Kidney end, elliptic front (shape 23)			13.6		4.4								2.3
15. Square, elliptic front, half elliptic ends (shape 24)		4.4		4.2									0.4
16. Square, elliptic front, canted corners (shape 26)	12.5												0.4
Percent, rare shapes	12.5	4.4	31.9	12.5	4.4	18.2	12.5	10.0	6.7	10.6	9.4	40.0	11.0

Chart IV
Regional Frequencies of Popular and Rare Shapes of Turned-Leg Card Tables with Folding Tops*
(Expressed as percentages of each region's output)

	RMNH	Nbry	Sal	BoAr	NY	PhAr	All Tables
Number of tables*	13	11	24	32	12	16	108
Popular shapes							
1. Square, serpentine front, serpentine ends, ovolo corners over colonnettes (shape 7)	69.2	18.2	66.6	59.4			42.7
2. Square, elliptic front, half-elliptic ends, ovolo corners (shape 8)	23.1	9.1	8.3	15.6			10.2
3. Square, elliptic front, serpentine ends (shape 6)		18.2	16.7	9.4			8.3
4. Square, elliptic and hollow front, half-elliptic and hollow ends, ovolo corners (shape 9)	7.7	45.4					5.6
5. Double elliptic (shape 10)					33.4	12.5	5.6
6. Treble elliptic (shape 11)					50.0		5.6
7. Square, elliptic front, serpentine corners (shape 12)						56.4	8.3
Percent, popular shapes	100.0	90.9	91.6	84.4	83.4	68.9	86.3
Rare shapes							
8. Square, ovolo corners (shape 2)			4.2				.9
9. Square (shape 3)					8.3		.9
10. Square, elliptic front (shape 4)		9.1		6.3		6.2	3.7
11. Kidney end, serpentine middle (shape 5)						12.5	1.9
12. Square, serpentine front, serpentine ends, canted corners (shape 13)				3.1			.9
13. Square with round corners and ¾ colonnettes (shape 16)				3.1			.9
14. Square, canted corners (shape 17)					8.3		.9
15. Square, with serpentine and round middle front, serpentine ends, ovolo corners, and ¾ colonnettes (shape 22)						6.2	.9
16. Kidney end, elliptic front (shape 23)						6.2	.9
17. Square, elliptic front, half-elliptic ends (shape 24)			4.2				.9
18. Square, canted and ovolo corners (shape 25)				3.1			.9
Percent, rare shapes	0.0	9.1	8.4	15.6	16.6	31.1	13.7

*One Philadelphia table (cat. 50) has been omitted from this chart because of its nonfolding top.

Chart V
Mean Number of Places on Tables
with Relief Ornament, Mean Number of Pieces of Veneer on Front Apron, and Mean Number of Places on Table with Plain, Patterned, and Pictorial Inlay, by Region

	UNH	RMNH	Nbry	Sal	BoAr	Nwpt	Prov	Conn	NY	PhAr	Balt	Ann	All tables
Number of tables	8	36	33	48	101	11	16	10	27	36	43	5	374
1. *Relief ornament*													
Straight-leg tables	0.13	0.39	0.43	0.09	0.12	0.10	0.13	1.20	0.07	0.32	0.40	2.00	0.32
Turned-leg tables		0.54	2.00	0.33	0.84				1.92	2.25			1.05
2. *Veneer, front apron*													
Straight-leg tables	2.38	2.05	1.53	2.91	2.48	1.60	1.81	1.50	2.21	1.11	1.57	0.60	1.98
Turned-leg tables		3.30	2.18	3.55	4.00				2.42	1.13			3.03
3. *Plain inlay*													
Straight-leg tables	5.13	4.61	4.86	3.52	5.05	5.50	6.00	4.50	8.33	6.55	6.12	3.60	5.38
Turned-leg tables		1.31	0.36	1.88	2.19				0.08	0.63			1.37
4. *Patterned inlay*													
Straight-leg tables	2.00	1.74	0.91	2.42	2.14	0.20	0.94	0.80	0.60	0.28	1.50	0.40	1.45
Turned-leg tables		2.54	1.00	1.67	1.53				0.00	0.06			1.24
5. *Pictorial inlay*													
Straight-leg tables	1.38	1.04	0.50	0.21	0.64	1.90	1.19	1.60	2.13	0.22	1.74	0.60	1.01

Chart VI
Regional Frequencies of 100 Patterned Inlays Used on 374 Straight- and Turned-leg Card Tables

	UNH	RMNH	Nbry	Sal	BoAr	Nwpt	Prov	Conn	NY	PhAr	Balt	Ann	Total
Number of tables	8	36	33	48	101	11	16	10	27	36	43	5	374
1. *Number of different patterned inlays*													
A. Total number used	7	33	17	31	47	2	14	4	8	6	29	3	
B. Total number used uniquely	0	8	2	7	12	0	2	1	1	3	16	2	54
C. Number used in common with other centers	7	25	15	24	35	2	12	3	7	3	13	1	
2. *Number of same patterned inlays common to centers*													
Rural Massachusetts–New Hampshire	6												
Newburyport	2	6											
Salem	5	12	9										
Boston area	6	20	12	20									
Newport	0	0	1	1	1								
Providence	2	6	4	6	7	0							
Connecticut	1	2	1	2	2	0	3						
New York	1	5	3	2	3	0	1	0					
Philadelphia area	1	3	2	3	2	0	2	0	0				
Baltimore	3	4	7	9	8	0	4	0	3	3			
Annapolis	0	0	0	0	0	0	0	0	1	0	1		

Chart VII
Regional Frequencies of 162 Pictorial Inlays Used on 374 Straight- and Turned-Leg Card Tables

	UNH	RMNH	Nbry	Sal	BoAr	Nwpt	Prov	Conn	NY	PhAr	Balt	Ann	Total
Number of tables	8	36	33	48	101	11	16	10	27	36	43	5	374
1. Number of different pictorial inlays													
A. Total number used	12	18	9	9	33	15	17	10	12	5	55	3	138
B. Total number used uniquely	5	13	3	5	21	9	12	9	7	3	50	1	
C. Number used in common with other centers	7	5	6	4	12	6	5	1	5	2	5	2	
2. Number of same pictorial inlays common to centers													
Rural Massachusetts–New Hampshire	2												
Newburyport	2	3											
Salem	1	1	2										
Boston area	5	1	4	3									
Newport	0	1	0	0	1								
Providence	2	1	0	1	2	2							
Connecticut	0	0	0	0	0	1	1						
New York	0	1	0	0	0	1	1	0					
Philadelphia area	0	0	1	0	0	0	0	0	0				
Baltimore	0	0	0	0	1	0	1	0	3	1			
Annapolis	0	0	0	0	0	0	0	0	0	0	2		

Chart VIII
Regional Frequencies of Straight-Leg Tables Ornamented with Pictorial Inlay at Various Places and of Types of Pictorial Inlay Used Any Place on the Table
(Expressed as percentages of each region's output)

	UNH	RMNH	Nbry	Sal	BoAr	Nwpt	Prov	Conn	NY	PhAr	Balt	Ann
Number of tables	8	23	22	24	69	11	16	10	15	19	43	5
1. Places on tables												
A. Pilasters	63	26	29	4	31	82	56	30	60	16	58	40
B. Shaft	38	48	5	4	10	82	25	50	47	0	62	0
C. Front apron, center	36	26	10	14	24	18	38	30	14	16	7	0
D. Top, center	0	4	5	4	0	0	0	0	36	0	38	20
E. Apron areas adjacent to ovolo corners	0	0	0	0	0	0	0	10	0	0	2	0
F. Top corners or top perimeter	0	4	0	0	0	0	0	0	0	0	5	0
G. Cuffs	0	0	0	0	0	0	0	10	0	0	0	0
H. Front apron, corners	0	0	0	0	1	0	0	0	0	0	2	0
I. Interior leaves	0	0	0	0	1	0	0	0	0	0		
2. Type of pictorial inlay												
A. Plain, single unit	9	41			33	33	29	33	25		4	
B. Engraved, single unit		12		11	14	34	24	11	17		9	
C. Simple integrated	41	29	25	11	15	27	6	22	8	20	24	
D. Inset integrated	50	18	75	78	38	6	41	34	50	80	63	100

Chart IX
Regional Frequencies of Different Kinds of Ornament
at Various Places on Card Tables (expressed as percentages of each region's output) and Regional Means for the Use of Ornament

	Straight-leg tables												Turned-leg tables					
	UNH	RMNH	Nbry	Sal	BoAr	Nwpt	Prov	Conn	NY	PhAr	Balt	Ann	RMNH	Nbry	Sal	BoAr	NY	PhAr
Number of tables	8	23	22	24	69	11	16	10	15	19	43	5	13	11	24	32	12	17
Percentage frequencies of each region's total production																		
1. *Top of table*																		
A. Wood																		
i. Veneer	12	4	9	0	0	27	12	20	79	10	30	0	0	0	0	6	83	0
ii. Solid wood	88	96	91	100	100	73	88	80	21	90	70	100	100	100	100	94	17	100
B. Center or rear ornament																		
i. Pictorial inlay	0	4	5	0	0	0	6	10	15	0	38	20	0	0	0	0	0	0
ii. No ornament	100	96	95	100	100	100	94	90	85	100	62	80	100	100	100	100	100	100
C. Perimeter ornament																		
i. String inlay only	0	4	5	0	4	64	6	30	64	5	45	40	0	0	0	0	8	0
ii. Crossbanding or banding and string inlay	0	0	0	0	0	0	6	0	14	0	26	0	0	0	0	0	0	0
iii. No ornament	100	96	95	100	96	36	88	70	22	95	29	60	100	100	100	100	92	100
2. *Top leaf edge*																		
A. Top corner ornament																		
i. String inlay	12	0	0	0	2	18	19	10	100	5	53	0	0	0	0	0	0	13
ii. Bead	0	0	5	0	0	0	0	10	0	5	14	100	8	55	8	25	0	74
iii. No ornament	88	100	95	100	98	82	81	80	0	90	33	0	92	45	92	75	100	13
B. Contour																		
i. Round	0	9	9	0	0	0	0	30	0	5	0	100	15	36	0	6	0	12
ii. Hollow	0	0	0	0	0	0	0	10	0	5	14	0	0	0	0	6	0	0
iii. Square	100	91	91	100	100	100	100	60	100	90	86	0	85	64	100	88	100	88
C. Ornament																		
i. Plain string	38	48	81	41	51	45	59	10	0	80	29	20	15	9	21	28	0	0
ii. Patterned string	62	22	5	45	41	0	27	20	0	0	2	0	62	18	41	38	0	0
iii. Crossbanding or banding	0	0	0	0	2	45	7	40	79	5	31	0	15	0	8	3	83	19
iv. Relief	0	9	0	0	3	0	0	10	0	0	2	0	8	64	8	22	0	69
v. Other and no ornament	0	21	14	14	3	10	7	20	21	15	36	80	0	9	22	9	17	12
3. *Interior of top*																		
A. Perimeter ornament																		
i. String inlay only	0	0	0	0	2	9	6	10	21	0	21	0	0	0	0	0	0	0
ii. Crossbanding and string inlay	0	0	0	0	0	9	6	10	21	5	14	100	0	0	0	3	17	0
iii. No ornament	100	100	100	100	98	82	88	80	58	95	65	0	100	100	100	97	83	100
B. Surface																		
i. Baize	0	0	4	0	0	9	6	10	14	5	12	100	0	0	0	3	17	6
ii. Solid wood or veneer	100	100	96	100	100	91	94	90	86	95	88	0	100	100	100	97	83	94
4. *Lower-leaf edge, lower corner*																		
A. Shape																		
i. Chamfered or hollow	12	4	14	9	23	0	25	0	0	5	19	0	46	18	29	69	8	0
ii. Square	88	96	86	91	77	100	75	100	100	95	81	100	54	82	71	31	92	100
5. *Aprons, front and end*																		
A. Placement of panels of string, crossbanding, banding, and veneer																		
i. Front apron only	37	44	33	64	43	0	25	50	0	0	2	0	23	36	29	31	75	0
ii. Front and end aprons	63	44	19	27	50	73	50	10	100	74	86	60	69	9	50	56	0	6
iii. Neither front nor end aprons	0	12	48	9	7	27	25	50	0	26	12	40	8	55	21	13	25	94
6. *Skirt*																		
A. Ornament																		
i. Plain string inlay	62	22	43	50	47	82	66	30	57	79	41	0	8	0	17	25	0	24
ii. Patterned string inlay	38	52	48	32	47	9	20	20	36	10	57	60	54	27	42	44	0	0
iii. Crossbanding or banding	0	4	0	0	2	9	7	10	7	0	0	0	15	0	13	9	58	19
iv. Relief	0	13	9	9	3	0	7	30	0	11	2	40	23	73	25	22	25	57
v. No ornament	0	9	0	9	1	0	0	10	0	0	0	0	0	0	3	0	17	0
7. *Front pilaster*																		
A. Ornament																		
i. Panel of string inlay only	12	4	5	17	7	0	25	20	0	53	7	20	0	0	0	3	58	0
ii. Panel of veneer	0	40	62	54	53	18	13	40	20	5	21	0	0	9	8	13	0	31
iii. Pictorial inlay	63	26	29	4	31	82	56	30	60	16	58	40	0	9	4	0	0	31
iv. Relief	0	0	0	4	2	0	0	0	0	0	0	0	0	9	0	0	17	6
v. Other	0	4	0	0	0	0	0	0	7	0	7	0	0	0	0	0	8	0
vi. No ornament	25	26	4	21	7	0	6	10	13	26	7	40	0	0	17	3	17	57
vii. No pilaster	0	0	0	0	0	0	0	0	0	0	0	0	100	73	71	81	0	6

	Straight-leg tables												Turned-leg tables					
	UNH	RMNH	Nbry	Sal	BoAr	Nwpt	Prov	Conn	NY	PhAr	Balt	Ann	RMNH	Nbry	Sal	BoAr	NY	PhAr
Number of tables	8	23	22	24	69	11	16	10	15	19	43	5	13	11	24	32	12	17
8. *Rear pilaster*																		
A. Ornament																		
i. Any ornament	0	22	5	59	81	82	75	80	86	63	86	40	31	9	42	56	83	44
ii. No ornament	100	78	95	41	19	18	25	20	14	37	14	60	69	91	58	44	17	56
9. *Shaft*																		
A. Ornament																		
i. String inlay only	64	39	81	29	81	0	69	30	53	84	24	40						
ii. Pictorial inlay	36	48	5	4	10	82	25	50	47	0	62	0						
iii. Relief	0	9	14	4	2	0	0	10	0	5	7	0						
iv. Veneer, often with pictorial inlay	0	0	0	0	7	9	6	10	0	0	7	0						
v. No ornament	0	4	0	63	0	9	0	0	0	11	0	60						
10. *Cuff*																		
A. Ornament																		
i. Any kind	87	70	52	64	74	82	81	70	100	90	71	40						
ii. No ornament	13	30	48	36	26	18	19	30	0	10	29	60						
Means																		
1. Number of pieces of string composing plain inlay of apron panel	1.29	1.35	1.00	1.36	1.57	1.50	1.30	1.67	2.92	1.07	1.61	1.00	1.17	0.00	1.82	1.94	0.00	2.00
2. Number of sides of shafts of front legs ornamented	1.25	1.13	1.10	0.41	1.47	2.10	1.75	1.80	2.86	1.58	1.48	1.20						
3. Number of sides of shafts of rear legs ornamented	0.50	0.43	1.00	0.45	1.25	1.50	1.69	1.40	2.00	1.37	1.79	0.80						

Chart X
Regional Frequencies of Facade Designs on Card Tables (Expressed as percentages of each region's output)

	Straight-leg tables												Turned-leg tables					
	UNH	RMNH	Nbry	Sal	BoAr	Nwpt	Prov	Conn	NY	PhAr	Balt	Ann	RMNH	Nbry	Sal	BoAr	NY	PhAr
Number of tables	8	23	22	24	69	11	16	10	15	19	43	5	13	11	24	32	12	17
One-unit designs																		
Facade 1		13.0	47.5	8.3	4.3	27.2	25.0	30.0		26.3	11.9	40.0		54.5	20.8	9.4	15.4	93.8
Facade 2	12.5	13.0	9.5	4.2	17.4	36.4	18.7	20.0	20.0	47.3	42.7	60.0	7.7		4.2	3.1		
Facade 3	12.5		23.8	4.2	2.9	9.1			13.3		16.7				4.2	3.1		
Facade 4	12.5		4.8	4.2	8.7				33.3		2.4							
Facade 5A																		
Facade 5B	25.0	26.1	4.8	12.5	7.2	18.2	6.3	20.0		5.3								
Facade 5C																		
Facade 5D																		
Facade 6A		4.4			5.9		12.5											
Facade 6B																		
Facade 7											4.8							
Total, one-unit designs	62.5	56.5	90.4	33.4	46.4	90.9	62.5	70.0	66.6	78.9	78.5	100	7.7	54.5	29.2	15.6	15.4	93.8
Two-unit designs																		
Facade 8		4.4												9.1		3.1		
Facade 9					2.9					5.3			15.4					
Total, two-unit designs		4.4			2.9					5.3			15.4	9.1		3.1		
Three-unit designs																		
Facade 10A																		
Facade 10B																		
Facade 10C		8.7		16.7	4.3		12.5				4.8		7.7	18.2	4.2	12.5	61.5	6.2
Facade 10D																		
Facade 10E																		
Facade 11					1.5	9.1							7.7		20.8	34.4		
Facade 12A																		
Facade 12B																		
Facade 12C	25.0	13.0	9.6	45.7	39.1		25.0	10.0		10.5	7.1		53.8	18.2	45.8	34.4	7.7	
Facade 12D																		
Facade 12E																		
Facade 13		4.4							13.3									
Facade 14					1.5				6.7		2.4							
Facade 15									6.7		2.4	5.3						
Total, three-unit designs	25.0	26.1	9.6	62.4	46.4	9.1	37.5	10.0	26.7	15.8	16.7		69.2	36.4	70.8	81.3	69.2	6.2
Total, miscellaneous designs	12.5	13.0		4.2	4.3			20.0	6.7		4.8		7.7				15.4	
Total	100	100	100	100	100	100	100	100	100	100	100	100	100	100	100	100	100	100

Chart XI
Regional Frequencies of Straight- and Turned-Leg Card Tables Constructed with Primary Solid Woods and Secondary Woods
(Expressed as percentages of each region's output)

Straight-leg tables (UNH–Ann)   *Turned-leg tables* (RMNH–PhAr)

	UNH	RMNH	Nbry	Sal	BoAr	Nwpt	Prov	Conn	NY	PhAr	Balt	Ann	RMNH	Nbry	Sal	BoAr	NY	PhAr
Number of tables	8	23	22	24	69	11	16	10	15	19	43	5	13	11	24	32	12	17
1. Primary woods																		
A. Mahogany	87.5	8.7	100	100	97.1	100	100	80.0	100	73.7	97.6	100	76.9	90.9	95.8	100	100	100
B. Walnut										26.3								
C. Cherry	12.5	69.6			2.9			20.0			2.4		15.4					
D. Birch		13.0											7.7	9.1	4.2			
E. Maple		8.7																
2. Secondary woods																		
A. White pine	100	95.7	100	90.0	97.1	90.0	100	100	100	57.9	33.3		100	100	95.8	100	91.7	93.8
B. Taeda pine										26.3	61.9	20.0					8.3	6.3
C. Birch or maple	12.5	47.8	66.7	63.6	58.8	60.0	56.3	20.0	28.6	10.5	4.8		46.2	72.7	70.8	93.8		18.8
D. Cherry	62.5	52.2	4.8	9.1	25.0	30.0	31.3	40.0	42.9	26.3	9.5		38.5	9.1	8.3	6.3	58.3	31.3
E. Oak										78.9	92.9	100					8.3	62.5
F. Chestnut			14.3		1.5	30.0	18.8	10.0								4.2	25.0	
G. Tulip poplar				4.5	1.5	10.0			21.4	21.1	31.0						16.6	
H. Oak and/or Taeda Pine										81.2	100	100						62.5

Chart XII
Regional Frequencies of the Construction of Six Parts of Card Tables (Expressed as percentages of each region's output)

Straight-leg tables (UNH–Ann)   *Turned-leg tables* (RMNH–PhAr)

	UNH	RMNH	Nbry	Sal	BoAr	Nwpt	Prov	Conn	NY	PhAr	Balt	Ann	RMNH	Nbry	Sal	BoAr	NY	PhAr
Number of tables	8	23	22	24	69	11	16	10	15	19	43	5	13	11	24	32	12	17
1. Curved rails																		
Single board		31	48	39	16	9	12				2	20	84	82	67	66		12
Kerf		17	4		6		7	10							4			
1 Lamination	76	17	29	44	60		12			5	22	20	8	9	29	19		
2 Laminations	12	13	15	13	13	37	38	10	20	11	19		8	9		9	10	7
3 Laminations		9	4	4	1	36	19	20	20	31	41	20				6	70	69
4 and 5 laminations		4			3	9	12	20	33	48	14						20	12
Vertical laminations									27									
Rails not curved	12	9			1	9		40		5	2	40						
2. Hinged rails																		
Design 1: 1 fly, 3 fixed legs	100	96	95	78	98		81		7	100	31	100	100	100	100	97		87
Design 2: 2 fly, 2 fixed legs		4	5	22		46	19				64					3	86	13
Design 3: 1 fly, 5 or 6 fixed legs					1	54		100	93		5						14	
No hinged rail					1													
3. Back																		
Filler	50	70	57	78	62		19			21	33	60	85	73	62	88		12
Flush	50	30	43	22	32	100	81	100	93	79	67	40	15	27	38	12	83	88
Other, replaced					6				7								17	
4. Flyleg																		
Plane	100	91	100	100	97	9	6		7	47	21	40	100	100	100	100		12
Overlapping		9			1	36	94			53	74	60						70
Additional					1	55		100	93		5						83	12
Other or none					1												17	6
5. Rear leaf-edge tenons																		
None	25	74	62	61	46	36	31	10		5	14		69	73	67	59	8	6
One	63	26	33	35	52	36	56	80	33	69	74	100	31	27	29	38	17	63
Two	12		5	4	2	28	13	10	60	26	7				4	3	50	6
Three									7		5						25	25
6. Medial brace	13	4					6	20	29	11	60				4	3	17	6

Chart XIII

Regional Frequencies of Card Tables with Various Combinations of Straight-Leg Shapes and Flyleg Construction
(Expressed as percentages of each region's output)

	UNH	RMNH	Nbry	Sal	BoAr	Nwpt	Prov	Conn	NY	PhAr	Balt	Ann
Number of tables	8	23	22	24	69	11	16	10	15	19	43	5
1. Single taper shape and A. Plane flyleg	63	52	100	64	39		6		7	47	14	40
B. Overlapping flyleg		9				36	81			53	62	40
C. Additional flyleg						55		100	93		5	
D. Slide leg					1							
2. Pointed double taper and plane flyleg	37	39		31	48							
3. Squat double taper and plane flyleg					11							
4. Single taper with spade foot and A. Plane flyleg					5						7	
B. Overlapping flyleg							13				12	20
5. Single taper, five sided, and plane flyleg							9					
6. Single taper with knopped foot and overlapping flyleg							1					

Chart XIV

Regional Means and Ranges of Construction Points of Straight- and Turned-Leg Tables Calculated on a Scale of 0–13

	Straight-leg tables												*Turned-leg tables*					
	UNH	RMNH	Nbry	Sal	BoAr	Nwpt	Prov	Conn	NY	PhAr	Balt	Ann	RMNH	Nbry	Sal	BoAr	NY	PhAr
Number of tables	8	23	22	24	69	11	16	10	15	19	43	5	13	11	24	32	12	17
Mean number per table	2.50	1.57	1.57	1.32	1.84	5.50	4.50	5.90	9.20	5.84	5.57	3.60	0.69	0.73	1.08	1.16	7.50	5.94
Range of points, all tables	1–3	0–4	0–4	0–4	0–8	1–7	0–6	4–7	7–13	3–8	0–10	1–6	0–2	0–2	0–5	0–4	1–10	2–8
Range of points, ready-made tables	1–3	0–4	0–4	0–3	0–4	6–7	4–6	4–7	7–13	3–8	0–10	1–6	0–2	0–2	0–5	0–4	5–10	2–8

Index of Cabinetmakers and Other Craftsmen

The abbreviation "no." refers to the List of Tables Included in the Study.